# A SHATTERED IDOL

The Lord Chief Justice

& his

Troublesome Women

Photograph of Lord Coleridge

# A SHATTERED IDOL

## The Lord Chief Justice
## & his
## Troublesome Women

TOM HUGHES

Foreword by Sir Paul Coleridge

Marble Hill

First published in 2025 by Marble Hill Publishers
Flat 58 Macready House
75 Crawford Street
London W1H 5LP
www.marblehillpublishers.co.uk

A CIP catalogue record for this book is available from the British Library.

ISBN: 9781738497010
E-book ISBN: 9781068360831
Typeset in LDN Garamond Royale
Printed and bound by Biddles Books.
Text and cover design by Paul Harpin

# CONTENTS

# FOREWORD

# "You couldn't make it up"

BY THE STANDARDS of any age, this is a truly extraordinary saga. Even assuming the standards and mores of high Victorian society, if this tale had been written as a pastiche on the behaviour of family life in the second half of the nineteenth century it would be written off as rather poor and far-fetched family drama. But in fact from first to last every detail is true. And to say I too was jaw-droppingly surprised when Tom Hughes first approached me with the whole story during the early stages of his research for the book, would be a gross understatement.

I am the great, great grandson of the chief character in the narrative; the Lord Chief Justice of England, Lord (John Duke) Coleridge (1820-1894) who was undoubtedly the stand out and revered celebrity judge of the day. During my lifetime in any oral retelling of family history, from one generation to another, his status and reputation were/are unmatched. His name tended to be uttered in revered and hushed whispers. There were many pictures and faded sepia photos of him dotted round the house not only where I was brought up but in the houses of other relatives we visited as children (some reproduced in this book). Indeed long before I was old enough to know what a Lord Chief Justice was I knew about John Duke. Similarly I knew about his father, the first judge (Sir John Taylor ) and the Lord Chief's two sons , my feckless great Grandfather Stephen and his more sombre elder brother, the third Judge and second Baron, Bernard Duke. All were part of the colourful family narrative and mythology which I reckoned I knew reasonably well. With the exception of the global reputation of the poet Samuel Taylor Coleridge, the Lord Chief's great-uncle, the very fact of three Victorian judges happening in three successive generations was regarded, especially in legal circles, as noteworthy. Indeed, when I first started at the Bar in 1970 there were still senior practitioners and judges who had known Bernard and Stephen during their lives.

So when Tom first approached me in 2015 to find out what I knew about the Lord Chief's only daughter (Mildred) and the family shenanigans and goings-on surrounding her life and revealed in this book, I am ashamed, and the first to admit, that I effectively knew nothing. But why was that? I have since wondered. The answer I am sure is simple. After the death of the LCJ, Mildred was swiftly and effectively airbrushed out of the family history so that the family reputation could be allowed to recover. The waters of history were left to close over the whole sorry period and it is only now by Tom's unstinting and skilful literary archaeology that she has been properly reborn and reinstated.

What his research has revealed is a Trollopian family, apparently and to all intents and purposes, flawlessly embedded in the higher ranks of Victorian society but in fact deeply traumatised and divided by the Lord Chief's inability to cope with firstly, his highly intelligent and suppressed daughter Mildred, and secondly, Amy, his young and very glamorous second wife (but with distinctly dodgy antecedents). Indeed, it seems that such was the family falling-out over these events that by the time of the Lord Chief's death in 1894 the family was in every sense truly broken; neither his daughter nor his two sons were on speaking terms with him. As for poor Amy, she was swiftly consigned to family history as the beautiful temptress who went off with effectively all the Lord Chief's hard-earned fortune. Apart from her acknowledged glamour surviving in high quality portraits her reputation has never properly recovered.

For centuries, the newspaper-reading public have always been greedy for stories about celebrity families, not only their public lives and great public achievements but much more their scandalous private lives and behaviour. Internal family discord makes excellent copy reminding us, as it always does, that the great and good suffer from domestic schisms like us ordinary mortals. When it spills out onto the front pages we revel in it. Magazines like "Hello", the tabloid newspapers like the late News of the World and nowadays social media, justify their existence and make their living from gossip about figures in the public eye. It all enlivens our humdrum lives. However, when these domestic disputes find their way into the Royal Courts of Justice in the form of salacious libel trials which dominate the media for weeks at a time, we positively salivate with glee. The stories and trials in this book are no exception.

Back then the Private Eye of the day was Vanity Fair magazine. Men and women of renown were the subject of cartoon, lampoon and satire. This is how in 1887, accompanied by a colour cartoon, they summed up Lord Coleridge following the notorious libel trials:

"Lord Coleridge is a very moral man. He throws off without an effort the most beautiful moral platitudes. In cases which require hard sound law he is less admirable but his morality is superior to and compensatory for all shortcomings in this respect. He is sentimental; he is pious; he is literary; and he is distinguished by great humility, and an apostolic innocence of the wicked ways and men of the impious, unsentimental common world....... .......He is a classical

Caricature of Lord Coleridge
Vanity Fair (1887)

scholar, a metaphysician, a High Churchman. But unfortunately he also thinks himself a wit. Anything so superior and refined as Lord Coleridge was never known; anything so inferior as Lord Coleridge's jokes was never heard not even from the Bench.

Lord Coleridge has three sons. He also has a son-in-law, Mr Adams, who has ventured not without a certain success, to encounter his eminent father-in-law in the Law Courts on domestic questions of great delicacy. It was in this case (sic) when under examination as a witness that the Chief Justice rose perhaps to his highest point of dignity and worthy bearing.

Personally and in private life Lord Coleridge is a charming man. He is very thrifty. He is a ready diner and an excellent talker, and he is much admired in the small circle of his personal friends. He never reads any newspaper except the Times."

Once again I am ashamed to disclose that I had never really fully understood the references to "Mr Adams" until this book shed a full light on the stories behind the cartoon with its rubric, which so dominated the front pages in the last years of the 19th century. However, what is clear is that the Vanity Fair columnist perfectly captured the personality now fully exposed by Tom Hughes' book.

The storylines revealed by Tom's brilliant research and writing have it all. The only daughter of England's most senior (widowed) judge caught in a compromising situation "in a darkened room" with a gold digger, unemployed journalist leading inexorably to not one but two libel trials. And then the denouement of this frenzied legal and forensic activity finds the Lord Chief Justice of England himself being cross examined IN HIS OWN COURT ROOM (still Court 4 in the Royal Courts of Justice) by Mildred's supposed lover, Charles Adams, in person and without legal representation of any kind. Surely this tale itself could comprise a unique if far fetched TV drama. However, when to this story is added the seduction by the 63 year old Lord Chief of his 37 year old future second wife on the long voyage by ocean-going-steamer back from New York (itself leading to threats of a breach of promise of marriage case) surely the icing is truly on the cake.

I do not do proper justice to the detail of the two intertwined stories so stylishly revealed by Tom Hughes' diligent research and contemporary illustrations, all sewn together by his colourful and compellingly, readable style. Even making allowances for the fact that I am part of the family to which these events relate, I couldn't put it down. I am left finally with this question; how would this all have turned out if the Lord Chief's first wife had not died leaving a motherless, unmarried daughter to be brought up by a somewhat unimaginative, stuffy father bereft for years of female company?

Honestly, as you will see, "You just couldn't make it up."

Sir Paul Coleridge
*(The fourth "Coleridge" judge, 2004-2014)*

# ACKNOWLEDGEMENTS

FROM THE BEGINNING, the Coleridge family has been interested in and supportive of my efforts to tell this family saga. I first approached Sir Paul Coleridge. As with his great-great-grandfather, the Lord Chief Justice, and his great uncle, Bernard, he had completed a distinguished career on the High Court bench. I have appreciated our conversations and "zooms," as well as his guided tour of the Law Courts where Lord Coleridge's elaborate self-designed robes remain on display. He also shared essential letters and photographs handed down through generations. His great-grandfather, Stephen Coleridge, as you can see, was a most interesting figure. Paul has kindly written the foreword, as well. My gratitude also goes to the present (5th) Lord Coleridge who hosted my wife and me for tea at the Manor House in Ottery. Heath's Court – then Chanter's House, just over the wall, was then in other hands and unwelcoming visitors. It has been a great pleasure to work with Gill Coleridge, for many years a director of one London's most respected literary agencies, and another great-great descendant of the "Chief," who has offered her advice, encouragement, and unstinting assistance to find a home for this story. Thank you one and all.

I also wish to thank Sir James Munby, former President of the Family Division of the High Court of England and Wales, who read the manuscript and whose insights were invaluable.

I thank the staff of the Manuscripts Reading Room at the British Library, St. Pancras. To carefully hold and read 150-year-old letters (illegible, mostly, in his lordship's case) is a privilege. The Library's Newsroom is home of the essential British Newspaper Archive, the contemporary newspapers, magazines, and society journals of the day. Gone are hand-cranked squeaking machines with dodgy focus cameras, replaced by millions of digitised, *searchable (!),* pages on new (still dodgy at times) equipment. I wish to express my great appreciation to the Library staff. In the final stages of my preparation, the Library was dealing with the aftermath of an unfortunate cyber-attack but they were able to address my research needs under trying circumstances. The foreign press coverage relied on Newspapers.com, and Trove (Australia) and Papers Past (New Zealand). Elsewhere, The Ransom Library, at the University of Texas in Austin, holds the papers of Ernest Hartley Coleridge, Lord Coleridge's "official" biographer. Dr. Stephanie Coane, Deputy Librarian at Eton College provided some last-minute information from the Mary Coleridge papers. Anne Barrett at the archives of the Imperial College, London, and Jennie de Protani, archivist at The Athenaeum, were also helpful.

The National Archives at Kew hold the original English census records. Researchers at Roots-Chat.com provided remarkable details on the Davies-Ezcurra menage in Devon. The staff at the Royal Archives, Windsor Castle, assisted greatly, confirming there is no record that the second Lady Coleridge was ever presented to Queen Victoria.

The late and much-respected Sally Mitchell of Temple University, Philadelphia, biographer of Francis Power Cobbe, was very interested in my idea to tell Mildred's story. Her knowledge of the VSS and the "darkened room" remains essential. Professor David Brown, at the University of Southampton, deciphered the execrable hand of Lord Shaftesbury. The Royal College of Ophthalmology answered questions about the likely causes for Mildred's lifelong vision problems. Other helpful scholars include Julia Courtney, Ginger Frost, and Lesley Hall.

The village of Milford-on-Sea and the nearby hamlet of Keyhaven remain remote and ever beautifully situated. I have enjoyed my visits and conversations with the active membership of the Milford-on -Sea Historical Record Society. Bob Braid, Jim Butterworth, and others, have been eager to share village memories of "Mr. and the Hon. Mrs. Adams" of Harewood

House. I do hope the "calvary cross" will long stand near their unmarked graves in Milford.

As always, the opinions within and errors, (few, I hope) are mine.

Finally, it is an honour to be working with Francis Bennett, my editor and publisher at Marble Hill, well known for his many years in publishing, and this exciting new venture. And, lastly, my wife, Kathleen McGraw: counselor, driver, graveyard searcher, and grammarian; she is, as in all things, nonpareil.

# A NOTE ON MONEY

SINCE MONEY MOTIVATES much of the drama in our narrative, we should grasp the money nettle straightaway. For example, in 1883, Mildred left her father's home with £300 a year. Readers may want to have a sense what that sum in 1883 would be worth today. There are many sources. The methodologies are complicated, inexact, but fascinating, I guess. I have chosen *measuringworth.com*

Based on the inflation rate of the British pound, £300 in 1883 was equivalent in purchasing power to about £32,150 in 2021, the last calculated year. Too simple, *measuringworth.com* admits. A better way is to look at what income a person would need today to have the wealth and influence of someone with £300 a year in 1883. That figure, so it happens, is much higher: £246,500.

Let's look at Lord Chief Justice Coleridge's pay packet. At his peak, he earned £8000 per annum. To match that wealth today (what *measuringworth. com* calls his "relative income value") would require a salary of £6,574,000. Not quite a top Premier League salary but a very good living. For perspective, the salary of Dame Sue Carr, the first-ever *Lady* Chief Justice of England and Wales, is £294,821. Please don't tell her.

"Five Ways to Compute the Relative Value of a UK Pound Amount, 1270 to Present," MeasuringWorth, 2023.
URL: www.measuringworth.com/ukcompare/

# PREFACE

FRANKLY, IT PASSED me by when the British Library acquired the Coleridge papers in 2006. Lorries rolled up to historic Chanter's House in Ottery St. Mary, Devon, to remove 350 bound manuscripts and 29 cardboard boxes of correspondence from "the family of Samuel Taylor Coleridge." The immortal Romantic poet was someone to whom I had the slightest (long-ago) schoolboy introduction. Who doesn't recall the *Ancient Mariner*? "For all averred I had kill'd the bird." At the Library, however, an excited curator touted the "vast cast of eminent Victorians" also found within the larger collection. The trove included the letters and journals of three generations of Coleridges, one of whom rose to become Lord Chief Justice of England and Wales.

The Lord Chief Justice, John Duke Coleridge, is the idol of my title. He was a different man from his great uncle. The despondent poet once wrote in his diary, "I am not worthy to live ... I have done nothing!" Decades later, at the same age, John Duke, a rising barrister in a hurry, would have none of that moodiness. "The year has ended very well with me. I am within a little of £12,000 and, I dare say, I shall touch it before the 31st."[1]

A series of legal triumphs led to a peerage and, in 1880, elevation to sit as the Queen's leading judge.[2] "How well, too, he looked the part of Chief Justice, with his tall and stately figure, smooth, benignant face, winning smile, and beautifully modulated voice." Yet John Duke Coleridge never quite grasped why so many people disliked him. While he received many votes in the occasional ranking of England's "greatest living men," he also made the shortlist for England's "greatest humbug."[3] Much of this was the result of bad press of his own making. He feuded with the "red tops" before that trope was a thing. He put one powerful editor in gaol and assailed the rest. As a result, with malignity, the newspapers revelled in "lampoons on his private family history [which] were received by the English public with delight."[4] And that is what we shall be about.

I came to the Coleridge papers not for the "Chief," as he was commonly known, nor for the politicians and poets, scholars and sages, with whom he exchanged hundreds of letters. Rather, I sought traces of Mildred, his only daughter, eldest of his lordship's four children. Born in 1847, her first thirty-five years can be followed quite easily: a happy childhood despite diffident health. "Not as others," she was petted by the large Coleridge family and welcomed in her father's august circle. By the early 1880s, she was motherless, unmarried, described as unattractive, and, in her thirties. She was on the glide path to her future as "one of those necessitous, pitiful, relatives who so often make life difficult for a great family."[5] Circa 1883, Mildred disappears, rinsed from the family papers. This followed closely her attachment with the singular Charles Warren Adams.

Modern readers about to enter this Victorian world may well, at first, find it worthy of a hearty lampoon. It seems scripted for a successful period rom-com: the preposterous widowed *Paterfamilias* desperate to separate his devoted daughter "of many summers" from her infuriating swain, an unctuous intruder professing disinterest in her fortune whilst calculating it to the farthing. Lord Coleridge, however, devoid of a sense of humour, despaired for his "besotted child." Remember, she was 36. Everyone took this quite seriously and we, as interested onlookers, must too. How else to understand the facts behind "one of the most despicable scandals ever enacted in an English household?"[6]

*A Shattered Idol: The Lord Chief Justice & His Troublesome Women* presents the first full-length account of the obsession with the Coleridge family that enthralled Britain for more than a decade. And, we haven't even mentioned the second baroness. From Act II, Mildred would be upstaged by her dazzling, so much younger, stepmother, a "chirpy, piquante, little bit of white pique with the appetising bottines." [I had to look that last bit up and must admit to some disappointment to discover *bottines* were merely ankle boots in the day.] It was with real regret, then, that I realised Mildred – meant to be our focus – would have to share the stage. Two sensational confrontations unfolded concurrently, jolting the "celestial peace" of the Coleridge home: first Adams, then the mysterious second Lady Coleridge (nee Amy Baring Lawford, a "supposed" widow). As we will see, the resulting estrangements embittered the family long after Lord Coleridge passed away in 1894.

It took a decade for his late lordship's discreet nephew to produce one of those Victorian relics, the fat two-volume set, the *Life and Correspondence of John Duke Lord Coleridge*. Mildred was barely mentioned. As the author explained, "I am doing what he would himself have wished." As for the second baroness, the "Old Man's darling" early on won over her late husband's biographer. His remit seems to have been, "You could not do better than ignore the family life."[7] Winners write the history and so it was done.

Nevertheless, defying clear efforts from all sides to expunge these two women from their historic family record, enough remarkable letters and references remain to tell a story that has been hidden for a century and a half. It is an account of a domestic unravelling that led a friend to conclude, the Coleridges were "a family which has gone to ruin itself."

1   21 October 1804, *Coleridge's Notebooks: A Selection* (2002) The poet was 32. Christmas Eve 1854, John Duke to his father John Taylor Coleridge, *Life & Correspondence*, Vol. 1, 154. John Duke was 34.

2   For more details, "Builders of Our Law," The Law Times, Vols 111-112, (14 September 1901), 428-9, 445. Charles Kingston, Famous Judges and Famous Trials (1923) 104-135

3   Pall Mall Gazette, 19 January 1885, 6. The newspaper defined humbug as "a man who pretends to be more than he is, or a windbag."

4   "Malignity": "Lord Coleridge and the Newspapers," Central Law Journal, Vol. 21, 444.

5   Arnold Bennett's description of Aunt Maria in The Old Wives Tale (2019 ed.) 50.

6   25 November 1884, The World

7   Ernest Hartley Coleridge, Life and Correspondence of John Duke Lord Coleridge, Vol. 2, 345-6.

A photograph of Heath's Court after the architect William Butterfield's
1882 expansion and redesign.

# 1. OTTERY AND THE COLERIDGES

THERE HAVE BEEN Coleridges in Devon since the 1500s, mainly settled between Exeter and Dartmoor.[1] In 1760, the Rev. John Coleridge was the first to arrive in the village of Ottery St. Mary to be the new headmaster of the boys' school. Soon, he became vicar of the church, a "singularly imposing" 13th century pile. John Coleridge married twice and produced eleven children; the youngest boy (Samuel Taylor, born in Ottery in 1772) would live to be the great poet. Another son, "Colonel" James, followed a more lucrative military career and, in 1796, he returned to Ottery and purchased the 16th century "Chanter's House," beside the church. Oliver Cromwell had stayed in the house in 1646, while hunting down the last of the Royalists in the West. Prior to the Coleridges, the Heath family resided there for many generations, thus the locals knew the place as Heath's Court.[2] Until 2006, it remained the seat of the Coleridge family.

In 1838, Heath's Court (and the expenses that went with it) were passed down to the poet's wealthy nephew, John Taylor Coleridge, a successful and respected London barrister, and later a judge of the Court of Queen's Bench. John Taylor had four children. The eldest son, born in 1820, was the future Lord Chief Justice, John Duke Coleridge. Another son, Henry, and two daughters, Alethea, and Mary, followed.

John Duke (Duke was a family name, not a title, confusing nonetheless) retraced his father's path to Eton and Oxford, succeeding brilliantly. His reputation for vanity was established at university. The

Master of Balliol famously declared: "Mr. Coleridge, I have a very high opinion of you; your tutor has a high opinion of you; everybody in the college has a high opinion of you; but nobody has so high an opinion of you as you have of yourself."[3] Yet John Duke made numerous lifelong friends, among them John Henry Newman. These were years of religious turmoil at Oxford, highlighted by Newman's bolt to the Roman Church (taking with him Henry Coleridge, John Duke's younger brother, who became a Jesuit priest.) The friendship of John Duke and the future cardinal survived. Some of Coleridge's critics would later suggest "God intended him to be a Bishop but by accident he became a judge." There was no great Coleridge fortune and thus John Duke eschewed the clerical life for the bar. He admitted he had no particular aptitude or passion for the law but assessed his chances thusly: "Certainly, stupider fellows than I affect to think myself, get on very well." And he certainly did.

While at Oxford, at the deathbed of a favourite schoolmate, he met the poor fellow's sister, Jane Fortescue Seymour. Jane was four years younger, daughter of the Rev. George Turner Seymour, a wealthy, landholding, clergyman. From her portrait, Jane seems to have possessed middling good looks. Nevertheless, Benjamin Jowett, that future celebrated Oxford don, curiously congratulated his friend on his selection, "I am very glad you have chosen for something better than outside display." Jane's father thought she was a "simple and sensible girl." She was certainly quiet, refined and given much to sketching and painting. On 11 August 1846, John Duke and Jane were married in the "wind-worn" church of All Saints, Freshwater, on the Isle of Wight. The guests adjourned to the Rev. Seymour's nearby home at Farringford for a reception surrounded by glorious views of the Solent.

John and Jane moved in with his parents at their London home at 26, Park Crescent, just below Regents Park. Before his marriage,

John Duke had finished reading for the bar and set about earning his living on the Western Circuit. There, he hoped the Coleridge name might bring some reassuring familiarity in the struggle for briefs. Jane would remain in London with their first child, Mildred Mary Coleridge, born on November 6, 1847. Three boys followed, Bernard in 1851, Stephen in 1854 and the youngest, Gilbert, in 1859. In the manner of countless barrister wives, Jane Coleridge raised her growing brood in the rather overtaxed quarters of her mother and father-in-law. John Taylor admitted it was "a trial for us all." It was a plus when John Taylor came into the Coleridge estate in Ottery; Jane and the children spent summers and holidays in Devon. The boys, of course, once out of their rompers, would be sent away to school. Mildred would remain home with her mother.

In the early 1850s, John Duke's career at the bar took off. By legend, it began with the "Clayhidon murder."[4] Coleridge defended a young man from that Devon village who was accused of killing a tax collector. It may be apocryphal but the story was told that while Coleridge stood before the jury to make a final plea for mercy, a gust of wind swept the courtroom in Exeter and blew out all the candles. While the tapers were being relit, in semi-darkness, Coleridge, dramatically and from memory, quoted from Othello's candle speech as the Moor stood over Desdemona's bed. Coleridge reminded the jurors of the finality of their verdict. Unlike a candle, a man's life can never be relit. It would make for a better story if the man's life was saved but, for all the Shakespearean flourish, the wretched defendant went to the gallows all the same. Still, Coleridge's theatrics established his reputation as a "silver tongued" advocate. Briefs and fees poured in. In 1858, the Coleridges were finally able to afford a home of their own at 6, Southwick Crescent, in Paddington. In 1854, he was elected to the House of Commons for Exeter as a Liberal.

"The Rode Murder," "The Great Convent Case," "The Wicklow Peerage," and more, John Duke Coleridge played a role in many of the sensational legal cases of the 1860s. As each year ended, he would report to his father on his earnings. At Christmas in 1867, for instance, he wrote, "The year has ended very well with me. I am within a little of £12,000 (£1.6 million in 2022.) I dare say, I shall touch it before the 31st." He was among the wealthiest and best-known barristers in Britain. In 1868, the Liberals, under Mr. Gladstone, took power at Westminster. The new Prime Minister chose the rising Devon lawyer with the famous name to be Solicitor General. The post came with a knighthood.

Sir John Duke Coleridge's rise had been a rapid one. Too rapid for some. While pleased to be caricatured in *Vanity Fair*, John Duke could not have appreciated the editorial comment that he was "far too egoistic."[5] But his greatest triumph was still to come. Coleridge must have gone to his grave blessing the day the butcher from Wagga Wagga got off the boat in London proclaiming himself to be the long-lost Sir Roger Tichborne.[6] In perhaps the greatest trial of the Victorian era, Coleridge relentlessly prosecuted a perjury charge against the *soi-disant* Sir Roger.[7] Lady Coleridge, occasionally accompanied by Mildred, sat in court, sketching the principal figures in the case. The claimant was in the witness box for days while Coleridge, without shouting (too often), sleekly prodded and challenged. As he leaned in to the claimant or one of the supportive witnesses, Coleridge so often used the expression, "Would you be surprised to hear," it became *the phrase* of the hour in print and on the stage.[8] Coleridge's 28 day (!) closing speech "certainly must be regarded as the high-water mark of nineteenth century legal oratory."[9] The claimant was found guilty. Arthur Orton (his real name) went to gaol. Sir John Duke Coleridge went to the bench. A timely death leaving a vacancy, Coleridge was named Chief Justice of the Court of Common Pleas, and with that, came a peerage. He was now John Duke, the first *Baron* Coleridge of Ottery St. Mary.

The Coleridge's London home (from 1869) was No. 1 Sussex Square, just north of Hyde Park, described as "a capital and superior built mansion adapted for the residence of a family of distinction." Perfectly suited then. The aristocracy may have clustered in Belgravia and Mayfair but Paddington was attracting the better class of professional men. The neighbourhood was sneered at by some critics for its "pretentious grandeur."[10] Number 1 was at the southeast corner of the square; it was a substantial cream-coloured stucco mansion on six levels. The interior had been completely refurbished by William Butterfield, the celebrated "High Church" architect and longtime Coleridge friend.[11] There was a large dining room, communicating drawing rooms, a morning room, fourteen bedrooms and a library for Lord Coleridge's books. Prominently displayed were Lady Coleridge's sketches and "frescoes." The Coleridges gave a dinner to show off their new home and invited Dean Stanley of Westminster, politicians and notables including Robert Browning. Later in the evening, the doors were opened for a more general reception, "everyone admiring the beautiful rooms." It was "a free and pleasant" evening, a female visitor recalled, the "dresses really beautiful...nothing extreme in the way of décolleté-ness." There was some musical entertainment provided. "Mildred Coleridge played small things very nicely." Mildred was 22.

1  Ottery/Coleridges: *Life & Correspondence*, Vol. 1, and Bernard Coleridge, *The Story of a Devonshire House* (1905).

2  Heath's Court - the use of the apostrophe is inconsistent. The apostrophe is used in the "*Life & Correspondence*" and, therefore, here.

3  Thomas Seccombe, *In Praise of Oxford*, Vol. 2 (1912) 641.

4  Clayhidon legend: In 1853, tax collector William Blackmore was murdered in Clayhidon. Coleridge represented the accused, George Sparks. Life, Vol 1, 200. Coleridge did use the Desdemona speech but the windblown candle drama is not mentioned. See the *Exeter Flying Post*, 23 June 1894, 8: "It's strange how such tales are concocted and repeated from hand to mouth until they are believed."

5  *Vanity Fair*, 30 April 1870.

6  The Claimant: Lord Coleridge said he quickly knew the man was a fraud: "Sir Roger Tichborne was proficient in music; when I handed the claimant a music-book, and he held it upside down, I thought no further evidence was needed of his being an ignorant pretender." Ellis Yarnall, *Wordsworth and the Coleridges: With Other Memories* (1899).

7  More reading: Douglas Woodruff, The Tichborne Claimant: A Victorian Mystery (1957) Robyn Annear, The Man Who Lost Himself: The Unbelievable Story of the Tichborne Claimant (2002).

8  Would it surprise you to hear/know/learn/discover? Would you be surprised to hear there were many variants? Seriously. The most frequently quoted was "Would you be surprised to hear?"

9  "Legal oratory:" Joseph Meisel, *Public Speech and the Culture of Public Life in the Age of Gladstone* (1999).

10  Sussex Square: Joseph Smith Fletcher, a mystery writer of the "Golden Age" set one of his stories amid the "pretentious architectural grandeur" of Sussex Square.

11  Butterfield: his contributions to the dining room included some bizarre wallpaper of his own design he titled Worms. Coleridge was not impressed. "We shall have to put up with the "worms," which in time, I dare say, we shall get to endure, perhaps even like." Quoted in Paul Thompson, *William Butterfield* (1971).

# 2. A SOMEWHAT OVER-TRAINED BRAIN

WHEN MILDRED WAS born in Park Crescent on 6 November 1847, her mother described her proudly as her "fat angel." The neighbours made approving remarks. "She was much admired and not thought small," reported Jane to her husband away on circuit. But, by Mildred's fourth birthday, a close family friend, the novelist Charlotte Yonge, wrote to John Taylor, asking about his grand-daughter: "As you do not mention Mildred, I hope she is better."[1]

Mildred was raised amidst great privilege. Her brothers arrived at roughly three-year intervals through the 1850s.[2] At Park Crescent, the children scampered through the "Nursemaid's Tunnel" under the busy New Road to play in Regents Park. She and her brothers got on well. Bernard remembered, "We had our elementary dramatic performances. My sister, of course, took the female parts. I generally was the tragic or comic hero." Mildred and Bernard were quite like their father, intellectually curious, studious, and earnest. The two youngest boys, Stephen and Gilbert, were less so, more given to silliness and troubles in school. The three lads would follow the male track of tutors, a good public school, and university. But there were no such facilities for girls. Mildred, though, was afforded excellent "home-schooling." Miss Yardley, the governess, was tasked with providing the required grounding in various subjects and a smattering of art and music. Mildred was an unusually intelligent child. Her mother wrote, "She is so knowing. I love my hubby's child."[3] She learned Latin and Greek, studies generally thought to be too difficult for the female brain. She was devoted to her grandfather and wrote to John Taylor constantly, addressing him as Socrates, and signing herself as Kebes (one of the philosopher's Theban disciples). Of course, the Coleridge home would have that Victorian mainstay, a pianoforte, and Mildred would learn to play. But few girls in London were tutored by Sir Sterndale Bennett of the Royal Academy of Music. John Stainer, later the organist at St. Paul's Cathedral, was another of her mentors.

Alas, Mildred's health was never strong. Years later, Bernard recalled their nurse used to make Mildred roll around where the sheep would lie in Regents Park, "because the scent was thought to be wonderfully strengthening." From the available evidence, it is more than likely Mildred had rheumatic fever as a child. Patients who survived the feared disease suffered consequences meaning "lifelong delicacy." Typical effects were general weakness and lack of stamina, stiffness or lameness in the joints, and - in many cases - vision problems. As will be seen, Mildred had all three.

Mildred was regularly sent away from London's soot and dampness to the freshness of Devon. She spent much of her time in Ottery staying with her aunt, Mary Frances Keble Coleridge, at Manor House, Mary's residence near the church. Like Mildred, Aunt Mary, or "Maymie," had various afflictions of her own, mostly headaches. She lived quietly. "Milly" was her favourite and she kept the girl busy in Devon helping at church and working with charities. Keeping with her Greek, Mildred called Maymie, "Pheme," the goddess of rumour, as her aunt knew all the latest town and family gossip. Maymie never married. There was a convention at the time "for an English family life to be perfect there should always be a dear old-maid aunt in the domestic circle." Maymie certainly filled that role for the Coleridges; was Mildred destined to be next in her line?[4]

As Mildred turned 12, Maymie was quite worried about her niece. Mildred was "an exceptionally brilliant and clever child," but with few outlets for her talents. Mary pressed her friend Charlotte Yonge, who wrote religiously-themed stories, to set up a writing group for Mildred, and girls like her, "wealthy, intelligent girls with time on their hands." Yonge established an essay society where the girls, using pen names (Mildred's was Lady Bird) made contributions to a journal, *The Barnacle*, published semi-regularly and shared among an extended network of families and readers.[5] Miss Yonge was called Mother Goose and her girls were "the Goslings." In early 1861, the group of "eager, merry schoolgirls," gathered around Miss Yonge at the Coleridge home (still, at the time, in Southwick Crescent). Yonge sent a note to John Duke with an update on the Goslings, adding her brief concern, "I grieve over Mildred's lameness."[6]

Still, Mildred was the leader of the Goslings. The other girls idolised her. Sophia Lonsdale recalled: "Mildred was a very brilliant and entertaining girl, and I can well remember the sort of hero worship I had for her. She wore a red cloak, which as she was very tall, made her a conspicuous object. A sight of her red cloak made me perfectly happy for the entire day!"[7] To *The Barnacle*, Mildred contributed poetry, song lyrics, and translations of Dante and Schiller. In the Christmas issue of 1865, a contributor wrote: "The Lady Bird ... [is] a very superior being, let me tell you. Our Lady Bird has a clear, penetrating voice, and is decidedly musical [with] a most cultivated taste in all sorts of subjects...quite a prodigy of learning...She is a very remarkable insect." The Gosling period ended suddenly. In 1866, Miss Yonge reported to a friend, "Goosedom has had a shock and a revolution, chiefly induced by Mildred Coleridge having no time for it, and her aunt (Maymie) therefore losing interest in it."[8]

This change in Mildred's level of interest may well have been the natural course of things as she was in her late-teens, older than many of the other girls. She was also increasingly interested in the political world and shared her opinions frequently, writing to her father and grandfather. That year, a crowd tore down the fences in Hyde Park, demanding action on the Reform Bill. Mildred, who was in Ottery at the time, wrote to her father, ("Dear Pippie!") to say how sorry she was to miss "the ruckus." She blamed the riots on the Tory government's "silly" decision to send the police in to clear the Park. The Coleridges were a decidedly Liberal family.

Mildred's parents had long been concerned about their daughter's fragility. Her brothers would later tell the world she was a spoiled hypochondriac. George Ernest Herman, the leading gynaecologist of the day (who did not treat Mildred) would have called it neurasthenia. "Women whose nervous systems are weak notice trifling symptoms, and go to doctors more readily than women who are strong."[9] Mildred's headaches, nervousness, peevishness, sensitivity to noise and light, emotional swings etc. were typical.[10] Victorian doctors believed "nervous disorders" were hereditary. Those who knew the family would have agreed. "The eccentricity of character which distinguished Samuel Taylor Coleridge would appear to have descended to some of his posterity." This has been well-chronicled in the lives of the great poet and his children.[11] There were similar issues in Mildred's direct line; her (paternal) grandmother is worthy of mention. John Taylor married a clergyman's daughter, Mary Buchanan. By all accounts, she was a difficult woman.

> From the first year of her married life to the end of her days she was an invalid, a real, and, what was worse for herself and others, an imaginary sufferer. Nervous and highly-strung, she made life extremely difficult to an over-taxed, over-conscientious husband ... she was neither a happy nor a happy-making woman.[12]

Of her four children, two, John Duke (Mildred's father) and (Maymie, her favourite aunt), were throughout their lives susceptible to breakdowns. In his years on the bench, Lord Coleridge's frequent absences were subject to comment. Sudden attacks of lumbago were commonly blamed. Many professional men, under stress, were thought to be particularly susceptible. They worked and suffered until a breaking point, usually leading to a physical event, such as the stabbing back pains of lumbago. Bed rest and, if possible, a change of air, were the best thing for it.[13] There was no curing tonic; the famous Dr. Treves once said, "You cannot pour strength down the esophagus."

In upper class women, like Mildred, such complaints were often grouped under the heading of hysteria.[14] Little was known but much was suggested about women of Mildred's age, moving through puberty into young adulthood. Victorian doctors worried about those girls who over-worked during their formative gynecological years. "What Nature spends in one direction, she must economise in another direction," wrote Dr. Maudsley, the leading "alienist" of the time.[15] A woman who gave herself over to strenuous studies would find her sexual and reproductive organs atrophying, her "pelvic power" diminished or destroyed, and her fate one of "sexlessness and disease." This repression of sexual feelings could be a cause for hysteria. Dr. Herman, again, warned that a girl inheriting a weak nervous system might easily be spoilt by over indulgence and idleness. Such precocious girls were too often encouraged by their parents in books and arts "to force her brain and neglect her body."[16] As a younger man in the House of Commons, Coleridge had worked closely with the liberal writer and MP, John Stuart Mill. In his book, *The Subjection of Women*, Mill also worried for the girls raised as "hot-house plants."

Mildred's mother was very concerned and fashioned a plan. On her behalf, John Duke consulted Thomas Huxley, the eminent scientist. Huxley also had a daughter, younger and, by accounts, prettier than Mildred, but similarly shy and "depressive." Perhaps Huxley would have some advice. In his letter to Huxley, Coleridge explained that his wife "thinks that without letting [Mildred] know the object (which we do not want to do), she (Lady C) could act for you." For starters, what should they be looking for? Huxley's reply and any results of his second-hand diagnoses do not survive.[17]

John Duke would attribute some of his daughter's issues to what he called her "somewhat over-trained brain."[18] Regardless, Mildred's intensive habit of reading and study gave rise to a more tangible medical issue: her vision. By 1868, it had become a serious concern. Mildred wrote to her mother, "[my eyes] are rather blinder than usual & I had a wee return of the pain over them yesterday." They talked of "double-seeing" but the exact nature of Mildred's problem cannot be stated. Her parents consulted with two of London's leading oculists, William Bowman and George Critchett, ophthalmic surgeons known for their work with cataracts.[19] Just the descriptions of Victorian cataract surgery were terrifying; although chloroform had replaced crushed ice as a sedative. Mildred underwent several operations. At one point, she wrote her grandfather, "I never had such a bad operation" and it left her wanting to "tear my eye out." Sadly, there was little improvement. John Duke wrote to his father, "Sweet Mil, I fear, will be no better. Poor darling, it makes my heart sink."[20] Mildred wore thick spectacles all her life. She was quite self-conscious about her eyes and her eyeglasses. One evening, she and her mother attended a diplomatic assembly at the Gladstone home in Carlton House Terrace. She wrote to her grandfather, "I did not want to go, for those things are so confusing to me, I can see nothing & am in danger of blindly charging against some great swell. But Papa wished it and I got through it somehow."[21]

Three weeks after stumbling about the Gladstones' drawing

room, Mildred would face a much greater challenge. Her essential presentation at court would take place in the Queen's Drawing Room at Buckingham Palace on 10 March 1869. Mildred had turned 21 the previous November. Typically, a girl was presented to court after her eighteenth birthday but too much cannot be read into Mildred's tardy presentation. In December, her father had joined Gladstone's cabinet and received his knighthood. The daughter of Sir John Duke Coleridge could now dare present herself at court, to be introduced to the monarch by her mother, newly styled as Lady Coleridge. Unmarried, Mildred wore the required headdress with two white feathers in her hair. In procession, the invited ladies shuffled through a series of unheated rooms. When at last it came Mildred's turn, a page took command of her train and spread the fabric with practiced care. A card was handed to the Lord Chamberlain. "Your Majesty, Miss Mildred Mary Coleridge, presented by her mother, Lady Coleridge."[22] Once in the "Presence Chamber," Mildred faced the daunting curtsey. A bow practiced at home and so gracefully executed under mamma's eyes was no easy physical act when fully gowned. Her "lameness" notwithstanding, Mildred apparently curtseyed without incident. Even with a tedious line of a hundred such ladies passing before her, the Queen likely took note of this young lady. She knew Mildred's father was an associate of that hateful man, Gladstone, who had just vanquished her favourite, Mr. Disraeli.[23] But there was no time for political chat or gossip. Others were waiting, the line moved along.

Mildred was "out." All the "lady's" books proclaimed this as a most important day for any young woman. "She has been emancipated from the dullness of domesticity and the thralldom of the schoolroom." She may now enter the round of balls, concerts, and other gaieties, "which will play so large a part in her life." But the gaieties would have to wait, as Mildred's eyes continued to trouble her. That fall, Mildred and her mother went to Paris for more consultations (M. Desmarres was the cataracts specialist) but Mildred returned only with yet another new pair of eyeglasses, the lenses were blue as the latest science recommended. The French doctors thought Mildred's "general health" was the greater concern and recommended "she is to be out of all excitement and not in a town." Charlotte Yonge thought the trip had been a failure and it was "very sad for (Mildred) and Jane both." Let others worry; Mildred was not complaining. She began 1870 writing to her grandfather, "No one could possibly have a happier life or lot in life than mine is."

Her presentation at court had started an unofficial clock. It was generally thought a young woman from a good family should find a husband no longer than three seasons after coming out. It wasn't as if Mildred was hidden away in a room. "Sir John Duke and Lady Coleridge and Miss Coleridge" were regularly seen in the social columns attending teas, receptions, and balls. "Gentlemen, as a rule, are always ready to make new friends and acquaintances; like butterflies, they like to flit from flower to flower among the pretty faces." She was not conventionally attractive; she was also shy, lame, and wore prominent eyeglasses. Mildred could dance; she much enjoyed the *Sir Roger de Coverley*, the dance for eight couples apparently mandatory in today's Victorian period mini-series. Her most frequent partners were her brothers. At dinner, she could well converse with the man to either side but young ladies were warned, "if interrogated upon any subject with which they are acquainted, they should modestly show their knowledge." Her parents entertained regularly but it was generally an older crowd at Sussex Square. One evening, Mildred and Butterfield, the architect, got away from the group to have a private "confab." She said he became "quite affectionate." Nothing came of it, the "austere bachelor" never married.[24]

If her letters are indicative, Mildred had the usual interest in young men. As a girl of 17, while visiting a friend, Mildred wrote her mother about one young gentleman who paid a social call. He was "such a handsome man with a fine head but he has not yet spoken once so I don't know what he is like." Another time, at Heath's Court, "a nice young American" was brought round for a visit. She wrote to her father, he "is extremely nice! Rather handsome too."

Mildred was hardly alone. "The proportion of girls who not only never marry but never receive an offer is now very great."[25] No offers had come her way. Why was that? Despite everything, she was a baron's daughter possessing a famous name and good expectations. Her father's income at the bar (by then, approaching £20,000 p.a.) was among the highest in the profession. In 1873, he took a pay cut to become Chief Justice of the Court of Common Pleas, but the appointment brought with it a place on the Privy Council and a peerage, the first Baron Coleridge. Her father, however, was an additional challenge for any young suitor. John Duke Coleridge's reputation for haughtiness, severity, and sarcasm would certainly dissuade all but the boldest junior members of the bar from daring to approach his only daughter. Perhaps a suitable country curate might have been flushed out for Mildred amongst the rustic parishes around Ottery. Would such a curate have the income to offer Mildred a suitable home and establishment? Unlikely, however an ambitious curate might well know that, in time, marriage to a peer's daughter was the temporal path to a better "living.".

At his father's death in 1876, John Duke inherited Heath's Court. We have a view of life in the Coleridge household from a visitor to Ottery in the late 1870s. Lord Coleridge was a devoted letter writer (as we shall see) and had numerous American correspondents. Invitations to visit England were generously offered and regularly accepted. Richard Henry Dana III, son of the author of *Two Years before the Mast*, came to Heath's Court in September 1875, enjoying his first exposure to "delicious Devonshire cream." Of more interest were his opinions of his host and hostess. Lady Coleridge was "quiet and reticent... she hasn't much small talk." But Lord Coleridge was an impressive man: "The most striking thing about him to me is his fine shaped head and broad forehead, over deep-set, large, and handsome eyes. His nose is a trifle long, his upper lip short, with a beautifully moulded chin and mouth and very expressive lips, and he has an almost boyish freshness of complexion, though he is nearly fifty-five years old." Dana enjoyed the family ambiance; after dinner, "Bernard and Mildred played piano duets." Miss Coleridge was twenty-eight.[26]

1  "I hope she is better:": Yonge to John Taylor Coleridge, 27 Sep 1851, *CFP* Add MS 86206.
2  Coleridge childhood: Bernard Lord Coleridge, *This for Remembrance*, (1925).
3  Jane Fortescue Coleridge (nee Seymour), wife of John Duke Coleridge; 1847-1877. *CFP* Add MS 85927-85929.
4  "Dear old maid aunt:" Annie Thomas, *A London Season*, Volume 2 (1879) 97.
5  Goslings-Barnacle: Julia Courtney, "The Barnacle: A Manuscript Magazine of the 1860s," from *The Girl's Own: Cultural Histories of the Anglo-American Girl, 1830-1915* (2010) edited by Claudia Nelson, Lynne Vallone. For more on Yonge, Christabel Coleridge, *Charlotte Mary Yonge, Her Life & Letters* (1903). Mildred's Gosling papers, etc. CFP Add MS 86151-52.
6  Lameness: Yonge to John Duke Coleridge, 23 May 1861, *Letters of Charlotte Yonge*, Newcastle.edu.au.
7  "Recollections of Sophia Lonsdale" (1936)
8  Yonge to Frances Mary Peard (undated 1865/6) *Letters of Charlotte Yonge*, Newcastle.edu.au.
9  George Ernest Herman, *Diseases of Women: A Clinical Guide to Their Diagnosis and Treatment* (1907)
10  Herman described symptoms closely matching Mildred's complaints: "Often the patient complains of giddiness and faintness. The power of accommodation of the eye is weakened and the retina is more sensitive, and hence there is asthenopia. The patient says things swim before her eyes; she cannot read or sew in the evening; she cannot bear a strong light. (*Diseases*, 16.)

11  Coleridge insanity: JF Nisbet, *The Insanity of Genius and the General Inequality of Human Faculty* (1893) Lady Eastlake wrote to Miss Cobbe, "a Coleridge mind thrown off its balance will account for much." 13 January 85, Sheldon ed., *Eastlake Letters*.

12  Lord Coleridge's mother: *Life & Correspondence*, Vol. 1, 11.

13  "A Manual of Medical Diagnosis" (1870) quoted in Nick Howlett, *The Medical Casebook of Sherlock Holmes and Doctor Watson* (2023) 406ff. "In many cases, it is one of the forms of hysteria ... nothing can be more deplorable than the permanent mischief which has frequently ensued from confining such persons to a recumbent posture."

14  "A nervous disorder in which the nervous system is deranged without the existence of any organic disease." Wilks, *Diseases of the Nervous System,* 362.

15  Maudsley: Elaine Showalter - The Female Malady - *Women, Madness, and English Culture* (1985). Maudsley quoted in, Lisa Appignanesi, Mad, Bad, and Sad: A History of Women and the Mind Doctors (2009)

16  Education for women: "Sex in Mind Education," *The Lancet*, 9 May 1874. "The best system of education for woman has not yet have been devised; but the worst system is that which, in attempting to improve the mind, eventuates in the destruction or the perversion of the sex." For more, see Janet Oppenheim, *Our Shattered Nerves: Doctors, Patients and Depression in Victorian England* (1991)

17  Coleridge to T.H. Huxley, 19 December 1869. The Huxley Papers 12.276 Archives Imperial College London.

18  Over-trained brain, *CFP* Add MS 85915.

19  Eye doctors, *CFP* Add MS 85880. George Critchett & son, were leaders in surgery on the eye and invented new surgical instruments such as Critchett's cataract knife, Critchett's scissors, and Critchett's fixation forceps.

20  *CFP* Add MS 85915.

21  [Mildred's] Letters to her grandfather John Taylor Coleridge, her grandmother Mary Coleridge, and her aunt Mary Frances Keble Coleridge, CFP Add MS 85973.

22  Presentation experience: "A Drawing Room in the Reign of Queen Victoria," *Time: A Monthly Miscellany*, (1880) 43-48.

23  Disraeli (Tory, of course) never cared for Coleridge; he referred to him as a "silver-tongued mediocrity."

24  Butterfield: "He never married and lived austerely in Bloomsbury in grim discomfort, without carpets." Stephen Coleridge, *Memories* (1913) 83.

25  "Matrimonial News," *The Spectator*, 5 November 1870, 11.

26  Dana's visit: Dana, Hospitable England in The Seventies - *The Diary of a Young American 1875-1876* (1921).

# 3. YOUR DEAR MILLIE

LORD COLERIDGE'S MARRIAGE was a happy one and he was the unchallenged *Paterfamilias*. Reputedly one of the great talkers in all London, he easily dominated the table at home and out.[1] To a fault. "It is sometimes a little sad to know that people who can talk well miss, as the Lord Chief Justice did, the point of conversation, which is that it is a game which must be played by more than one." Beyond his professions of politics and the law, Lord Coleridge knew and hosted most of the luminaries of literary and intellectual life: Arnold, Jowett, Newman, Browning, and their ilk. His wife, Lady Coleridge, on such occasions, would likely say nothing at all. If the subject sometime veered toward art, she might offer a comment or two. Her great interest was portraiture. Her sketches of her children, including Mildred, were hung in the Royal Academy. No less a critic than John Ruskin thought Lady Coleridge's portrait of Cardinal Newman was the best done, much better than the one by Millais (that home-wrecker.)[2]

In late January 1878, Lady Coleridge attended the Winter Exhibition at the Grosvenor Gallery on New Bond Street. The next morning, she complained of a sore throat. Soon, "pleuritic" symptoms of an ominous nature developed and despite the attention of some of the finest physicians in the city, she sank and died in the early morning of February 6. She was just 54. Her death was "as sudden as it was sad," Only the day before, Lord Coleridge had advised the parties in the case before him that he would need time to address "a private matter." What was thought to be a simple winter cold proved fatal in less than a week.

Lady Coleridge's body was shipped to Devon by a special train of the London & South Western railway. From Sidmouth Junction, a local train bore her body one last time down the Otter Valley to the station west of the town. Ottery itself was completely shuttered. "Seldom has a deeper, more sorrowful feeling of bereavement been felt outside the family circle." Her ladyship was well-beloved. "There was no pride in her," a local told the papers, "She was a lady you could speak to." Few would have said the same of her husband, Lord Coleridge. "He affected a humility which some say he did not possess."

The rain held off. Still, the twelfth of February 1878 was dark and cold when they buried Jane, Lady Coleridge. John Duke, supported by Mildred, his eldest child and only daughter, led the mourners two-by-two, as they walked the short distance from Heath's Court to St. Mary's. Respectful Otteregians stood caps in hand as the mourning party entered the ancient church. As the coffin was carried in, the choir sang "Our Heads are Bowed with Woe." Lord Coleridge's brother-in-law, the Bishop of Oxford, presided. Jane was laid to rest in the Coleridge vault, "near the ivied wall over which is Heath's Court."

Tributes and condolences poured in to the family. One of the most touching came from the Rev. Richard Church, Dean of St. Paul's, who eulogised Lady Coleridge in the *Guardian*:

> She was so singularly unworldly. Guileless, simple, modest—with great gifts, and frankly delighting in their exercise and their achievements, she had the power to make her home and its daily life bright, animated, pure; and this, apart from any personal thoughts about herself, seemed her work for this world. And she shone in it.

A longtime friend of the Coleridges, Dean Church made a final and keen observation, "In (Jane's) conversation, there was ... an almost timid and self-retiring humility, half afraid of having spoken too boldly or too much." To some, Jane was altogether "un-Coleridgean." Mildred was devoted to her mother and would also show the same "timid and self-retiring humility" to a troubling degree

The Coleridge family returned to Ottery in September to dedicate a memorial to Lady Coleridge. Butterfield had finished his renovations at Sussex Square and Lord Coleridge next employed him to expand and modernize Heath's Court. But all work ceased on that job until the memorial was completed. The church organ was relocated from the south tower transept, and there beneath a five-light east window, room was made for a recumbent effigy sculpted by Frederick Thrupp of the Marylebone Road. New windows were installed and the surrounding walls were decorated in Butterfield's trademark mosaics. The memorial read:

> To the fair and holy memory of Jane Fortescue, Baroness Coleridge, her husband dedicates this marble, thankful for his happiness, sorrowing for his loss, steadfastly hoping, through God's mercy, to meet her, when the night is past, in the perfect and unending day.

The project cost £2100 and was paid for entirely by Lord Coleridge. He also used the opportunity to remove several shabby cottages adjoining the church "to improve the area."

The memorial service for Lady Coleridge was a moving one. The family grief was still fresh. John Duke's sister, Alethea, married to Bishop Mackarness of Oxford, was thankful Mildred would be there for him. "Your dear Milly must be, I am sure, a comfort to you [with] her gentleness and forgetfulness of self. I only hope she is not overstraining herself in her thought for others." And what of Mildred's own grief? Among the letters of condolence was one from a Mrs. Thomas Bishop, "I trust Maymie is with darling Mildred, we so much fear for her after this great tension of mind and body. May God support and comfort you all, my dearest friend." (Mrs. Bishop will soon feature in the Mildred drama.) When Miss Yonge visited Heath's Court in the autumn, she reported, "I found Mildred pretty well, but her father very poorly though he seemed to be getting better."

Following his wife's death, Lord Coleridge instructed his solicitors to draw up a new will.[3] Lady Coleridge had no particular fortune and left several small bequests, paintings, and personal items to her children. Lord Coleridge, on the other hand, was a wealthy man; he anticipated serving on the bench long enough to receive an annual pension of £4000. His fortune from his successful days at the bar was considerable. He wished to make the right provision for Mildred and "the dear boys."

Lord Coleridge's eldest son and heir, Bernard, neither physically nor socially ever matched his father's standing in the world. He was a "mild radical" politically and thought by some to be a dry stick.

Lady Coleridge with her two oldest sons, Bernard on her left and Stephen on her right. The photograph of Lady Coleridge is from a *carte de visite* in the Coleridge family papers.

Stephen Coleridge, the second of Lord Coleridge's three "dear boys" was frequently a trial for his father. Stephen early gave up the law and turned to (luckless) money-making schemes.

Bernard, the eldest boy, was now 27. He would inherit the peerage, Sussex Square, and Heath's Court. Bernard married his first cousin, a daughter of the Bishop of Oxford. They had one daughter and a second child was expected. Bernard had followed his father to Eton and then to Oxford, although he enrolled at Trinity, where he captained his college rowing club. He was an avid walker and a vehement foe of all "blood sports." Bernard was studious and well-read and marked out for the law. He was called to the bar at Middle Temple in 1877 and as a junior barrister, again like his father, he sought to make his name on the western circuit. He even moved into his father's old Temple chambers in King's Bench Walk. Yet Bernard never had the imposing courtroom presence of his father. His voice was never as melodious as the pater's, nor did he have the physical stature, standing only five-foot-nine.[4] No one expected Bernard ever to reach his father's standing as an "exquisite ornament" of society. In truth, Bernard was thought to be a dry stick. He had an eye for politics and had given some well-received speeches with a "radical" flavour in Exeter where he hoped one day to stand for his father's old constituency.

Stephen Coleridge was 24. He was, by far, the handsomest member of the family. But unlike his sister and elder brother, he had no particular scholarly aspirations. He struggled as a schoolboy and was sent out to be tutored in Honiton by "a monster of cruelty named Izod."[5] There would be no Eton for Stephen. Instead, he went to a little-known school at Bradfield and then to Cambridge, another break with the family track. He flirted briefly with the bar but withdrew, choosing to follow his new interest: the theatre - or, at least, the leading lady of the day, Ellen Terry. Stephen became so ardent in his attentions to Miss Terry, sending flowers, waiting at the stage door, and the like, that she soon employed him, *in her words*, as her "toy boy." He watched her son, ran errands, and fended off rival importuners. Terry was then "married" to a hard-drinking lout, but Stephen helped her conspiratorially manage her other affairs, employing a system of coded letters. She said he was "a naughty boy."[6] All of this backstage drama was expensive and "Steevie," to the great frustration of his father, had no income. But "Steevie" was full of plans, the latest to get a business going in Cyprus, the Mediterranean island newly "discovered" by investors.

Finally, Gilbert Coleridge, the youngest child, was finishing out his difficult years at Eton.[7] He was 19. A delicate, musical child, he had not done well at school either. He remembered Eton favourably enough, however, to write a chatty memoir, *Eton in the 70s*. The book was full of the usual jolly recollections of tutors and caning, "applied smartly to the tight trousers of a bent figure."[8]

In his Lordship's new will, provisions were made for the three boys and any future families of their own, but what about Mildred? Motherless at 31, spinsterhood seemed to be her fate.

1  A great talker: J.H. Balfour Browne, Recollections Literary & Political (1917), 134.
2  Lady Jane: her Newman portrait was much praised, "the best rendering we have seen of that face," The Times, 1 May 1875, 12.
3  The 1879 will as pertains to Mildred: Lord Coleridge left her £12000 (in effect, £300 a year for 40 years) in trust for her sole and separate use for life without power of anticipation. If she encumbered or aliened the life interest it was to go over. She could, in her will, appoint a life interest for any husband who survived her. (This was written two years before she met Adams). Her father also left another £5000 for her absolute use during his lifetime. If she died before him, that too would lapse. The combination of the two big numbers clearly gave Adams the figure of £17000.
4  Bernard had a curious physique: "He is not a very tall man but he has the legs of a very tall man ... he has a very distinct superfluity of leg in proportion to body." Exeter/Plymouth Gazette 29 March 1887, 4.
5  Stephen wrote about his father in Famous Victorians I Have Known (1928). For his childhood, see Memories (1913)
6  "Toy boy," see Michael Holroyd, A Strange Eventful History: The Dramatic Lives of Ellen Terry, Henry Irving, and Their Remarkable Families (2010)
7  On Whitsun Monday 1878, Mildred wrote to her father with news Gilbert had failed at Eton; she recommended he be pulled from the school. He stuck it out. CFP Add MS 85973.
8  Gilbert Coleridge, Eton in the Seventies (1912). Arthur Duke Coleridge (q.v.) had written Eton in the Forties. (1898).

# 4. THE HOMEBIRD AT SUSSEX SQUARE

MRS. MARIA HAWEIS enjoyed a late Victorian vogue as an expert in feminine beauty, dress and decorum – not necessarily the field for a clergyman's wife. In her 1878 book, *The Art of Beauty*, Mrs. Haweis separated the young ladies moving in proper Victorian society into two classes - the Visible and the Invisible. Mildred Coleridge, rather proudly, would have seated herself among the latter. Here is the author's description of an "invisible" spinster:

> She is not pretty and never was. She has never been engaged and seems to think she has only to accept cheerfully her role of old maid of the family. It is no doubt her destiny never to be cared for by anybody and she was intended for one of the useful ones. So, she goes in for being fearfully useful. She is an admirable daughter. She despises amusements as 'nice for the young ones but rather frivolous.' She wears her soft brown hair scraped down on each side of her face and prefers tidily high unfashionable dresses in the evening. She thinks of everyone's comfort and happiness but her own and refuses to dance.[1]

But for her enthusiasm for the odd country dance, Mildred was spot on for the category.

There was no date certain when an unmarried young lady passed over into the dreaded category of spinster. The thirtieth birthday, however, was certainly an ominous one. In the simplest mathematical terms, once all the marriageable young men and women were paired off, there was a surplus of women left alone. This was especially true among the upper classes and the aristocracy.

The mid Victorians exercised a great deal of thought and worry over what to do with "the odd women" or "the redundant women." Deportation schemes were organized and financed to send excess females out to the Antipodes, South Africa, India, or the Americas. The goal was to export as many as 10,000 women a year. This was all well and good for those women hoping to find a mate in the goldfields, or live a life in service with some American family. Still, the fact remained about 30% of Englishwomen in the upper classes would never marry. In 1862, Miss Frances Power Cobbe published a much-discussed article "What to do with our Old Maids?"[2]

Miss Cobbe was speaking directly to the plight of women like Mildred Coleridge, "the condition and prospects of women of the upper classes who remain unmarried." Too many women in Mildred's situation were pressed by their family or driven by the fear of living alone into making a "marriage of interest," an arranged marriage for money, position, or simply to have a home. Miss Cobbe insisted the assumption that marriage was the sole destiny for such women must be abandoned. Let the doors of the professions, the arts and music, be opened to these unmarried, well-educated women (like Mildred). To allow these women to assume their full role in society would "make the condition of celibacy as little injurious as possible." The single life for such women could yet be "free and happy." In 1862, Miss Cobbe was well ahead of her time. She and women like her were ridiculed as "the shrieking sisterhood." The true era of the "New Woman" would not arrive until the 1890s but by the early 1880s women were pressing for "constructive roles in society."

In fairness to Lord Coleridge, on most social issues, he held rather advanced views for the time. He was a strong Liberal voice in

Parliament. In the Commons, Coleridge tried (unsuccessfully) to reform the law of primogeniture, by which a nobleman's title and estates passed – in the normal order of things – to his eldest surviving son. Coleridge called it "a gross injustice to widows, daughters, and younger sons." On one of the great issues of the 1870s – the Married Women's Property Act – Coleridge was an early advocate for the protection of a wife's income and fortune that traditionally fell under the control of her husband. In the House of Lords in 1877, he rose to describe himself as the father of a daughter: "There is not one of your Lordships who would, on the marriage of his daughter, leave her unprotected, and to the tender mercies of the English Common Law."[3] This rhetorical record would be of some interest when Lord Coleridge's theories met the practicalities within his own family.

After the death of Lady Coleridge, the expectations for Mildred were to remain at home and care for her father. The eldest unmarried daughter's role was "to enliven, to cheer, to amuse, the latter moments of her parent's declining age."[4] She would also take on the responsibility of managing the household or households, as the Coleridges lived grandly in both London and Devon. The Coleridge establishment at Sussex Square was a large one with a dozen servants. Additionally, the family moved back and forth between London and Heath's Court according to the time-honoured "vacations" built in to the legal calendar. Mildred would command the servants in both

A rare photograph of Mildred, in her twenties, from a *carte de visite* found in the Coleridge family papers.

settings and work with "cook" on meal planning. Her father's friends were numerous and he entertained frequently.[5] The dining room at Sussex Square could be set for 24. Mildred would assume her late mother's place opposite her father "across the mahogany" in the dining room. These were duties that should not burden her brothers. Mildred was perfectly typecast to fill the role of what a modern feminist writer describes as the Victorian practice of "immolating daughters on the altar of their siblings' careers and their elderly parents' needs."[6]

To be sure, with servants at her call and in two very elegant residences, Mildred lived a much more comfortable life than the usual "old maid daughter." Lord Coleridge provided her with a yearly allowance of £80 in "pin money" for her own needs.[7] This little fund obviated the need for Mildred to run to her father any time she wanted a new bonnet; she could use it to "deck her person suitably to her rank." Plus, Mildred would be a very wealthy woman at her father's death. As Mildred understood her father's will – and this would be much disputed – her inheritance would be nearing £17,000. Invested "in the consols," it would afford her £300 a year. At the time, a working family in London could live "comfortably" on 80 quid.

There was never any question as to Mildred's ability to plan a menu or make the needed household arrangements. She'd observed her mother do it for years. The fiddly bits at Sussex Square were all capably in hand: Westaway, the butler, Hannah Knott, the housekeeper, and Mrs. Butler, the cook, were longtime family servants. And so, Mildred settled into her new responsibilities in her father's home. Bernard and his young family moved out of Sussex Square, but not far away, taking a small house in Paddington's Talbot Square. Stephen and Gilbert were still living at home.

The family letters reveal, at first, Mildred delighted in her new role. As Mrs. Haweis would have predicted, Mildred made herself "fearfully useful." She fretted over her father's always precarious health, especially his use of opium for his lumbago.[8] "The fact is he devastates himself with pills till diarrhea sets in! So stupid of him & so wrong."[9] She became her father's sounding board regarding the two younger boys. Gilbert struggled at Eton and Lord Coleridge despaired of the boy's chances ever to succeed at Oxford. But Mildred was more hopeful, "He is not such a silly as Stephen about young ladies, you know. Too childish for that."

Lord Coleridge's many friends also grew to rely on Mildred's domestic skills. Matthew Arnold, prior to an upcoming visit, asked Lord Coleridge if Mildred could find a bed for Mrs. Arnold's maid who'd be coming. On another occasion, Cardinal Newman wrote to his Lordship suddenly, "Can you lodge me on Tuesday? And, should I, in the midst of my jobs, find myself in want of food, would Mildred give me something?" Of course, selfless, reliable, Mildred would set a humble table for the prelate.

It helped greatly that father and daughter were quite simpatico. Lord Coleridge was a serious man who did not show his best in the frivolous "fashionable entertainments" common to London "Society." On that subject, Mildred was right in line. During one August vacation, Mildred accompanied her father to Scotland where they stayed at New Hailes, a fine country house outside Edinburgh. The other guests included a couple of pretty 19-year-old girls, Miss Carry Millais, the painter's daughter, and Miss Ethel Playfair, daughter of a wealthy Liberal MP. Mildred, more than a decade older, thought the duo of giggly, flirtatious young ladies, all done up in the latest finery, were "very affected" and their conversation was "indecent." Her father fully agreed, she reported. He thought the girls were insufferable and Mildred worried he might "explode" at some point. Mildred wrote to Aunt Maymie it was all she could do to remain civil. "I wish I had the pluck to 'go in' at girls of that sort. I haven't, can't, or don't." To be sure, Mildred and her father were delighted to leave New Hailes to stay with Matthew Arnold in the Lake District where the conversation with the Victorian "sage" was certain to be of more consequential matters. Father and daughter saw life very much the same.[10]

Mildred and her father were not inseparable. He was frequently absent on his assize travels. The Coleridge "network" was a wide one. Perhaps Mildred's dearest friend was a younger second cousin, Mary Elizabeth Coleridge. Mary's father was Arthur Duke Coleridge, who trained as a lawyer but served in the legal bureaucracy. He was better known as an amateur tenor and organist. It was Arthur who taught Mildred the piano and who recognized her abilities. He introduced her to Sterndale Bennett and others who furthered her playing. Mildred often stayed at "Uncle" Arthur's home in Cromwell Place. Mildred was fourteen years older than her cousin; Mary was another delicate and shrinking child, but highly intelligent. Like Mildred, she grew to be tall, reed-like, and pale. Mildred would tutor Mary in languages, especially Italian, and, when Mary was old enough, the two toured Europe together. They were very close.

Travel abroad was always stressful for a woman of Mildred's delicate health. In June 1879, for example, Mildred accompanied Dean Church and his wife on their annual holiday in the Alps. It did not go well. The trip began in Pontresina amid the "wonderfully fragrant pine forests" in the Engadines. The dry, bracing, glacial air at nearly 6000 feet was touted as "very invigorating to invalids." Mrs. Church had promised to write Aunt Maymie regularly; she reported Mildred seemed happy. "I suppose she never has much colour but she is not so pale as usual." Meanwhile, Mildred was also writing to her aunt with the real story. She fell on one of their walks and twisted her elbow. She was also "crippled up with rheumatism." Pontresina was unpleasant:

"the horrible 'bracing' atmosphere made life an effort as it always does to me."[11] The guidebooks did warn visitors to be aware of the signs of mountain sickness: a tightening in the chest, palpitation of the heart, headache, giddiness, sleeplessness. Which was exactly how Mildred explained it to Maymie. In a letter marked PRIVATE, Mildred reported "an attack of the miserable giddiness and powerlessness for which I know nothing but keeping quiet is any good." In most tourists, these symptoms are temporary. "In some rare cases, however, they are so obstinate, that it becomes necessary for the sufferers to go away to the lowlands." The Churches were looking forward to seeing Zermatt, even higher in the mountains, but they graciously cut short their holiday at Mildred's request. She pleaded with Maymie not to tell her father. Mildred realised she was being a "drag and a marplot" on the friendly Churches but she could not bear the conditions any longer. The travellers returned to England. Mrs. Church reported to Maymie that she finally had to tell Mildred, in candour, "You are not fit to travel, my dear. I must say you will have to be a homebird."[12]

Mildred went to Heath's Court to recover from her "holiday." Arnold, who was again visiting Lord Coleridge, wrote to his wife Mildred "appeared all the better" for her travels. Everyone was always solicitous of Mildred.[13]

The Coleridges ritually stayed at Heath's Court from August to late October, returning to London when the courts reopened, and then it was back to Devon for Christmas and the New Year. When in London, Lord Coleridge attended the required law dinners and political functions but he had not yet fully re-entered society. After the period of mourning, the word was made known that for any purely social evenings, Lord Coleridge would accept no invitations not including his daughter. Stephen recalled his father would toss the invitations across the table to Mildred, declaring "I shall not go." She would write the required note. Soon, it was noted regularly the "Lord Chief Justice and the Honourable Miss Coleridge" were "among the company present" at many dinners and soirees. "At homes" resumed. Father and daughter were adjusting to their new routine of life. But Steevie was coming home.

Stephen Coleridge was returning to Sussex Square, accompanied by his young wife and their infant son. Over the scandal-marked years ahead, much of Mildred's correspondence with her family was destroyed. Curiously, however, the Coleridge papers include several letters between father and daughter discussing Steevie's imminent homecoming. The second son's life was ever full of interest, and his sudden marriage was typical. In March 1879, after a brief courtship, Stephen was engaged to marry Geraldine Lushington, from a most respectable Devon family of achievement in the church and bar. Just two weeks later, they were married at Christ Church, Down Street, a backwater sanctuary, tucked in a Mayfair lane near Shepherd's Market. The alleged reason for the hasty nuptials was Stephen's imminent sailing for Peru. His Cypriot venture had gone nowhere. Stephen was now keen on seeking his fortune in trade in the southern hemisphere.

Stephen and his new bride sailed for Lima, a voyage requiring a passage around the notorious Cape Horn. The ship was loaded with freight, including twenty upright grand pianos, which Stephen conceived to be in great demand in Peru. When the would-be merchant prince arrived, however, he found Peru at war with her larger and more powerful neighbour to the south, Chile. The reasons for the conflict are obscure but it was no less sanguinary. The British party was prevailed upon to remain aboard their ship, their cargo made useful only as barricades from the odd rifle shot. When word of this far-off war reached London, Lord Salisbury, the Foreign Secretary, actually offered to send a British warship to rescue Stephen and his party. It was not necessary. Stephen was able to get everyone on a departing ship, by way of New York, putting them back in London sometime in early 1880. He also sent a telegram home announcing the birth of his son on 5 November, in Lima. Certainly, given the perilous voyage and the warlike conditions found upon arrival, it is entirely possible Geraldine delivered the boy two months prematurely. Readers are free to entertain alternative theories. Regardless, Stephen, Geraldine and the baby were coming home to Sussex Square.[14]

Mildred was not pleased at news of the impending arrival of "the Peruvians," as she now dubbed them. Stephen was long a source of friction in the Coleridge home. He quarreled frequently with his father, usually over money. His Lordship more than once grumpily satisfied Stephen's creditors. As the young man was steaming home, Lord Coleridge was away in Lancashire. Mildred hectored her father about Stephen's homecoming. She urged him to be strong. "I think a firm hand must be made at the outset. And while they come to the house, we couldn't have a divided empire of course." Mildred feared her father would inevitably give in to Stephen. "It will end by you telling me you were 'too hard upon the dear fellow.'" Of course, Stephen could not be turned away and Mildred promised to have Sussex Square ready. "You always do see the very best of Steevie, he doesn't show his other side to you, and she is such a pretty little thing. I daresay we shall get on very well; I will certainly do my best to make them comfortable."

On 6 February 1880, "the Peruvians" docked at Liverpool and proceeded straight to London. Mildred informed her still-absent father, "The travellers arrived last night looking very much like themselves and not at all embarrassed. They have a French nurse for the baby. I think we shall do very well." Mildred's use of the word "embarrassed" would seem to indicate the child's early birth date had not escaped her attention. Maymie came up to London to give Mildred some moral support but it only took two days before Mildred was grousing to her father: "Steevie's talk is quite preposterous & what they say of their plans is perfectly mad but we shall 'fold our hands' and let them talk till you come home." Stephen attempted to mollify his tetchy sister by asking her to be the boy's godmother, an offer she accepted. But she could not abide her brother's indolence and frivolity. "Half past eleven is Steevie's time for starting now-a-days with a hansom to the door." The Peruvian venture proved another disaster resulting only in more debt. At this time, Mildred lost an expensive gold chain and her father offered to replace it but she replied "With the Stephens on your hands. I could not let you." The cache of letters ends there.[15] The problems, of course, did not.

Beyond Stephen and his mad plans to vex her, Mildred was also dealing with the new experience of the noise, smells and distractions created by an infant at Sussex Square. Mildred was always nettled by noise; disturbances of any kind brought on headaches and that giddiness feeling ("the muddlings," she called it). Stephen and Geraldine went out to the theatre two or three nights per week. Was "Aunt Mildred" supposed to watch the baby? Relations between Mildred and Geraldine became decidedly frosty. It did not help that Lord Coleridge, once back at Sussex Square, was predictably smitten with his new grandson. "Would it surprise you to know" Stephen named the boy, John Duke, to please his father? The toddler was carried out to meet the distinguished guests who came to dine. Soon, 80-year-old Cardinal Newman was writing his old friend Lord Coleridge, asking to be remembered to Mildred and "dear Johnny." It had been a tiring ordeal and Mildred – with Maymie – were thankful to escape to the continent, take in the passion play at Oberammergau and enjoy the restorative Bavarian baths.

On 20 November 1880, Sir Alexander Cockburn, the Lord Chief Justice of England died at his home in Mayfair. A brilliant lawyer and jurist, Cockburn led an irregular private life.[16] There was never any doubt the only man to succeed him was Lord Coleridge. A day after Cockburn's funeral, "as almost everyone expected," the announcement was made. *The London Daily News* declared, "It can be safely affirmed that no one objects to the appointment."

In 1880, Lord Coleridge was appointed Lord Chief Justice of England. This wonderful crayon drawing was done three years earlier by his wife, Jane, Lady Coleridge. She did not live to see her husband's achievement. This sketch was used to open the second volume of his lordship's biography, published in 1905.

In the old Westminster Hall, on 1 December, with "the Hon. Mildred Mary Coleridge, his lordship's only daughter," watching from the side galleries, the new Lord Chief Justice took the oath. "I, John Duke Coleridge, do swear that I will well and truly serve our sovereign lady, Queen Victoria, in the office of Lord Chief Justice of England, and I will do right to all manner of people after the laws and usages of this realm, without fear or favour, affection or ill-will. So, help me God." It was a brief ceremony. Once again, Lord Coleridge was admired for, what observers called, his *suaviter in modo*. He looked the part. He stood 6 foot 3 inches tall, though with stooped shoulders. He was wearing his full-bottomed wig; his robes were trimmed with ermine, around his neck hung the golden chain of office. "He is one of those men, rare in the present day, who can add impressiveness to the pomp and trappings of an historic office." Answerable only to the Lord

Chancellor, he was now the highest-ranking judge under the Crown. Mildred was justly proud of her elevated father and often wished to be one of his clerks. "Oh, dear, why was I not a boy?"[17]

A happy family Christmas was spent in Ottery. Heath's Court was still under scaffolding as Mr. Butterfield was back to work on the renovations of the Coleridge seat. The family stayed with Maymie at the smaller Manor House next door. Thus, to celebrate Gilbert's 21st birthday, the festivities were moved to the Ottery Town Hall. On 28 December, the family hosted a grand ball. More than 100 guests enjoyed an excellent supper and danced well into the new day. A band played no fewer than 21 dances. The whole family was there, including Mildred. It was a wonderful evening.

The holiday gaiety was welcome, as always. But Mildred was eager to get back to London to resume her increasing workload with the Victoria Street Society, the leading campaigners to halt the practice of vivisection. The perfect world of the Coleridges was about to come apart.

1  Mrs. Maria Haweis, The Art of Beauty (1878) 276.

2  Old maids: Frances Power Cobbe, "What Shall We Do with Our Old Maids?" Fraser's Magazine, November 1862.

3  Hansard, Vol. 235, Column 72, House of Lords, MWPA (1870) Amendment Bill, Second Reading.

4  "To enliven" quoting Patrica Wakefield in Bridget Hill, Women Alone: Spinsters in England, 1660-1850 (2001), 70.

5  "It had been his habit to give one dinner-party every fortnight - generally of twenty-four people at a time." Stephen Coleridge, Digressions (1925)

6  Immolating daughters: Claudia Nelson, Daniel Nelson, Family Ties in Victorian England (2007), 108.

7  Pin money: Sally Mitchell ed, Victorian Britain: An Encyclopedia. By prenuptial agreement, an affluent husband annually provided his wife for her free use, a figure usually set at 1% of her dowry. It began in the 14th Century when pins were quite costly and sold at fairs. Husbands gave their wives money to "lay in a stock of pins for the ensuing year." Pins rapidly became cheaper and more readily available and the "pin money" was diverted to other toilette needs, although the name remained. If the reader skipped over the Note on Money, it might be helpful to read it now.

8  Opium? Diligent friction with opium liniment is often serviceable in lumbago, crick of the neck, and other local rheumatic affections. An opiate plaster is also productive of comfort in this class of cases. E J Waring, A Manual of Practical Therapeutics (1871). Of course, Samuel T. Coleridge was a "great opium-eater."

9  Lumbago: Mildred to Maymie, 16 August 1881, CFP Add MS 85973.

10  Simpatico: Mildred to Aunt Maymie, 11 August 1881, CFP Add MS 85973.

11  The Engadines were too bracing for many English visitors, "The Engadines as a Health Resort," The Lancet, 14 June 1873.

12  Mildred's travel letters, including PRIVATE in CFP Add MS 85973.

13  14 August 1879; Arnold also reported that Ottery is a "horrid little town" but the countryside "pleases and soothes me." C.Y. Lang, ed, The Letters of Matthew Arnold, 1879-84 (1996).

14  Peru: In Memories (op cit), Chapter 4, Stephen provides a full account. "The history of twenty pianos was, from first to last, diverting."

15  Mildred's letters re: "The Peruvians," etc., CFP Add MS 85972-85973.

16  The Queen refused to grant Cockburn a peerage "upon the ground of [his] notoriously bad moral character." See, The Letters of Queen Victoria, (2014) 257.

17  "Not a boy?" Mildred to her father, 2 February 1880, CFP Add MS85973

# 5. CHARLES WARREN ADAMS

There is a well understood dictum:
The more a marriage is opposed the more likely it is to occur.[1]

THE SOCIETY FOR the Protection of Animals Liable to Vivisection was formed in London in 1875. Among the founders was the aforementioned Miss Frances Power Cobbe.[2] The footsteps of Miss Cobbe can be followed through most of the reform efforts in the mid-to-late nineteenth century: housing reform, women's rights, suffrage, and more. She quickly became the leading voice of the anti-vivisection movement. For a start, she sensibly simplified the name: The Victoria Street Society (VSS). Offices were established in Victoria Street, just a short walk from Parliament.[3]

Miss Cobbe was nearly sixty. "Round and fat as a Turkish sultana and face mature and pulpy, she could have passed more easily as a jovial grandmother than a saboteur of science."[4] She used a forceful personality and her social connections

Frances Power Cobbe (1822-1904) was the unchallenged leader of the Victoria Street Society. In 1881, she hired Charles Warren Adams to be Secretary of the society. Adams enjoyed early success, especially with his book *The Coward Science*, on which he worked closely with Mildred Coleridge. How closely became the question that changed Mildred's life.

to recruit vital and influential patrons. It was a great coup to have the Earl of Shaftesbury, another giant of Victorian reform, become the society president. So powerful was his standing with the British public, it was said Lord Shaftesbury didn't join the Victoria Street Society, rather the society joined him. The vice-presidents of the society were no less illustrious: several more peers, three Bishops, Cardinal Manning, and, from the arts, Lord Tennyson and Robert Browning.

The younger Coleridges, in a brief display of unity, all showed interest in the cause. Although their roots were in Devon, the family had become quite urban. At Heath's Court, they'd be up for a good walk but they never pursued any of the local field sports. Bernard and Stephen were first to join the anti-vivisection movement; at Oxford, Gilbert founded a student chapter. Richard Dana thought the Coleridge children were, at first, far more advanced on the issue than their father. Convinced, finally, by the arguments of his children, Lord Coleridge abandoned his earlier lukewarm support and agreed to become a Vice-President of the VSS. In 1878, with her father's assent, Mildred Coleridge also joined the VSS.

With her eagerness and ample free time, Mildred quickly made her mark: she wrote several topical leaflets, including "Fair Play" and "Sham Humanity." Miss Cobbe coveted women for the cause: "if my sex has a mission of any kind, it is to soften this hard old world." Their critics claimed the movement was in the hands of sentimental women. Mildred became a valued member of the executive committee, "a small corps of enthusiasts whose gratuitous labours were the heart and soul of the movement." The fancy names for the letterhead were well and good but it was at the committee level where the work got done. Mildred had found her "occupation" at last.

At its founding, the VSS had limited goals. The militants might have hoped for an outright ban but the consensus of the leading members was to demand the adoption of "well considered restrictions and safeguards" on the practice of vivisection. This early spirit of intellectual compromise produced the Cruelty to Animals Act of 1876. Let the valued research continue but with increasing attention to the minimisation of pain and suffering for the animals. By 1880, however, it was clear – at least to Miss Cobbe – the new law had failed. "By slow, very slow degrees, we learned that nothing could be much further than the truth," Cobbe wrote. The abolitionists were on the march.

The VSS was expanding rapidly with local chapters in most of the major British cities and even abroad. A large bequest from a Frenchwoman provided enough money for the society to launch its first regular journal. On 21 January 1881, Miss Cobbe employed Charles Warren Adams to be the first "paid" secretary of the society. For his salary of £200, Adams was to be at Victoria Street from 10-5 each day and handle all correspondence. A veteran journalist, Adams was also tasked with editing the society's new monthly, *The Zoophilist*. The first issue was dated 1 May 1881; at sixteen pages, it sold for sixpence. Adams gave readers the three essential principles of the VSS: 1) Vivisection is practically inseparable from cruelty; 2) It inevitably hardens the hearts and deadens the consciences of men; and 3) It is an unsound and delusive method of research.

On Saturday, 25 June 1881, carriages began queuing at noon in front of the Coleridge home at 1 Sussex Square. As it was raining steadily, the arriving guests clambered up the steps, if a Bishop or a Countess would ever be seen to clamber. The annual meeting of the Victoria Street Society was to be held in Lord Coleridge's library before "a large and distinguished audience" of 150 ladies and gentlemen. Miss Cobbe was in good spirits on the day. The society was flourishing: new members, new chapters, and a new publication. In her opening comments, she gave a great deal of the credit to the "paid secretary." Adams heard the applause as he rose to give his report. His comments were seconded with the usual murmurs of "Hear, hear." Adams submitted his report for approval and Cardinal Manning moved its acceptance. A sepulchral figure, the 73-year-old prelate vowed in what life was left to him, he would do his utmost to end vivisection.

As a courtesy, the day's host, Lord Coleridge, was asked to say a few words, a chore he would never decline. He reminded everyone he had come to the movement rather late. Once "reluctant and unwilling" he stood before them as a "complete and absolute convert." Coleridge was troubled, however, by the increasing harshness of the rhetoric on both sides, especially in the *ad hominem* nature of many of the attacks. The critics of the VSS had portrayed the opponents of vivisection as somehow effeminate, "weak-minded old women of both sexes." But Coleridge said, "There is nothing manly about defending cruelty to dumb animals." Still, he insisted tolerance, patience, and an informed campaign will succeed in the end. "The evils of Vivisection are so great and the good it professed to accomplish so doubtful, it should be abolished, as hateful to Almighty God."

To close the meeting, Lord Shaftesbury pronounced himself delighted. He wanted especially to recognize Miss Cobbe whose "vigour and perseverance" were greatly responsible for the successes to date and those that certainly lie ahead. She was undoubtedly a remarkable woman. Lord Shaftesbury declared he was "astonished" at the work being done by the women of "this generation." Miss Cobbe accepted the plaudits graciously, adding, "It is to Miss Coleridge our thanks are due. For many months she has been a strong help to me, and all that can be said in gratitude is due to Miss Coleridge for her goodness, and labour and trouble, in preparing this meeting for us." Mildred blushingly accepted the tribute and applause. At which point,

"Lord Coleridge and Miss Coleridge terminated the proceedings." It had been a great day for the society, for Mildred and, certainly for Mr. Adams. In the next issue of the *Zoophilist*, the editor fulsomely thanked Lord Coleridge for his hospitality and the use of his "spacious drawing room." The meeting had gone off "with great *éclat*."[5] This controversial gentleman needs to be more clearly introduced.

Charles Warren Adams was 48. His family ancestry was well-established: he was "of the Adams of Ansty Hall," near Rugby, in Warwickshire.[6] His late father had also been prominent at the bar; John Adams was a Serjeant-at-Law, a once prestigious but now, in 1881, largely defunct title.[7] Charles was the second son of his father's third wife. His two brothers were clergymen. He'd grown up in Paddington, not far from the Coleridges.

As a youth, Adams was well over six feet tall, of "towering height and distinguished appearance." By the 1880s, he had grown rather stout, broad-shouldered and bearded, with a tendency perhaps to overdress. His adult bulk belied his sickly youth. As a boy, he was sent from London to live with a clergyman's family in Somerset. At the age of 18, he went out to New Zealand to join a new "pilgrim" colony: "an ideal society sustained by an ideal Church of England."[8] Plainly, it didn't suit Adams' ideals and, after two months, he returned to London and joined the Army. Within a year, he cashed out of the 49th Foot. The next year he tried his hand at the study of law, entering the Middle Temple. Curiously, given his litigious future, Adams did not finish that off, either. He left for an appointment in the Ordinance Office that was again short-lived. Charles' doting mother was Charlotte Priscilla Adams who wrote numerous, if rarely read, children's books with titles like *The Useful Little Girl*. She encouraged her son's literary aspirations and he published a couple of novels and a book of drawing room charades. The books were kindly noticed but

Charles decided his next career move would be to seek his fortune in South Africa.

In 1861, Adams boarded the *Castle Eden* at Gravesend but the ship got no farther than Plymouth, putting in amid complaints of inedible food and filthy conditions. In what was likely the first display of his lifetime propensity to litigate, Adams sued on behalf of the first-class passengers, winning the case.[9] He took another ship to Cape Town and arrived safely and in love. He hastened to marry Georgina Polson, a clergyman's daughter he wooed on the voyage. But unemployment and his wife's ill health soon brought Adams back to London, where their first child, a daughter Charlotte, was born. In 1863, Adams' mother purchased for him the struggling London publishing house of Saunders & Otley. George Meredith, no less, was one of his "professional readers." Adams was still writing on his own, using the pseudonym of Charles Felix. His book, *The Notting Hill Mystery,* is arguably considered to be the first "detective novel" and Adams' identity as the author has only latterly been established.[10] Alas, it was so typical of the luckless fellow that any success in life came posthumously. Meanwhile, his publishing house went bankrupt in 1869.

Adams moved into journalism but again found success elusive. He edited newspapers (briefly) in Cardiff and Bradford. In the 1870s, he was back in London, writing free-lance articles. In 1873, he joined the staff of a new conservative daily, *The Hour*, serving as the paper's drama critic and leader writer. Disraeli, the Tory leader, touted the paper as his favourite but the *Hour* struggled to find readers. When Adams was let go, he promptly went to court claiming wrongful dismissal and the case was actually heard by Lord Coleridge, although the plaintiff seems not to have made any lasting impression on the bench at that time!

Adams was enterprising. In 1877, he tried to gin up interest in the first round-the-world cruise, aboard a first-class yacht leaving from London for nine months.[11] "For persons to whom time and money are no object, it will offer a splendid opportunity for enjoyment. Mr. C. Warren Adams has been engaged to accompany the expedition." Enterprise does not always lead to profit. Adams' idea sank without a trace. By 1880, he was desperate and out of ideas. He had no steady job. He wrote a new "three-decker" novel but it drew savage reviews and disappeared.[12] And his wife was mortally ill with cancer. Their daughter proved to be a troublesome teenager and, with her mother desperately ill, the girl was moved from home to home among her mother's family. She was living with an aunt when her mother died in the autumn of 1880. Thus, Charles Warren Adams was rather in need of a job when the opening was announced for a "paid secretary" at the Victoria Street Society.

In harness once again, Adams brought new energy and organization to the VSS. One of those he early on impressed was Mildred Coleridge who said his "vigour" was exactly what they lacked. Adams arrived from the world of advocacy journalism and was used to the kind of attack prose well-suited to the newly aggressive tone in favour at Victoria Street. He shaped up the various provincial chapters, establishing new ones, and increasing their financial support to London. He even gave Mildred a new title: "Subscriptions and donations were to be made payable to the Hon. M. Coleridge, Hon. Treasurer." This was flattering and all new for Mildred. She was outside the home, for the first time working beside and conversing with men, in what people had already begun to call "the office." Heretofore, the only men she associated with were her father's male friends, mostly much older, many of them married or committed bachelors. At Victoria Street, the relationship Mildred began to develop with Adams was entirely different.

Adams worked closely with Miss Cobbe and the central executive committee, Mildred among them. In a note to Lord Coleridge, Shaftesbury "rejoiced" at how Adams was so reliant on "your amiable daughter." Adams needed Mildred because of her knowledge of foreign languages. Adams had none. Mildred, beyond her childhood Latin and Greek, also mastered French and German. Much of the research and publication - for and against vivisection - was being done on the continent. To keep readers of the *Zoophilist* current in the debate, Mildred's role was vital, reviewing such works as *Uber den Wissenschaftlichen Missbrauch der Vivisektion.* Adams praised her work; without Mildred, the *Zoophilist* was nothing. She was quite pleased. Even her father was impressed; Mildred knew he "was aware of it, we frequently spoke of it, and he was pleased, too."

On 3 August 1881, the Prince of Wales opened the International Medical Congress at St. James' Hall in Piccadilly. 3000 physicians and scientists had come to London. On the first working day of the congress, one of the most anticipated lectures covered the latest experiments on the brain, using animals. Dr. David Ferrier, of London's King's College Hospital, a leader in the field, preferred monkeys. He claimed to have made significant advances in cerebral localisation, determining which areas of the brain controlled which motor functions. Ferrier invited all interested researchers to his Physiological Laboratory and Anatomical Theatre, near Lincoln's Inn Fields. The tiered gallery was soon filled. Ferrier, a "dapper little Scotsman," presided. Assistants brought out two live monkeys. Ferrier explained that a portion of the brain in each monkey had been cauterised. One monkey had been left paralysed; the other monkey deafened. A biscuit was offered to the paralysed monkey but the animal could not reach for it. The deaf monkey, however, happily snatched his treat. A percussion cap was then placed between the two monkeys and soon exploded with a loud bang. The paralysed monkey screamed in terror while the deaf monkey showed no reaction whatsoever. As the smoke cleared, Ferrier continued with his lecture, declaring he had now determined "the auditory cortex [was located] in the region of the upper part of the superior temporal gyrus." The two monkeys were subsequently destroyed. The congress, before leaving London, overwhelmingly approved a resolution that, while deprecating the infliction of unnecessary pain, experiments on animals were indispensable.[13]

On 3 November, Mr. Adams presented himself at Bow Street Magistrate's Court and obtained a summons for Dr. Ferrier on a charge of violating the Cruelty to Animals Act. Two weeks later at Bow Street, Adams and Bernard Coleridge were seated at the prosecution table. Bernard was there to assist Samuel Danks Waddy QC who argued the case for the VSS. Miss Cobbe and Mildred were among the "several ladies" present. The crowd was enlarged by dozens of medical students, spilling into the hallway and street, noisily defending their chosen profession.

The key witness for the VSS was a doctor who attended Ferrier's simian exhibition as a "secret" observer. Ferrier had told his audience that lesions were made on the brains of the monkeys with "the application of red-hot wires." One of the monkeys had been kept alive since January of that year. Waddy reminded the court that, under the law, a researcher might operate on a monkey, but the animal must be given chloroform and, then, the animal must be destroyed before the drug wore off. To keep an animal alive required a "Certificate B." Waddy charged that Ferrier failed to get that certificate and was thus liable to be fined £50. There was a problem with the Society's case: Ferrier had not actually operated on either monkey. The cauterisations were done by a Dr. Yeo (who apparently had a Certificate B). After lengthy arguments, the magistrate decided there was no case to answer.

All Ferrier had done was to comment on the results of a controversial operation done legally by someone else.

Dr. Ferrier left amidst "disorderly howling and cheering" from the supportive student section. *The British Medical Journal* paid his legal bills. The secular press suggested that well-meaning "shallow sentimentalists" should understand the vital need for medical research conducted as humanely as possible. Critics said the VSS aimed too high; hoping to bag a big-name target. Miss Cobbe felt they'd been hoodwinked like rustics at a country fair. "You lay your money that Professor Ferrier is under that cup. The cup is lifted to reveal, Hocus-Pocus, only Professor Yeo!" For the VSS and all anti-vivisectionists, it was an embarrassing defeat.[14]

1   Dictum: The Age (Melbourne) 6 Jan 1885, 6.

2   The leading source on "the Cobbe" is Sally Mitchell's *Frances Power Cobbe: Victorian Feminist, Journalist, Reformer* (2004.)

3   For the movement, Richard D. French, Antivivisection and Medical Science in Victorian Society (1975).

4   "Turkish sultana," Derek Hudson, Munby, *Man of Two Worlds* (1972).

5   The Times actually gave Mildred co-credit with her father for hosting the meeting. 28 June 1881, 10. A full discussion of the meeting, the speeches, in The Zoophilist, 1 July 1881, 51-58.

6   For the Adams of Anstey Hall see Burke's *Genealogical and Heraldic History of the Landed Gentry*, look for Mildred's name.

7   "Old Adams would convict his own mother," 15 September 1855, Punch, Vols 28-29 112.

8   Adams' stay in New Zealand was quite brief, hence the title of his memoir, *A Spring in the Canterbury Settlement* (1853). The author, "C. Warren Adams, Esq." was 20.

9   Adams' first lawsuit: "The Rights of a Passenger," Western Daily Press, 17 June 61.

10   "The Case of the First Mystery Novelist," Paul Collins, New York Times Book Review, January 7, 2011. The claim is somewhat disputed but Collins continues to have many scholars on his side.

11   "A Pleasure Tour Round the World," Illustrated Police News, 17 Feb 1877, 3.

12   Ram Dass. Tinsley Brothers 3 vols. The Morning Post: "This is a bad subject for fiction, and, in Ram Dass, that bad subject is badly treated."

13   For more on Ferrier, *Medical Science and the Cruelty to Animals Act 1876*. See Whiterose. ac.uk 83097.

14   Trial coverage: "The Charge against a Vivisectionist," London Daily News, 18 November 1881, 2; British Medical Journal (anti-VSS biased) 19 November 1881.

# 6. THE ONLY TWO[1]

THE FERRIER DEBACLE was hardly reason to give up. The vivisection controversy was not over. New bills were being readied for Parliament. The push for greater public support was heightened. Lord Coleridge was asked to write an article for the prestigious *Fortnightly Review*. Mildred was a great help to her father, bringing to his writing desk the relevant source material from Victoria Street; her father called it, "repulsive literature," reading it "made me sick." In his typically wordy, elegant style, quoting classical, literary, and scriptural thought, Lord Coleridge described how his feelings on the issue had evolved from moderation into his present hard-line support for "absolutely forbidding the practice." In part, he was motivated by "the ostentatious contempt" of the medico-scientific communities for any criticism of their vile work. No one may question their bloody trail of "baked dogs and mutilated cats, gouged frogs, nail-larded pigs and brain-extracted monkeys." So much for toning down the rhetoric.[1]

Entitled "The Nineteenth Century Defenders of Vivisection," his lordship's article was the most important piece in the *Fortnightly's* issue of February 1882. Early that month, Mildred proudly carried her copy as she sat in a compartment on the Great Western's *Flying Dutchman* train as it steamed out of Brunel's vaulted glass shed at Paddington bound for Exeter. There was a meeting in Torquay on the 10th to rescue the faltering local chapter of the VSS. Mildred's Coleridge relations – the Martyns - were among the local activists. Sophie Martyn, the daughter of a clergyman's widow, knew Mildred from the Gosling days. Mildred told her father she would be staying with the Martyns in Torquay. She did not tell him, apparently, that her carriage companion on her Devon journey was the secretary, Mr. Adams.

The "Down Dutchman" did the non-stop four-hour run to Exeter in well-upholstered comfort – in first class. Adams had not planned to attend the Torquay meeting; he originally intended only to visit his wife's grave in Plymouth. As Exeter was on the way, he could escort Mildred. Because of several sensational incidents, many women were uneasy about traveling alone on trains. The Great Western did set aside a compartment in all classes for women but they found their lady passengers reluctant to avail themselves of it.[2] Adams could also help with the necessary change in Exeter, for the South Devon line for Torquay. In Adams' mind, since he'd come that far, he might as well go to the meeting, too. The Martyns were at Torquay station to meet Mildred who introduced them to the secretary of the VSS who had come down from London for this important event. Adams found lodgings in the town. He later billed the VSS for his expenses; it was just a business trip.

The Secretary's decision to make the detour for Torquay wasn't entirely gratuitous. The importance of the meeting was signalled to all when Lord Haldon, the resort town's builder and patron, graciously offered to host the event at his Gothic "Manor House," set in the lush hills over the town and claiming the finest panorama of the Channel. It was February but Torquay's attraction was its mild winters; the magnolia and camelia were already in bloom on the villa-studded slopes. Still, the massive fireplace in the "grand but gawky" hall was lit when over 100 leading residents voted to revive and fund the Torquay branch and elected Lord Haldon as President and Chairman. Mrs. Martyn was named co-secretary. While Adams never expected to speak, the distinguished visitor from London was asked to make a few remarks. He referred to Lord Coleridge's article which he commended to all.[3] The evening had been a great success. Mildred was to stay on for a few days more with the Martyns and then go to Ottery. She and Adams were seen in Torquay the next morning attending services at St. Michael's church, prior to his afternoon departure for London.

In London, Adams returned to find the *Fortnightly* article under critical assault. It must have pained Lord Coleridge to read in the monthly science journal *Nature* that his arguments were "childishly weak."[4] Worse, the octogenarian legend of Victorian science, Professor Richard Owen, publicly accused the Lord Chief Justice of a "wholesale insult to my profession." Let "puffed up" lawyers stick to the law, Owen howled. No matter how elegant the prose, Owen said the *Fortnightly* article simply repeated "stupid and ignorant" lies about doctors baking cats. A biologist and paleontologist, Owen gets the general credit for coining the word *dinosaur*. The Natural History Museum is his legacy. But he was never a popular man. He feuded with Darwin and was generally disagreeable. He was a man "who did not take criticism well, who seldom acknowledged his own mistakes, and who did not always give credit where credit was due."[5] Nonetheless, when he spoke, people still listened.

In the *Zoophilist*, Adams defended the "splendid article by our Noble Vice President (Lord Coleridge) ... a man whose gifts and character have lifted him to the summit." Owens wouldn't descend to a debate with a man like Adams. The man was a paid journalist, not a scientist. Adams required tutoring (from people like Mildred). Adams churned out articles preying on the "compassionate credulity" of the public, "a tempting field to the venal knave for raising and garnering a harvest of subscriptions." No one did "ostentatious contempt" quite like Owen.

Much ink was spilled in 1882. Owen published his book-length defense of vivisection entitled *Experimental Physiology: Its Benefits to Mankind*. Experiments with animals had led to the essential discoveries of the circulatory and nervous systems. He cited the newest work on ovarian tumours. The opposition would halt everything. Owen even coined a new (if less lasting) word: *Bestiarian*.

> The consistent Bestiarian may say, let those women with such complaints get rid of them as they can. Their mission, with the help of a Lord Chief Justice of England ... is to haul up to Bow-street every experimental advancer of physiological and healing sciences, as an immoral offender, an unfeeling, inhuman wretch, a displeaser of Almighty God, a horrible torturer of His creatures.[6]

Mildred and Adams were enraged at the direct attacks on Lord Coleridge. As with the *Zoophilist*, they worked together alone on a rebuttal. The colleagues spent long hours, in the reading room at the British Museum and in Adams' office at Victoria Street. Mildred recalled the feeling that they were the "only two" in this fight. The 300-page result of their work was entitled, *The Coward Science: Our Answer to Professor Owen* and published by Hatchard's of Piccadilly in late August. To be clear, "Our" was a reference to the Society and not to Mildred. In her mind, they might have been "only two" but there was "only one" name on the title page. The title page identified the author as Charles Adams, "Paid Secretary" of the Society for the Protection of Animals from Vivisection. (The "venal knave" struck back.) Again, Mildred went uncredited or mentioned within. The book received a good deal of attention, much of it positive. "So far as the discussion has at present gone, Mr. Adams appears to have had decidedly the best of it," wrote *The Monthly Review*. *The Literary*

*World* thought Adams' attack on Owen was merciless, "but whether or not it will help the cause he has espoused remains to be seen." Miss Cobbe, of course, was thrilled with the book. "How splendid. It will be the death of that old impostor."[7]

What an exciting time it must have been at the offices of the VSS but Mildred wasn't present for any of it. It was feared the intense research of the preceding months had taken its toll on her always delicate health. Between her father's article, the Owen response, and the monthly work for the *Zoophilist* - said to contain "some of the most sickening things" in print - Mildred needed a respite. Her father's annual "Long Vacation" began in August and it was well-timed for Mildred to retreat to Heath's Court and put away all disturbing thoughts of "brain-extracted monkeys."

In Devon, Butterfield's redo at Ottery was finally finished, albeit slightly delayed by a workman's torch that set fire to the place in June. The old Coleridge home, thought to have been "inconveniently small," had been restored and enlarged at great expense (£16,000!) The masterpiece

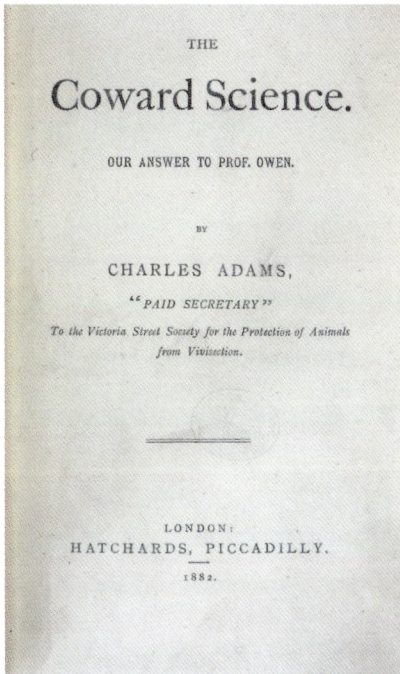

THE

# Coward Science.

OUR ANSWER TO PROF. OWEN.

BY

CHARLES ADAMS,

"*PAID SECRETARY*"

*To the Victoria Street Society for the Protection of Animals from Vivisection.*

LONDON:
HATCHARDS, PICCADILLY.
1882.

Mildred remembered how she and Adams were the "only two" who collaborated on *The Coward Science*, published in 1882. Adams, however, took sole credit on the title page. Mildred and Adams had frequently worked together in the secretary's private office. Lord Coleridge most definitely would not have approved.

51

was his Lordship's new library, filling the entire west-facing wing looking over the great lawn to the river Otter and beyond to distant Dartmoor.[8]

One of the first "new" books for the collection arrived from London on 31 August. Adams, employing his most ingratiating tone, inquired for Mildred's health and enclosed a first edition of his book:

> My Lord, Miss Coleridge has told me of her promise to abstain for the present from all "A.V." work. I hardly think that a perusal of the accompanying volume, which has no horrors in it of any kind, will come under that designation, but I would rather be on the safe side. I, therefore, take the opportunity of enclosing for your Lordship a copy of which I will ask your acceptance, in the hope that you may permit it to reach her hands.

Lord Coleridge mentioned to Mildred he had received the book and a "charming" letter from Mr. Adams which he acknowledged with a brief note. The volume, on which his daughter had worked so diligently, went directly (and apparently unread) on to the shelves.

In Ottery, Mildred was once again kept active by dear Aunt Maymie. They made the usual social calls of a country summer. They went to Lady Kennaway's garden party at Escot. Lord Selborne (the Lord Chancellor) and his two pretty daughters came to Heath's Court for a short stay. Mildred joined her father for the re-consecration of nearby Alfington Church, restored by Lord Coleridge with a memorial to honour Bishop John Coleridge Patteson who had been murdered by islanders in the Pacific. One of the church windows still bears the inscription: "Gift of Mildred Mary Coleridge 1882."[9] In late October, Mildred was among the local ladies who sorted through the second-hand clothing and shoes for the annual jumble sale in Exeter to benefit the Additional Curate's Society. Good work all, but she was eager to be back in London.

Full instructions were left behind with the staff for the approaching Christmas celebrations in the new Heath's Court. In early November, the local papers reported the Lord Chief Justice and the Hon. Miss Coleridge were returning to Sussex Square. Mildred went directly to Victoria Street. She wired ahead to Adams to expect her early that afternoon.

1  Coleridge's article *Fortnightly Rev.*, 1882, 225-236.

2  The GWR provided 1000 female-only seats, but claimed only 248 were used, while more than 5000 women chose to sit in the smoking carriages! Gillian Reynolds, *Gendered Journeys* (2016).

3  A letter from Lord Coleridge was read at the Haldon meeting. Western Times, 13 February 1882.

4  "Childishly weak," "Vivisection," *Nature*, 9 March 1882, 433.

5  "Sir Richard Owen, the Archetypal Villain," FriendsofDarwin.com

6  Bestiarian: Wordnik - an advocate of the kind treatment of animals; specifically, in Great Britain, an antivivisectionist. The OED, however, declares: This word is now obsolete. It is last recorded around the 1890s.

7  "Old impostor," FPC to CWA, quoted in The Times, 8 December 1884, 4.

8  Heath's Court: Butterfield's Ottery work is the subject of a recent study by the architectural historian Nicholas Olsberg. Youtube: https://drawingmatter.org/writer/olsberg-nicholas/ (viewed 4 September 2023).

9  Alfington Church visit 2014.

# 7. THE DARKENED ROOM

LONDON PLANNERS CONCEIVED of the new Victoria Street as a Parisian-style boulevard connecting Buckingham Palace with Westminster. Acres of notorious slums were razed and tons of material carted in to elevate the new street made 80 feet wide. The lower end was lined with large mansion blocks and "chambers" and became popular with trade groups and lobbyists. From the doorstep at number 1, a visitor could see the pinnacled towers of Parliament.

The offices of the Victoria Street Society were on the first floor. Miss Cobbe described the suite of rooms: "an ante-room (piled with our papers), a large airy room with two windows for the clerks, a secretary's private room (Mr. Adams worked within), and a spacious and lightsome committee-room with three windows." The committee members worked around a long oak office-table. Miss Cobbe's private office was decorated with "various little feminine relaxations." There, she entertained those callers who might have been squeamish owing to "the frightful character of our work."[1]

A cascading series of events began on a bright, pleasant Friday afternoon, 3 November 1882.[2] Mildred Coleridge, a few days short of her 35th birthday, came directly to Victoria Street from Waterloo Station arriving at about 1 p.m. She found the place quiet. Early in the month, things were slow. The latest *Zoophilist* had gone out; bundled copies of the new issue were in the ante-room. As always, though, "the secretary," Mr. Adams was in his office. He was expecting her. Mildred arrived that day filled with questions about the new book and the favourable response it received. She and Adams worked closely on the project and most often in his private room. The main committee room was, as we have read, "spacious and lightsome," with those three windows. It was most often too bright in daytime for Mildred's worrisome eyes which were always sensitive to glare. Further, the committee room was sort of a day-to-day gathering place and not where she could necessarily concentrate on her work. Mildred took to retreating to the secretary's room, where the light from a single window could be softened by shutters.

At about two o'clock that same November afternoon, Miss Cobbe arrived. The usual clerk at the door was not about. She called out, at first getting no reply. Then, the door to Mr. Adams' office slowly opened. Miss Cobbe, though she said nothing at the time, got the sense she had interrupted something. Adams and Miss Coleridge both appeared flushed and unsettled by her arrival. Yet, they gathered themselves and the three engaged in some small talk and their interaction seemed to end pleasantly. It most definitely would not. What followed, according to Sally Mitchell, Cobbe's biographer, was a "complex melodrama." For Mildred, it was a life-changing afternoon.

It would be understandable if Miss Cobbe had become jealous that Mildred, her erstwhile devoted young colleague, had fallen under the spell of the charismatic Adams – a man she had come to distrust and dislike. It was inevitable that two such contentious personalities would clash and relations between Miss Cobbe and her paid secretary were already nearing the rocks. Adams was a difficult man. He received a pay rise at the VSS to £250, but sought more. Enrollment was up, the *Zoophilist* was thriving, and Adams thought his new book, so well-received, was worth a "bonus." He suggested £100. Cobbe had praised *The Coward Science*, but she deemed it a private book, written "off the clock," hence deserving no additional stipend. Adams began lobbying other members for support. This was taken as a challenge by Miss Cobbe who did not appreciate challenges. While "her whole aspect suggested cheerfulness, she was not always ready to listen with urbanity to opinions she did not share."[3] If she thought Adams to be a rival for leadership of the VSS, she would not hesitate to crush him. The case of Anna Kingsford, driven off by "vicious gossip," was fresh in many minds. Cobbe could be a "formidable hater." She was completely capable of using her suspicions of "a budding romance" between Adams and Mildred Coleridge to get her way. In the words of a modern critic, Miss Cobbe's ensuing conduct was a "piece of madness."[4]

The exact date is not known but, about this time, Miss Cobbe welcomed to the office, Dr. Charles Drysdale, president of the Malthusian League, proponents of "the limitation of families." He edited *The Malthusian*, which very carefully offered information on contraception - intended for "married couples only," of course. Drysdale may have been accompanied at the VSS by Thomas Bonser, another controversial figure.[5] Whatever, Adams claimed Cobbe personally introduced Drysdale to Mildred and they spent some time in conversation. The observant secretary scurried back to his room and immediately dashed off a letter to Lord Coleridge. Although he neglected to mention the "incident of the darkened room," Adams alerted the ailing Coleridge about Drysdale's visit. Lord Coleridge should know his daughter had been introduced to "this person" by Miss Cobbe. He hoped his Lordship would agree that the anti-vivisection cause could be damaged by association with such notorious characters. Coleridge replied to Adams (who saved the letter), "I entirely approve of the course you have taken in the matter on which you have written to me." It would not be wise for the VSS to "raise up enemies unnecessarily." A footman left from Sussex Square to Portman Square, bringing Adams' letter to Lord Shaftesbury. The 81-year-old Earl, although devoted to "the Cobbe," as he called her, was beginning to question her increasing militancy. He recently forbade her from stalking vivisectionists on the Sabbath. Notes were soon being carried to and fro, with instructions to wait for a reply. At Miss Cobbe's "dear little house" in Hereford Square, she received a note from Lord Shaftesbury cautioning her to avoid mixing her causes together.

In that atmosphere, the 25-member "Central Executive Committee" met on Saturday. Mildred expected trouble, knowing the "good deal of friction" between Adams and Miss Cobbe. Mildred would, no doubt, have been there to support Adams but she was kept at home at Sussex Square. Her father's lumbago had recurred and three weeks of bedrest were recommended; Mildred's duty was clear. She was disappointed but Adams would keep her *au courant*. The 18 November meeting demonstrated the VSS was firmly under Miss Cobbe's control. If she didn't think Adams deserved more in his pay packet, the committee would not challenge her. The debate was brief; Adams was denied. He made noises about a lawsuit but was urged, in the best interests of the society, to let it drop. Instead, Adams turned on Miss Cobbe, suggesting if the "best interests" of the VSS were at issue, she should reconsider bringing people like Dr. Drysdale into their midst. Cobbe had her opportunity. If Adams wished to pose as Mildred's protector, he would do better than be found alone with her in a "darkened room." A professional disagreement became a proper row. Adams demanded Cobbe apologise for her innuendo. He challenged the others present to raise any issues they might have about his conduct with Miss Coleridge. Things had gone too far. Amid "words of excitement," the meeting adjourned.[6]

What did the darkened room mean for Mildred? What was Miss

Cobbe implying about her conduct? Adams was eager to brief Mildred during the few minutes she was allowed away from her father's sickbed. She had a half-hour every morning after church. Adams met her and they walked back to Sussex Square as he filled her in on the raucous meeting and Miss Cobbe's insinuations. In front of their numerous colleagues, he (and, of course, Mildred, in absentia) had been accused of being discovered in some improper intimacy in the secretary's private room. Mildred was aghast. At home, she went into to her father's sickroom hysterical and in tears. She assured him nothing improper had occurred. The "darkened room" was no darker than any room would have been on a November afternoon in London. The door to the secretary's office was ajar. They had heard someone in the outer office. Adams said, "That must be Miss Cobbe. I'll fetch her in." Any "emotions" Miss Cobbe claimed to observe were also explainable. Mildred had been consoling Adams as he wept over a photograph of his late wife. The second anniversary of Mrs. Adams' death had just passed and he hadn't yet got over it.[7] "My heart is in her tomb," he once told Mildred. So much for the prescribed rest and quiet Lord Coleridge sought at Sussex Square. Mildred was incensed and vowed to resign from the VSS. She would never work with or meet Miss Cobbe ever again. Coleridge wrote again to Shaftesbury (the titular president of the VSS) to report Mildred was "in a considerable agitation having been falsely accused of undue familiarity with Mr. Adams."

What in the world was going on at Victoria Street? While his lordship may have accepted his daughter's explanation, he well knew she had to be more careful.[8] A woman's reputation was "like the bloom on a newly cut peach, touch it ever so lightly and it is gone." Moreover, this "Mr. Adams," whoever he is, should also appreciate the peril of such a potentially compromising moment. As a gentleman, in Mildred's interest, he ought not allow it to happen. Reputations could be questioned or destroyed by a single misstep, even if the intention was entirely innocent. But what if it wasn't "innocent?" A cad of lower rank or fortune might plot to "compromise" a wealthy young lady so her "only way out" was to get married, with the prize being not the young bride but her dowry. This was not only the stuff of bad novels. It was a most unsettling situation. "A woman's reputation needs jealous guarding."

Lord Coleridge, as well he should, begged to see Miss Cobbe as soon as possible. She would please explain her comments which so upset his daughter. At Hereford Square, Miss Cobbe was "demented with worry." Nevertheless, she informed his lordship she could not see him until after her pre-arranged tour of the Midlands escorting Elizabeth Cady Stanton and Susan B. Anthony, the American suffragettes. What a busy woman. She did, however, share her belief that Adams, for several months, had curried a relationship with Mildred which did not go unnoticed. Thus, her reaction when she walked in on them that afternoon in Adams' darkened office. She would explain everything on her return. In the meantime, Dr. Channing, of the VSS executive committee, would call at Sussex Square in the morning.

The daily newspaper reports on the Lord Chief Justice's health were promising and on 20 November, the interested public was informed Lord Coleridge was doing better and "able to sit up at short intervals." Therefore, in his bedroom, he met William Channing, Miss Cobbe's emissary. Boston born, Harvard educated, Channing had been in England for many years. A churchman, he was a founder of the Social Purity Alliance. He assured Lord Coleridge he had no personal knowledge of any impropriety between Adams and Miss Coleridge, but he and others at the VSS were struck by the clear familiarity between them. They were on terms of "Charles" and "Mildred." Was that all? Remember, however, the use of Christian names was appropriate only between people "intimately acquainted" and, of course, with servants. Channing believed the amount of time Mildred spent in the secretary's private office unfortunately gave rise to comment. Mildred was not present that morning; she refused to see Channing, dismissing him as "one of Miss Cobbe's hangers-on" who was hardly ever in the building. When her father asked if people at Victoria Street might suspect Adams was "making love" to her, Mildred snapped, "No, of course not."

Not for the first time, Lord Coleridge missed the counsel of his late wife. While he and Mildred were very close, nothing could replace a "mother's touch." This was a novel situation in his world. But, pending Miss Cobbe's return, he determined Adams must keep away from Mildred. Coleridge wrote to the secretary:

> My dear sir, I have had a long letter from Miss Cobbe and a long interview with Mr. Channing and with my daughter. I will not trouble you with going into the details of the letters and conversations. Neither do I desire to cast blame upon or find fault with anyone. But my daughter is my only daughter and she has no mother. I must see, therefore, that she is not intentionally compromised by conduct even the most innocent, which yet may, from want of consideration, be mischievous to her. Her intercourse with you has, I dare say quite inadvertently, assumed this character, and I must therefore request that for the present it shall cease. I write this with her knowledge and at her request.[9]

Despite the last sentence, Mildred was not in agreement at all. She surely felt ill-used. Through no fault of her own, she faced a vicious accusation. She was disappointed her father had not seen it that way. She and Adams were merely collaborators whose only shared passion was the cause of anti-vivisection. Instead, her reputation had been slandered before many of her friends. The cause for which she devotedly worked for five years, even at risk to her own fragile health, was now closed to her. Overwrought by the injustice, Mildred secluded herself in her room at Sussex Square. Adams, meanwhile, sent a curt reply asking his lordship to consider the source for these unfair and untrue allegations. He and Mildred had done no wrong; rather, he held her in the highest respect and regard. For that reason alone, Adams would agree to end all communication between them, for the moment.

As promised, Mildred resigned from the VSS in a letter to Shaftesbury. The Earl forwarded the "deeply to be regretted letter" to Miss Cobbe, demanding an explanation for the "astounding and novel statements by yourself about Miss Coleridge." As for Adams, he had to go. Shaftesbury thought the man was "self-seeking, ambitious, deceptive and wicked." On 25 November, even with Miss Cobbe still away, the executive committee sacked Adams. "All communications concerning either the general business or the editing of *The Zoophilist*, must be addressed till further notice to the Hon. Sec. Miss Frances Power Cobbe." No public reason was given. On his way out of the door, Adams declared he would sue the VSS for his unpaid wages and "other costs."[10] In his diary, Shaftesbury blamed "the Cobbe" for her "unprecedented imprudence." The good news was that Adams, the "jellyfish," was gone. Still, Shaftesbury worried, "We are in a very serious mess."[11]

Lord Coleridge was strong enough in early December to join the Queen for the opening of the new Royal Law Courts in the Strand. He would never miss such an elaborate ceremonial occasion. He had a "bias toward showiness, he wore his robes with the air the Englishman loves." His clerks thought he was "as particular about his lace ruffles and cuffs as a young girl." For the occasion, observant court watchers noticed he had added a sash of his own design, embellishing his scarlet gown with ermine trim.[12] It was a festive day. Judges, court workers, and their families, fanned out exploring the massive new building and its bewildering maze of corridors. But Mildred remained at home.

The depth of his daughter's reaction to the Adams row surprised Lord Coleridge quite a bit; he'd been totally unaware of the extent and nature of this relationship. From sources he later described as "various people at various times," he learned it had been going on without his knowledge for nearly a year, at least. Mrs. Martyn in Torquay, for instance, reported to her "Cousin Johnnie" that Adams showed up with Mildred for the VSS meeting as far back as February. Apparently, they had travelled together by train, alone, from London, which the woman thought curious. She also described seeing Mildred and Adams in the same pew at church. Lord Coleridge was growing more convinced he'd done the right thing. Mildred tried to explain; she'd gone to Torquay (where she was well known and had many friends) to attend "an influential meeting" to launch the new branch of the VSS. Adams, who was on his way to the West to visit his wife's grave in Plymouth, thought he might accompany her. Those who knew their Bradshaw's as well as the Lord Chief Justice, would know the Great Western's "Plymouth trains are run for Plymouth alone." As for the church pew meeting, Mildred assured her father, it was entirely by coincidence.

Miss Cobbe was back in London on 15 December and met by appointment Lord Coleridge at Victoria Street. His lordship had never visited the office where his daughter worked for several years, the last two with Adams. He respected Miss Cobbe but, other than on vivisection, the two were not particular allies. Their greeting was formal. Miss Cobbe took her visitor directly into Adams' former office. The afternoon was grey and cold following a dense fog for most of the morning. The light from the single window was not helpful. It met the description of a dark room. Cobbe tried to assure Coleridge she never wished to imply any fault on Mildred's part. Adams was solely responsible. It was her sense – and shared by many others at the VSS - Adams had encouraged his special relationship with Mildred. He asked her to call him "Charles." He urged her to use his office and they were frequently together within. Cobbe had grown to distrust Adams and she knew Mildred was not accustomed to men like him. She became worried. Thus, on 3 November, when she arrived unannounced to find the office empty and the two of them behind closed doors, she quickly concluded Adams had been up to something. And Cobbe provided an important new detail; she'd subsequently learned the clerk at the door had been sent off on an errand. "Would it surprise you to know," Adams gave that order? What was a father to think but that his daughter had been enticed into a compromising encounter, frustrated only by Miss Cobbe's fortuitous interruption? Home at Sussex Square, Lord Coleridge told Mildred she was not to associate with Adams any further. The man was gone from the VSS and there was no need to continue their acquaintance. There would be no discussion.

Mildred remained inconsolable. The tale of the "darkened room" would remain a closely-held family secret. Most of Mildred's friends were her father's friends and they would assume her seclusion was another bout with one of her allied "illnesses." If there was a "Team Mildred," the most prominent member was Mrs. Thomas (Cecilia) Bishop. She was a Northcote, her older brother was Lord Iddesleigh, a leading Tory politician but a longtime Devon neighbour and friend of the Coleridges. Mrs. Bishop's husband, a wealthy physician, preferred to live in Paris. Effie Bishop, their daughter, was another of Mildred's good friends. Mrs. Bishop also had a villa in Torquay and was present for the meeting at Lord Haldon's in February. She wrote to Lord Coleridge, assuring him she had observed Mildred and Adams closely and nothing she saw from their conduct in Torquay would indicate it was anything more than – essentially – a business trip. She warned his Lordship that forcing Mildred to abandon a cause which had become the great interest of her life was damaging her health. Mildred was in an alarming state.

In his lengthy reply, Coleridge thanked Mrs. Bishop for her concern but his position was firm: he did not trust Adams, a total stranger, and accused the man of plotting to compromise Mildred's character in such a way that she would not dare refuse any offer he might make.

> What do we really know of (Adams), of his life, of his antecedents? The true answer would be - nothing. His heart in his wife's tomb! Was the only day he could look after his wife's tomb (or something) at Plymouth the one day in the year when he knew that Mildred would be with you at Torquay? Is Torquay on the Plymouth line? Were there no pews in St Michael's church on a weekday for him to sit but the one Mildred was in? Well, I could ask questions of this sort enough to fill this sheet. I don't pretend to know a woman's nature; but I think I do know what is a gentleman's duty to a young woman with no mother. Understand, I believe Mildred absolutely, without reserve, but to a man his conduct can have but one judgment passed upon it. The crying over his wife's picture in a darkened room where he had got Mildred alone by appointment, the other man of the establishment having been sent by him off to the City, moves my indignation. I have not a word to say to anyone who likes a daughter so treated. I don't.[13]

Mrs. Bishop tried a second appeal and received her final rebuff:
> As to what Mrs. Bishop might have done, if she knew the facts as to Mildred as I know them, I do not care to inquire. I conceive that the honour of my daughter is as precious to me as her

daughter's is to her, and I need no help to take care of her.

Lord Coleridge feared he had been too frank in his comments, knowing Mrs. Bishop might well share his letters with Adams. "But I cannot help it." Those fears were well-justified.

Christmas 1882 had been planned to be a very special holiday at Heath's Court. Butterfield had finished, at last. The original 17th century Chanter's House was still there, somewhere, a "kernel" hidden within a new larger red-brick structure designed to accommodate all the required amenities of a late Victorian mansion, including an aviary, a skittles' alley, and a billiard room. One doesn't picture Lord Coleridge for snooker. The great new western elevation looked out from his lordship's 18,000 book library, windows opening to a terraced lawn rolling down to the road, for all passersby to admire. That was Butterfield's remit – according to the architect's most recent biographer – as if Coleridge was declaring, "This is how proudly I stand in the history of my family and our times and I am going to show it to you."[14]

Alas, it was a dreary fortnight in Devon.[15] The December weather was warm and wet. Adding to the soppy gloom was Mildred's continued heartbroken retirement. A Christmas fete allowed the locals inside the walls to poke about for a day and have some cake. The event of the season was a brilliant "Grand Ball" held on New Year's Night, 1883. Lord Coleridge's hospitality was unstinting. Dancing began in the library at 9 p.m. and the waltzes, galops, polkas and Lancers continued "with much spirit" until three in the morning, observed without comment by the tireless busts of Milton, Shakespeare, Wordsworth and, of course, the greatest kinsman, Samuel T. The *Exeter Flying Post* listed 150 guests: the leading gentry, locally and from across the West Country, associates from the bench and legal world in London, and the greater Coleridge family. Aunt Maymie, Mr. and Mrs. Bernard, "the Stephens," and Gilbert were all noted. Not so much as a Christmas cracker was heard from Mildred

Coleridge whose Devon presence went un-recorded.

The war of wills had been joined. Mildred's health was showing the strain. But her father would not bend. As 1883 began, Lord Shaftesbury wrote to the Cobbe, "This Mildred business is simply disgusting. What misery she will bring on her poor Father, and the family."[16]

1  The VSS office description, F.P. Cobbe, *Life of Frances Power Cobbe*, Volume 2 (1894) 276. The offices of the VSS were renumbered 20 Victoria Street in the late 1880's.
2  The most complete previous study of the darkened room incident can be found in Sally Mitchell. FPC, op cit.
3  Stephen Coleridge, "Miss Frances Power Cobbe," *The Animal's Defender & Zoophilist*, Vols 36-37, 73.
4  For Kingsford-Cobbe & "piece of madness:" Norm Phelps, The Longest Struggle: Animal Advocacy from Pythagoras to PETA (2007) 136-142.
5  Drysdale's Malthusian theories were "almost always seen as a code for free-love." See Sally Mitchell, Cobbe, 319. In one of her letters, Mildred referred to the "Bonser episode." T.O. Bonser was an eccentric Cambridge fellow who spent his summers distributing birth control leaflets among the "peasantry." He may have visited the VSS with Drysdale. For Bonser, see *Pioneers of Birth Control* (1919)
6  "Words of excitement, etc.," Sally Mitchell explains Shaftesbury's growing concern with Cobbe's activism. Shaftesbury letters: Add MS 86250. Shaftesbury's penmanship was deplorable. I credit the assistance of David Brown, Professor of Modern History, University of Southampton, who is preparing the diaries for publication.
7  Mrs. Charles W Adams died in Fulham on 11 October 1880.
8  Courtship rules: formal introductions, chaperones at all times, never alone. Rules "for the purpose of averting the mischief that unchecked intercourse and incautious familiarity might give rise to." debretts.com/courtship advice from the Victorians.
9  "My dear sir," Lord Coleridge to Adams, 20 December 1882.
10  Adams did sue the VSS: 7-8 December 1883: Adams v Adlam, Cobbe & Others, Adams scored a rare legal victory. The VSS agreed to pay him £158 11s for his extra work. It was clear they were just happy to be rid of him.
11  Mitchell, Cobbe, 289ff. Shaftesbury was furious that he'd been "left in the dark" on this.
12  Lord Coleridge's delight in the dress up part of his office was legendary. W.L. Woodroffe, "*Lord Coleridge and the English Law Courts*," James Parton (ed.) Some Noted Princes, Authors, and Statesmen of Our Time (1885), 238.
13  "What do we really know," Coleridge to Mrs. Bishop, 15 December 1882. This letter, suggesting Adams hoped to entrap his daughter, features prominently in the second trial (q.v.).
14  Butterfield's "masculine severity" did not please everyone, e.g. he created "a medieval jewel held firmly in a massive Victorian setting." Lord Coleridge clearly loved it, "This is how proudly," quoting Olsberg, (q.v.)
15  On 22 December, the Exeter & Plymouth Gazette called it "damp, muggy, and dispiriting." A week later, 29 December, the same paper went for "murky, wet, and miserable."
16  "This Mildred business," Shaftesbury to Cobbe. 16 January 1883. See Mitchell, Cobbe, 292.

# 8. THE WHITE ELEPHANT

WHILE THE COLERIDGES gathered amid festive holly and Christmas roses, Mildred sulked in her room. The family quietly palavered. How had matters come to this pass? Lord Coleridge frequently referred to his 35-year-old daughter as "motherless." If Lady Coleridge were still alive, he surely believed, this *mesalliance* would have been forestalled. The Coleridges believed, no, knew Mildred to be naïve; she had kept out of "the world." She was happiest and most useful in quiet Ottery. She travelled quite a bit; she was always welcome in the homes of her parents' friends. This work with the VSS, however, was a new experience and, to a point, it had gone well. All the Coleridges shared the "cause" and they must have believed the Victoria Street Society would be a "safe" space. The executive committee, where Mildred's work won such praise, was eminently respectable, with MPs, scientists, and physicians.[1] Prominent women lent their name to the effort; the VSS letterhead included sixteen women, including two countesses and several "Ladys." What harm might befall Mildred in such company? And yet, she found herself inveigled into the orbit of *the paid* secretary, that awful man, Adams. Lord Coleridge, as might be true of more than a few great liberals, was a confirmed elitist. At the very least, he would have expected any suitor for his daughter to be a gentleman. In Coleridge's eyes, Mr. Adams, by appearance and manner, was not of their caste. His lordship had asked, "What do we really know of him?" Adams came among them a stranger from down-market Hammersmith. It didn't help he wore a full beard.

Lord Coleridge had "an inveterate antipathy" to beards, believing they were a grubby, Bohemian affectation. Plus, Adams was a journalist, the occupation he listed in the 1881 census. Lord Coleridge abhorred (most) journalists, having been quoted, "I suppose these people must live."[2] Worse, Adams was now an unemployed journalist, sacked at the *Zoophilist*. The man's dress was another indicator. Rising men were advised to "adapt themselves to the manners of the class they desire to enter [and] ape the dress of the order immediately above them."[3] In the legal world of the Coleridges, a man could never go wrong with black. Nothing ostentatious or flashy would do. "To be overdressed is an offence in the eyes of the world, and justly so." Adams was known for his florid style and over-accessorising with rings, fobs, and pocket handkerchiefs. He looked like he slept in his clothing. His manner was off-putting. He was louder than thought necessary, argumentative, and reputed to have a wrathful temper. In sum, he was an entirely unsuitable companion for a rather gentle, sheltered, petted, "old maid" like Mildred.

As the holidays ended, the family left Devon for London with a new strategy. Rumours were not going to be enough. Facts were required. Mildred would listen to facts and understand her infatuation was unjustified. The net was cast for more intelligence on Adams. As for Adams, solely for Mildred's health, Lord Coleridge would relent, a bit. The initial ban on all "intercourse with Mr. Adams" was repositioned as a "suspension." He would permit letters to be exchanged. The Lord Chief Justice would not be long in London, leaving for a six-week assizes circuit in North Wales, Cheshire, and Shropshire. Upon his return at Easter, the situation would be reviewed. Mildred seemed mollified by this. At Sussex Square, Mildred was to enjoy the company of Aunt Maymie, who was clearly intended to be her designated minder.

Maymie was a semi-invalid herself and rarely accompanied Mildred on any of her housekeeping errands. "Would it surprise you to know" Adams contrived to meet Mildred on at least two occasions? He was seen in earnest conversation with Mildred one day after Sunday services at St. James, Sussex Gardens. In February, Bernard "happened" to observe them walking arm-in-arm along the wintry paths in Kensington Gardens. If he was spying, Bernard was not very adept at his tradecraft. He was caught out and there was an awkward little meeting amid the bare horse-chestnuts. The two men shook hands. When these rendezvous were reported to Lord Coleridge, he blamed Adams entirely. Mildred, again, insisted there was an innocent purpose for these meetings. Adams' daughter, Charlotte, had just turned 21 and lived unhappily with her mother's relations. Mildred agreed to use her family connections to get the young woman admitted to the Sydenham College of Art. She met Adams only to settle those arrangements. They had made no effort to keep their meeting secret, the gardens were just over the Bayswater Road from Sussex Square. Please stop spying on me, she begged her family.

At Easter 1883, Lord Coleridge made a new proposal. Rather than conspiring to meet in church-pews or leafy lanes, if Mildred wished to contact Adams, she could invite him to call at Sussex Square. His visits would, of necessity, be chaperoned by Maymie or Mildred's lady's maid. Meetings outside the home would require advance permission. Lord Coleridge trusted Adams "would not abuse this [privilege] and that he would remember the situation in which Miss Coleridge was placed by the death of her mother and [my] necessarily almost constant absence from home." The "by appointment only" plan seemed to work; Mildred's health and mood were much improved. She and Maymie went down to Devon in the spring. It was like old times; there was a concert at Ottery Town Hall and Mildred's pianoforte solo was "executed very tastefully." It was for the best she was out of London for the annual meeting of the Victoria Street Society with Miss Cobbe still running the show. Surprisingly, her father did attend and made "one of his profoundly impressive speeches."

Lord Coleridge had enjoyed merely a polite relationship with his late wife's family, the Seymours.[4] Mildred, alone, it seems, kept up with her mother's relations. 55-year-old Harriette Seymour, yet another unmarried aunt, lived in a small cottage in Porthleven, Cornwall, where she painted watercolours of shipwrecks and sunsets[5]. Harriette was in London for a June show of her works at *The Society of Lady Artists* in Great Marlborough Street. Mildred would certainly get no questions when she volunteered to assist her aunt's venture. "Would it surprise you to know," however, the nuts and bolt of the exhibition - the crating and shipping of the art, the hanging, the publicity, the tickets, were under the superintendence of C.W. Adams, Esq? Adams was meeting Mildred regularly at both Aunt Harriette's lodgings and Mrs. Bishop's home.

Mildred had lost count of the number of times her father asked her, "Are you in love with this man?" She insisted she wasn't, nor he with her. Nonetheless, if everywhere that Mildred went, Adams seemed to follow, people were going to talk. Two people could not be seen meeting "without some love-affair being gossiped about." By this point, all of the Coleridges not named Mildred were at their wit's end with this ubiquitous gentleman who was clearly defying the family. Confronted by her father, Mildred again bridled at being watched; it was intolerable. Why couldn't they be allowed to have their innocent friendship? Byron thought a man and woman made "far better friendships ... with this condition, they never have made, or are to make, love with each other."[6] To Mildred, that was exactly her relationship with Adams. The wisdom of a Byronic appeal to

Lord Coleridge seems dubious. Mid-Victorians, and that would include Lord Coleridge's generation, questioned the innocence of any purported "male-female friendship." The intimacy of such a relationship could lead only to one outcome. Men were not to be trusted; women - especially Mildred - were to be protected. A proper young lady must always have a chaperone while in a man's company; an older married woman, a "wedded protector," was preferred but "an elderly unmarried relative who knows the world" will serve. They must have a way of noticing everything that goes on without appearing to do so.[7] To be sure, it was 1883, "great latitude is now allowed to young ladies." The infamous "Girl of the Period" and her ilk were rewriting the rules. Not under Lord Coleridge's roof. There was a reason why his lordship was called "the oldest fogy in England."[8]

In desperation, Mildred (and Adams, for it was his idea) proposed their "nominal engagement." A befuddled Lord Coleridge invited Adams to Sussex Square. "The whole subject of the engagement with my daughter is so complicated and so entirely beyond the experience of any gentleman with 62 years' experience of life that further correspondence would be interminable." On 22 May 1883, Charles Warren Adams arrived at the Coleridge home. Mildred greeted him at the door; Westaway, the butler, took Adams immediately to the library where Lord Coleridge was waiting, along with Bernard. The greetings were cordial. Adams had been in the room before, introduced by Mildred to Lord Coleridge at the 1881 meeting of the VSS. With his customary conceit, Coleridge chose not to recall the moment. Adams knew Bernard but insisted straightaway he would not discuss Mildred in her brother's presence. "Bernard is my son and heir and has my complete confidence," Coleridge replied. Adams was unmoved. Bernard, with the merest bow, took his leave.

Adams and Lord Coleridge were in conversation for some time.

Their memories do not differ in any significant way. Adams freely admitted he had no more than sincere admiration for Mildred. They were "thrown together" at the VSS. She was smart and talented in languages; he admired her research and was grateful for her encouragement. They were working colleagues in the normal nature of things. Why should they hide a natural friendship? Adams believed Miss Cobbe was jealous of his growing influence over her former protégée. That explained her wholly false presentation of the "darkened room" afternoon. Don't go there, Coleridge interrupted. He accepted his daughter's account and believed her blameless. But Adams had placed Mildred in a very damaging position. As her father, Coleridge would not allow her name to be compromised. What were Adams' intentions?

It wasn't often a suitor made such a case as Adams suggested that afternoon. He was a man of 50, married once and with no desire to repeat the experience. "I am not in love with your daughter and have never pretended to be." Mildred, in truth, was a "plain woman" for whom he had no particular attraction. Nor she for him. Frankly, he could not afford a wife. Mildred, from a good family, used to a certain lifestyle, and who suffered from fragile health, was far beyond his means. He had the nerve to use the expression "white elephant." What a jarring and unkind choice. In mitigation, perhaps, the papers were full of news about the great showman Mr. Barnum who very recently "succeeded in overcoming the scruples of the Siamese Government" and obtained such a creature from King Thebaw.[9] Still, Lord Coleridge little expected Adams would so blatantly insult his daughter. Adams returned serve, accusing Coleridge of calling him a fortune-hunter. If you are, Coleridge warned, you'll be disappointed; it would be "absurd" to think he would give Mildred anything worth the while of a fortune-hunter. Why were they arguing? Adams insisted he didn't want to marry Mildred, thus the proposed "nominal engagement." The umbrella offered by the arrangement would allow them to meet without exciting comment. The engagement would be left open, *sine die* as the lawyers said. Call off the spies, dismiss the chaperones. The harassment could not continue. If it did, Adams assured Coleridge they would marry, against their wills. As it stood, it was intolerable and affecting Mildred's health. "For God's sake, give her a chance." He would allow Lord Coleridge some time to consider the proposal and he left.

On the plus side of Adams' plan, long, unconsummated, engagements were commonplace, not just in Victorian fiction.[10] Nevertheless, an announced engagement, nominal or otherwise, would inform the world Lord Coleridge had sanctioned the connexion; it made no difference whether the wedding ever happened. How could he face his friends knowing he'd allowed his only daughter – a peer's daughter with a sizeable inheritance - to betroth herself to a penniless, quarrelsome man like Adams? Any man approaching Mildred's father should have an income, or expectations, and some social standing. Instead, Adams boldly proclaimed he had nothing but an historic name. To quote one marriage book, "That the man should bring nothing is usually regarded as an unnatural circumstance attending marriage, and one not altogether to his credit."

In the normal course of things, Lord Coleridge would have been pleased to see his daughter happily wed. Upon her wedding day, he would settle upon her a good portion (if not all) of the money he planned to leave her at his death. After Adams left Sussex Square, on or about that evening, Lord Coleridge rewrote his will. Perhaps, this was merely precautionary; he was about to take a trans-Atlantic voyage. That was still two months away and about which, much more later.

Lord Coleridge rejected the "nominal engagement" gambit. It

was beyond unconventional and certainly unworthy of his daughter. He had been "entirely unconvinced" and the idea was a non-starter. Mildred was enraged and, off her own bat, demanded Adams reappear at Sussex Square. Before her father, she demanded to know what he had against Adams. Make a charge and he will answer it, Mildred pleaded. Coleridge mentioned the relatively minor Kensington Gardens incident. Adams scoffed; it was a quarter-hour conversation about his daughter's schooling. It wasn't that, Coleridge assured him; it was the way Adams convinced Mildred to disobey her father. He and Mildred always had a very close relationship, she would have never crossed him but for Adams' influence. No gentleman would behave in such a manner. Adams demanded Lord Coleridge make an outright charge, "For God's sake, say it out!" Coleridge would not be interrogated. "He, a peer and Chief Justice, could not stoop to justify himself against a man like me," Adams recalled. Exasperated, he exclaimed, "So who am I, then, Dr. Fell?" A reference to the nursery rhyme:

> I do not like thee, Dr. Fell, the reason why I cannot tell.
> But this I know and know full well, I do not like thee, Dr. Fell.[11]

Lord Coleridge had no more to say and Adams stormed out of the house.

Adams insisted that despite all this back and forth, he saw Mildred less than a handful of times during the summer of 1883. No one saw her, really. She retreated again into sullen seclusion. The family grew increasingly concerned. Her uncle, Father Henry Coleridge, a Jesuit priest at Farm Street in Mayfair, wrote to Maymie bemoaning Adams' "baneful influence."[12] Mildred refused to see anyone. Maymie confided in Lady Eastlake, who then wrote Lord Coleridge,

"I truly feel your ineffable trial in the strange conduct of yr child.

I loved her. I am sure she is not accountable & wd rather think her so than hold her responsible for conduct wh bears no defence & which is so much at variance with her own interests as with her duty. Your sister left me with a very heavy heart that day when she called & told me the terrible state of affairs. May God yet help her & you."[13]

On 11 June, Adams informed Lord Coleridge an engagement announcement had been prepared and was ready for release. Mildred was "still being persecuted respecting himself," forcing him to act:

It is with very great regret that I find myself compelled to make a communication that may not be agreeable. I have therefore to inform you that we have entered into a formal engagement. In doing this without your assent, I am not lacking in respect towards Mildred's father, and I now relieve you of all responsibility except the acquiescence in a *fait accompli*. If your lordship will recognize the position and enforce it upon the family, no further difficulty can arise. [Adams asserted the] "rights of intercourse and protection that a recognised engagement gives; and so long as those rights are respected, and Mildred herself remains happy and unmolested, I shall ask no more."

The following day, Coleridge responded:

I regret to learn that my daughter and you have taken a step, for which, as you correctly say, my sanction was not required. You declare yourself to "possess and to assert rights of intercourse and protection." I perfectly understand, as no doubt you wished I should, the threat conveyed to me in the last paragraph of your letter. I have only to observe that my daughter and you must act as you think fit. But you must distinctly understand that while she remains my daughter she is under my protection, and that I recognise in no one those rights of which you speak. As long as my daughter wishes to remain with her father, she will have as his daughter his tender love, and his watchful care to the very utmost of his powers. When she wishes to leave him, as she and you have both intimated to him, he is quite conscious of the fact that he has no power to retain her. Yours, &c., Coleridge

At Great Marlborough Street, Aunt Harriette's exhibition ("Landscapes in Pastels") was closing; with moderate reviews and tepid sales. One afternoon, when Mildred was there with Adams, Aunt Maymie arrived. She was full of talk about new information she had received. They'd heard from an (un-named) Adams' relation, who, when told of the engagement, chortled, "Good riddance. We're glad to be rid of him in the family." There was a painful scene in the gallery; Mildred shouted down her once favourite aunt, calling her rude and vulgar. The older woman left in tears, claiming there was much being found to Adams' discredit.

Adams immediately wrote a series of letters to Lord Coleridge defending his first marriage. Not to worry, Coleridge replied, "Six or seven and twenty years ago, a boy and girl did that which hundreds have done before and thousands will do again without any wise or kindly man who knows the facts of human nature thinking the least of them for it." From the Judge's Lodgings in Winchester, the Chief Justice continued:

It seems that my sister has imprudently repeated something to your disadvantage told her by someone who denies to be quoted. (A silly woman, who had much better have minded her own business.) I have implored my sister to abstain from any remarks whatsoever about you to any one, and I have no doubt that she will abstain. Your anger is very natural and very pardonable: but good sense will reassume its sway, and you will see things in their true proportion ... I can, I hope, honour and appreciate manly independence, but a man may be independent without constantly adopting a tone of menace and scarcely veiled insult toward a man older than himself, who is also the father of the woman for whose happiness he professes to be anxious ... By the course you are now pursuing you can no doubt succeed, if you count it a success, in making many of us very unhappy; but you cannot succeed in gaining our respect or regard.

Adams had also written that Mildred had been greatly shaken by the gallery clash, describing her as being "at death's door." Her father would not accept that diagnosis:

She is, and has, for years been delicate; my sister and I have seen with pain, long and long ago, how she has grown thinner and weaker slowly year by year. But there has been nothing in the opinion of the most thoroughly competent men to justify such an expression as "death's door." I am thankful to say that both her eyesight and her general health have distinctly and steadily improved, and that the improvement in both is not since her engagement. I will say no more of this. I am, sir, your obedient servant, Coleridge.

In his private moments, Lord Coleridge surely wondered if he was doing the right thing. A friend and brother judge, Sir William Brett, the father of three daughters, wrote him: "If what is contemplated is only imprudent, resist for a time. If it is wrong, resist to the last!"

In August, Lord Coleridge finalised preparations for his trip to America. The Lord Chief Justice was leading a delegation of British jurists invited to the United States. In happier times, Mildred would have sailed with him. To visit the great new American cities, New York, Boston, and Washington should have delighted her. Coleridge also hoped to put the ocean between her and Adams but she refused to go. Emissaries failed to sway her. The pernicious Adams was blamed, of course; everyone believed he had convinced her to insult her father. Mildred's absence was put down to her being a "bad sailor." Plus, there were security concerns.[14]

On 14 August, Lord Coleridge boarded the White Star liner, *Celtic*, in Liverpool. Leaving on the tide, the liner had hardly entered the "sulky swells' of the Irish Sea, when a letter was delivered to Lord Coleridge's state-room. He no doubt recognized the hand-writing:

> My lord, I have purposely postponed this letter until now as it does not call for any reply, being merely intended for your lordship's calm consideration during the weeks which must elapse before we are again thrown together. To the past, I do not propose to refer. If there be anything in it which your lordship considers to require explanation, I am quite ready to explain it. But I am not myself conscious of any such necessity, and think it better for all parties to deal now with the situation only as it stands. Your daughter has "engaged" herself to me. You will, I am sure, admit that unless there be anything unworthy in the connexion itself such an engagement is not a matter for complaint, still less for blame. Of herself, personally, I do not pretend to be worthy. With a woman so thoroughly good and pure and true he would be a bolder man than I who should venture such a

claim. But so far as birth and connexions are concerned, there is certainly no disparity on my side. For character, mine is open to investigation, and in the very small world in which I prefer to live such investigations are very easily made. In respect of pecuniary means, I readily admit that my position is one to which, were I proposing any immediate issue, objection might fairly be made. But, in the first place, even were it so, Mildred is of age to decide for herself after due caution and counsel how far the business of her present position might perhaps, if sacrificed, be compensated to her in other ways. And in the second, I am not proposing, nor have I ever proposed, anything of the kind. So far as her own wishes and happiness are concerned, her mind is, as you know, after many months of reflection, fully made up. I have but to speak the word and she would at once, as it is quite natural and right she would, give herself where her heart is already given. But I have refrained and do refrain from speaking that word, partly because I think with her that it is best for her to continue to set, as long as possible, her filial duties above all others; partly, I own, from that feeling, call it delicacy or pride, which you will, which must needs stand between a man of sensitive temperament and a woman richer than himself. That, my lord, is the footing upon which our relations stand and upon which we both propose that, so far as it with us, they shall for the present at all events continue to stand. It rests with your lordship to make the position comparatively easy or, as it has been hitherto, very painful, in truth, very difficult to us both. I leave it to yourself, to your own good feeling and generosity and fairness, above all to your own regard for her, to decide upon your future course. I am, your lordship's obedient servant, C Warren Adams.

1  A full roster of the VSS, including the executive committee can be found in the The Zoophilist, December 1, 1882.

2  Journalists. In 1881, Henry Labouchere, editor of Truth, a gossipy weekly, was defendant in a major libel action. Coleridge told him he would "rather starve or sweep a gutter than make £5,000 a year," out of a Society journal. Also, "A Judge on Journalism," The Speaker, 5 July 1890, 10.

3  Brent Shannon, *The Cut of His Coat: Men, Dress, and Consumer Culture in Britain*, 1860–1914 (2006) 123.

4  The Seymours: Mildred's "other" family, the family of her late mother. The relationship with the Coleridges was hardly close. Mildred's grand-father, (his lordship's father-in-law) the Rev. G.T. Seymour was a difficult man. He was Tennyson's landlord on the Isle of Wight; the poet called him "the most uncourteous animal I ever dreamed of." In 1863, widowed and 70, he married a young housemaid in St Petrox, Dartmouth. The Coleridges had very little contact with him after that.

5  Harriette Anne Seymour (1830-1901). Mildred's aunt. The exhibition featured her "pleasing and effective" collection of landscapes in crayon. Member of the Society of Lady Artists (from 1899, Women Artists.) "Whatever may be said of her paintings in oil and water colour, in her peculiar power of drawing in crayon she stands alone." More, Sara Gray, *The Dictionary of British Women Artists* (2009).

6  Byron: Letters and Journals of Lord Byron, Lord Byron to Lady Hardy, 1 December 1822. lordbyron.org.

7  "Chaperone" conundrum: "It is one of the greatest misfortunes to which women are liable, that they cannot, consistently with female delicacy, cultivate, before an engagement is made, an acquaintance sufficiently intimate to lead to the discovery of certain facts which would at once decide the point, whether it was prudent to proceed further towards taking that step, which is universally acknowledged to be the most important in a woman's life." Mrs. S.S. Ellis, *The Wives of England* (1843). For a late-Victorian perspective: "Chaperonage," The Spectator, 2 September 1893.

8  American newspaper reports, December 1886, newspapers.com. According to the unbylined London correspondent, Lord Coleridge's court rulings "smell of the Middle Ages."

9  White elephant: "Mr. Barnum and the White Elephant," Pall Mall Gazette, 15 Mar 1883, 11. Barnum (like Adams, perhaps) regarded it as the triumph of his career.

10  Engagements. "Long engagements are now (1869) extremely rare. Any engagement which lasts over two years is now called a long engagement; and one which lasts over two years is reckoned a melancholy and very middle-class affair." Saturday Review.

11  Dr John Fell (1625–1686) was Dean of Christ Church and Bishop of Oxford, a notorious disciplinarian.

12  Adams later tried to bring Father Coleridge in to his libel action, citing the "baneful nfluence" remark. The newspapers varied the word, sometimes baneful, sometimes baleful. They mean much the same thing.

13  "Your ineffable trial," Lady Eastlake to Lord Coleridge 15 July 1883 CFP Add MS 86270.

14  US trip/death threats: Irish militants had issued a "death warrant" for the Lord Chief Justice for his role in the trial of the "Dynamite Conspiracy," a series of bombings and attempted bombings in London. Four American secret service agents were assigned to protect him during his U.S. visit.

# 9. AN AMERICAN INTERLUDE

MILDRED WAS NOT on Mersey-side when her father left for America. Her place in the party was taken by her youngest brother, Gilbert. The 23-year-old lad earned his passage. "Quite proficient on the banjo," he enlivened the evenings during an unusually slow ten-day crossing. Lord Coleridge needed a touch of enlivening and this American interlude was to provide distraction from the maddening Adams. Yet, he could not know as he lay down in his stateroom that first night, as the *Celtic* steamed west, that he was leaving England with one domestic crisis to deal with. When he next saw the landing stages of Liverpool, twelve weeks later, he most definitely had two.

With that suggestive note in place, attention returns to the *Celtic* as it was met in New York harbor by a private yacht carrying a welcoming party including Morrison Waite, Chief Justice of the United States Supreme Court. The *Pastime* cruised around Manhattan Island, passing under the new Brooklyn Bridge on a bright and warm summer day.[1] There were many prominent members of the British bar and judiciary in the arriving party but none attracted America's attention as did Lord Coleridge. One paper pronounced him "England's Big Judge," and his standing "ranks very near to royalty." Physically, he was described as tall, "towering above the crowd," thin, slightly stooped, beard-less, with a stern face but an occasional pleasant smile. He carried himself with a "tone of high-breeding and unbending honour." Albeit his frock coat was described as "carelessly buttoned" which would have given our fastidious lordship great annoyance.

Lord Coleridge's personal tour had been arranged by William

Vanderbilt's son-in-law whose private New York Central rail car carried the Chief and his party through a dozen states - but not Canada which left those British subjects much aggrieved.[2] The reports sent home of the pomp and circumstance afforded to Coleridge's every appearance and speech began to seem a tad ludicrous. *Punch* mocked the tour of "The Learned British Legal Troupe" with some typical doggerel:

> A Lord Chief Justice, by common consent,
> Is Law's most lovely embodiment;
> And that is why the American Bar
> Have selected Me to travel afar.
> And furnish a capital holiday
> For a most mellifluous Lord Chief J.[3]

Lord Coleridge seemed to be on one of "Mr. Cook's package tours." He spent a full hour staring "in mute admiration" at Niagara Falls.[4] He watched sausage being made in a Chicago abattoir. His nights were a parade of dinners and speeches. "Coleridge Fed Again," read one headline. There were more murmurs at home. *The Fortnightly Review,* for which, of course, his Lordship had written, declared, "It may however be questioned whether it was altogether consistent with the dignity of the Chief Justice of England to be carried about America like Barnum's "Greatest Show on Earth." Lord Shaftesbury even wrote to Miss Cobbe; he thought Coleridge was making "a sad fool of himself."[5]

At home, Mildred remained under family pressure. Her childhood friend and ex-Gosling, Sophie Martyn, an unmarried second cousin, suggested Mildred join her for several weeks in Scotland (coincidentally far from Adams). "Cousin Sophie" was active in the VSS chapter in Torquay and knew Adams. At one time, Mildred hoped her relation might be a sympathetic family ear. But Sophie didn't like Adams either; in fact, Mrs. Bishop accused her of spreading "deliberate falsehoods." Mildred let her cousin know the Scotland trip was a non-starter. "I spoke to you openly, appealed to you to help me, showed you my whole heart. And Mr. Adams did the same. We both trusted you. And the result was not, as I think you will admit, such as to encourage either of us to do so again."[6]

Since so many of Mildred's letters were culled from the Coleridge papers, it is extremely fortunate this exchange survives. Included is one remarkable letter in which Mildred suggested her father's view of their relationship was purely his own.

> Of course, he has been so long accustomed to think of me as his unquestioned property about whom there was no need to be anxious, who was always the same & always there, ready to be counted on, without fear of objection from anyone on the ground of consideration for me. I have allowed you all to think that you might count upon me to have no self; to be merely the useful member of the family, who would keep the house & make things easy for everyone; whose home might safely be made uncomfortable [a reference to "the Stephens"], who would resent no sort of interference, & who would never have a wish, a plan, or a feeling on her own account.

Mildred felt herself alone, confronting her united family, all of them determined to crush her relationship with Adams, the first little bit of "unexpected and unsought happiness" she'd found in her life. She vowed to fight on.

> I am very thankful that a strong helper has been at last sent to

me. As long as my father needs me, it is my firm purpose to remain with him, & attend, so far as my strength will serve, to all his wants, and in this purpose, Mr. Adams, as yet, supports me. [But] If he sees it to be for my good that I should exchange my present work ... and be taken care of by him, I shall unhesitatingly obey him.[7]

The Martyn family shared Mildred's letters promptly with Maymie. Aunt Maymie forwarded them to Lord Coleridge. (The family, as with many Victorians, had a propensity for passing their letters around). Maymie was undoubtedly correct in divining the influence of Adams in the arguments Mildred used and the "newspapery" tone of her letters. She wrote to her brother in America. "It is all so utterly wretched and so hopeless that it makes me feel as if, never again, will I have a happy moment."

Meanwhile, Mildred, eschewing the moors of Scotland, headed for the familiar hills of Devon for a summer break. The Bishops had invited her to Torquay. The strain of dealing with her father's adamant opposition had become too much. She was weak and unfit to travel alone. Her lady's maid, Annie Woodcroft, who had been with the family for many years, would normally accompany her. But Annie had a bit of a problem. Her "habits of intoxication" had worsened to the point that several of Mildred's friends - including Mrs. Bishop - declared her unwelcome in their servants' hall. "Faithful" Adams stepped in. Of course, he did. Once again, he rode with Mildred from Paddington to Exeter making the change for Torquay. At his insistence, he refused to linger and surrendered his charge to Mrs. Bishop at the station and immediately booked his return to London. Even in Torquay, however, Coleridge observers were everywhere. Mrs. Martyn, unhappy that Mildred had snubbed her daughter's Scotland idea, made a full report to Aunt Maymie. "I felt so unhappy seeing her in church this morning. She is very white and thin, and looks unhappy and cowed." Separately, Paulina Martyn wrote, "I can hardly describe the pain of seeing Milly with those Bishops, ignoring me."

Adams was quite pleased with himself that he did not take advantage of Lord Coleridge's travels in any way. He one-off escorted Mildred to Torquay and saw her just once more in London. In his Lordship's absence, Sussex Square was closed "for the season," the blinds drawn and furniture covered. Mildred stayed with the Bishops and her other friends in the country for most of the time her father was in America. With his return looming, she returned to London and asked Adams to accompany her on a shopping trip to the West End.[8] When they returned with her purchases to Sussex Square, she invited him in for a meal. Adams demurred; he reminded her of his vow never to re-enter Lord Coleridge's home or presume upon his hospitality. "Don't be silly,' Mildred cheerily answered, 'it won't be much as we're all on board wages!" It was common when servants were left at home without their employers for any length of time, they would get "board wages." The kitchen would be closed and the servants would receive money in lieu of food, probably not quite a pound a week with the men getting a tad more for beer. The custom was to pool their funds, feed themselves cheaply, and pocket the rest for their entertainments.[9] Nonetheless, it would not add lustre to Lord Coleridge's reputation should it get out that he was pinching a few shillings by putting his daughter's comfort on the same footing as the kitchen help. Adams would have that card to play.

In late October, at last, it was time for the Chief Justice to return home. At New York's Academy of Music, before an audience of the great and good, he gave his most important speech in America.[10] He had often been asked whether he thought America was a great country.

Great in size and wealth, yes, he answered. Americans also fought a great war to end "the traffic in human flesh." But to be a great nation, he concluded, Americans must now strive for justice to every man, regardless of origin, race, or riches. His lordship's speech was politely reviewed but, typical of the whole trip, as many words were written about the dinner menu and Lord Coleridge's "jeweled shoe-buckles which glistened in the dazzling light."

Every Saturday, a White Star steamer left for Liverpool. The line "carried the cream of the first-class traffic." On Saturday, 27 October, a large crowd gathered at Pier 52 on the lower west side of Manhattan. Lord Coleridge deigned to sign a few autographs but absolutely no photographs were permitted.[11] He said good-bye to Gilbert who had decided to stay on and see a "bit more of the West." The *S.S. Britannic* was waiting; built in 1874, she was still a "marvel of elegance" and one of the fastest ships on the "Atlantic Ferry" route. Capt. Hamilton Perry personally welcomed Lord Coleridge aboard and, most generously, allowed his Lordship to have his stateroom. The splendid cabin was on "the upper deck forward" with the finest views and minimum effect from the waves. It was fitted out in black walnut and crimson

Lord Coleridge spent nearly two months being fed and feted in the United States. He left New York on October 27, 1883, aboard the White Star's luxurious *S.S. Britannic*. For the return crossing he intended to rest and re-read *The Aeneid*. He arrived in Liverpool a changed man.

velvet with all conveniences. Whilst Capt. Perry set about the process of swinging the 468-foot steamer out into the Hudson, the tall figure of Lord Coleridge was seen standing at the upper deck rail, in a black suit and top hat. A man of his breeding would do nothing as gauche as wave his hat in circles but he was observed to politely acknowledge his "adieus." He was also sporting a white rose in his lapel.

The trans-Atlantic tourist season began to wane as autumn settled in and the *Britannic* was not full when she steamed her way out of New York, "the Sandy Hook lightship abeam." The list of saloon passengers for Liverpool contained about 100 names; by any estimation, Lord Coleridge was the most notable figure. Among the others were a couple of MPs, a handful of "Honourables," an American Civil War general, several prominent physicians, and assorted wives and children. The list of eastbound passengers also included Mrs. A.M. Davies.[12]

It appears Lord Coleridge had little interest in mingling amongst his fellow travelers. Capt. Perry's kind offer was much appreciated. After 5187 American miles and almost 60 days of dinners, speeches, crowds, and varying levels of Yankee comfort in travel and accommodations, it would not have been unreasonable for his lordship to seek the seclusion which a cabin grants. It was time, if reluctantly, to take out again that impertinent letter from Adams. Mildred, the man dared to assert, had "engaged herself" to him. In his unctuous style, Adams wrote, "I leave it to yourself, to your own good feeling and generosity and fairness, above all to your own regard for her, to decide upon your future course." When Coleridge should have yearned for a return to Sussex Square, he found the prospect now distressing. Adams and Mildred would have to be faced and it would not be pleasant. To distract from those worries and to pass some monotonous hours of rolling seas, his lordship began re-reading *The Aenied*. As one does. This we know from a remarkable letter he wrote to a friend during the crossing. It was the letter of an old and lonely man who thought he had no more chance to find love. While reading Virgil always brought him great pleasure, the Roman was no match for Euripedes when it came to women:

> He does paint women, the only one of the Greeks who does, and what exquisite, pure, lovely women his are! There are no such lovely women as his in antiquity, and as, dear old friend, I am nearly sixty-two, and, the few years that are left, I shall go back more and more to these old fellows. They refresh me more, and give, I hope, a sort of glint of sunshine to me ... which nothing else can give.

Lord Coleridge found needed solace in re-reading Virgil's tale of Aeneas and Dido, which he called "the finest love-story in the world." He felt better having read it again. Enough even to dare leave his cabin. "And as the sun is bright and the sea blue, and the crest of the waves snow white, I will go out of my room and bask, yes, bask, on the first of November."[13]

Was that the very day, as with Dido, that Cupid's arrow found the Lord Chief Justice as he basked beneath a steamer-rug in his south-facing deck-chair? "Whoever has taken a long sea voyage aboard a great ship will remember that there is always a great deal of coupling off among the passengers." As her name was mentioned earlier, Mrs. A.M. Davies now graces our narrative. She was "understood to be the widow of an English officer." In the Lord Chief Justice's official "Life and Letters" published posthumously, the author - his nephew Ernest Hartley Coleridge - states that "it was on the homeward voyage that he made the acquaintance of his second wife." They met "as strangers but there had been a friendly acquaintance between his family and hers for more than thirty years." Mrs. Davies was born Amy Augusta Jackson Lawford; her uncle, now a clergyman, had been at Eton with

Lord Coleridge. Sadly, his lordship never had the pleasure of meeting Amy's father, Henry Baring Lawford, who had been a judge himself, serving many years on the Raj bench in Bengal until his recent death. It seems the slightest of acquaintances but, in transitory steamer company, it was certainly worth calling upon by way of introduction and then the lady's charm would take over. Amy was 30 years old, vivacious, attractive, with "a slender though perfectly molded figure."[14]

"There is something in the quality of sea air strongly conducive to flirtation." Two years later, those who claimed they were aboard the *Britannic*, recalled how the stately judge and the "fair and mysterious" young woman were soon inseparable. He "danced attendance upon her," in fact. There were some who believed the faster steamers would be hurtful to the "flirting classes." Others, and probably with merit, believed that as each hour passed and England got closer, with its prospect of a tearful separation at the dock, the pace of any romance would be that much more hastened.[15]

The last days of this crossing came in "rather ugly" November weather. The rain was steady as the *Britannic* reached her moorings at Liverpool at midday on 5 November. There was an invitation waiting for Lord Coleridge to attend a reception that afternoon for Princess Louise and her husband, the Marquis of Lorne. His Lordship declined, citing important engagements awaiting him in London. There was a special train steamed and ready for him at Lime Street station but, curiously, he asked that it be held. The Liverpool papers proudly reported Lord Coleridge, despite the weather, desired first to pay brief visits to historic St. George's Hall, the Art Gallery, and Museum. Only the *Liverpool Daily Post* dropped the morsel that the Lord Chief Justice made the rounds "in company with a lady friend."[16]

It had been – to a point - a mundane nine-day crossing. Yet, the powers of Virgil's pen on our lonely traveller cannot be underestimated.

The romance of Aeneas and Dido had flowered equally rapidly. The lovers were, as Virgil wrote, "unmindful of the realm, prisoners of lust."[17] As for Miss Lawford, we can choose to refer to the official biography which – two decades later – noted carefully "the acquaintance begun on board ship ripened into an ardent attachment." At home, however, Stephen Coleridge would put it to you more bluntly: "She met my father aboard ship from America – She became his mistress."[18]

The Mistress Note: In this handwritten note, found in his papers, Stephen Coleridge claims that Miss Baring Lawford had been his father's mistress until she was pensioned off. The arrangement broke down, Stephen asserts, when she regained her influence over Lord Coleridge, and threatening to mount a disastrous breach of promise lawsuit, he gave in and agreed to marry her. Courtesy of his great-great-grandson, Sir Paul Coleridge.

1  The Brooklyn Bridge, longest in the world at the time, had opened only that May, 1883.

2  Vanderbilts: Lord Coleridge dined at the home of W.H. Vanderbilt, the world's richest man. "The house is fabulously splendid, very magnificent, but no repose anywhere. It streams money down the walls, up the staircase." Life, Vol. 2, 334.

3  Punch, Vols 85-86, 107.

4  Niagara Falls: A few weeks earlier (24 July 1883), Capt. Webb, the celebrated British Channel swimmer, drowned in his attempt to swim the Whirlpool Rapids.

5  29 October 1883, Shaftesbury to Cobbe. Presumably, this is a reference to the whole "grand tour" and not other matters soon to be revealed.

6  Mary Sophia Paulina Martyn (1843-1887), apparently. The naming conventions in Victorian families - passing the same names down by all siblings to their own children - muddles modern genealogists no end. April 1, 2020, English Ancestors blog.

7  The Mildred/Sophie letters can be found in CFP Add MS 85973.

8  *Shopping escort? Women alone, even in the West End*, risked purse-snatching, insults, and worse. By the 1880s, however, escorts were beginning to be thought unnecessary. The "new women" began to travel in groups, deciding to "companion one another." E.D. Rappaport, Shopping for Pleasure: Women in the Making of London's West End (2000) 138.

9  "Board wages," see Dickens's *Dictionary of London* (1879).

10  Lord Coleridge's speech: New York Times 12 October 1883, 5.

11  Antipathy to portraits/photos: "He is, so to speak, equally ready to place in the pillory author, publisher, or artist, who presumes to deal with his graceful and gracious lineaments." Exeter & Plymouth Gazette, 24 February 1871.

12  I have relied on the thorough Britannic passenger list published in the Anglo-American Times, 9 November 1883. In addition, I have tried all the various sources, including Ancestry's UK and Ireland, Incoming Passenger Lists, 1878-1960. There are admitted gaps in that collection and, alas, this particular crossing and Liverpool arrival seems to be one of them. Anyone with knowledge of the Britannic passenger list, contact the author.

13  Reading The Aeneid, Dido & basking, etc., Lord Coleridge's letter to Sir M.E. Grant-Duff, Life, Vol. 2, 334-5.

14  HB Lawford, followed the usual route to the Indian Civil Service. After schooling at Haileybury, he went out in 1850, married an officer's daughter two years later. Amy was his first child. His career path began as a Magistrate's assistant and collector of the second grade. He retired in 1878 as a District & Sessions Judge, First Grade, Jessore, Bengal. Not much is known of his career, although when taking leave in 1871, a local paper reported his departure "was hailed with universal delight." Jessore correspondent of the Daily Examiner quoted in the Amrita Bazaar Puttak. 23 June 1871.

15  Shipboard romances: Before movies, there were novels: "I can conscientiously say that I never saw such an amount of unmistakable love-making within the same amount of space in my life." James Burnley, *Two Sides of the Atlantic* (1880).

16  "Lady friend," Liverpool Daily Post, 6 November 1883, 5.

17  "Prisoners of lust," Aeneid (Book I, l. 265).

18  Handwritten note in the possession of Sir Paul Coleridge.

# 10. OTHERWISE DAVIES

SOME BRIEF BIOGRAPHICAL details of the "lady friend" who would become the fascinating Baroness Coleridge are of great interest and essential to the second family schism that followed.[1]

Amy Lawford was born on 9 April 1853 in Krishnanagar, Bengal, the eldest child of Georgiana and Henry Baring Lawford. "Several generations" of Lawfords had served the Raj, in the military, civil service, and the law. Amy's father was Chief Judge of the High Court of Krishnanagar. She was a child of four when the Mutiny erupted; her father's region remained generally calm during that tragic period. Still, it was thought best that Mrs. Lawford take Amy (and her sister Flora and brother Egerton) back to England. At home, the Lawford children were placed with their mother's widowed sister, Aunt Sarah Davies, living in Portsmouth. Anglo-Indian families of means, like the Lawfords went back and forth quite often, rotating home usually for health reasons. In the 1860s, Judge and Mrs. Lawford were back in England, reunited with their children, and acquired a home in Upton Park, in a "salubrious" section of Slough offering magnificent views of Windsor Castle. Aunt Sarah also came to live there accompanied by her son, the majestically named John Augustus Seymour Morse Davies. In most of the contemporary accounts of *Davies (Otherwise Lawford) v Davies*, Davies is depicted as a caddish young officer along the lines of Jane Austen's Capt. Wickham. Fairly, perhaps, yet the man should get some credit for having an impressive CV. Davies had a B.A., he was a member of the Royal Institution, a fellow of the Royal

Astronomical Society, and a Lieutenant in the Royal Artillery. He also found the time to form an attachment with his pretty young first cousin, home from India, Miss Amy Lawford. Judge Lawford, alas, disapproved or, at least, believed Amy was too young for marriage. Davies was 28; Amy was just 17. His decision rendered, the jurist decamped again for Bengal.

With the disapproving pater soon 7000 miles away in Calcutta, Lt. Davies put a plan into motion. On 30 June 1870, Amy, her sister Flo, and Miss Cleaver, their governess, were at dancing school in London's Portman Square. Lt. Davies waltzed in and "by some specious pretext" was allowed to leave with Amy. They raced by carriage along the New Road to King's Cross for the 5:00pm train to Edinburgh. They reached the "auld grey toon" the next morning (July 1, pay heed, as these dates will assume a great importance.) Lodging was found in the upmarket *Edinburgh Hotel* in Prince's Street. The laws of Scotland in 1870 required anyone domiciled outside North Britain to reside in Scotland for 21 days before marriage.[2] Thus, patiently, on the morning of the 21st, having paid the twenty shillings fee at the registry office in Cockburn Street, John Davies and Amy Lawford "contracted a marriage by declaration" just before noon.

Waverley Station was a short walk down Cockburn Street and the newlyweds caught the first North British train south. They were back in Bucks the following day.[3] Amy was soon pregnant and John was busy with his new book, published in May 1871 by Longman's, *The Meteoric Theory of Saturn's Rings, Considered with Reference to the Solar Motion in Space*.[4] Who couldn't be impressed with the credentials of the author, Augustus Morse Davies, B.A., F.R.A.S., M.R.I., P.A.C., LIEUTENANT, ROYAL ARTILLERY? It was a thin volume, with "elaborate plates," in which Davies contended that our home planet, earth, will at some future date, get its own rings.

Described as the product of a "somewhat imaginative astronomer," the book transited the sky quickly and disappeared.

In August 1871, at Upton Park, their first child was born. Infant Evelyn Davies lived only seven weeks; she died that October.[5]

After that heartbreaking event, the story abruptly jumps ahead more than five years to 1877 when Miss Lawford ("Otherwise Davies") sought to annul her "pretended, irregular" marriage as it had not been contracted in accordance with Scottish law. The case was heard in London on 27 November 1877.[6] In the witness box, Mrs. Davies admitted going to Edinburgh with Lt. Davies for the purpose of arranging a "clandestine marriage." She provided dates and the trains they took. She recalled crossing the border at Berwick "very early in the morning," about 4am, on the first of July. They remained in Edinburgh until 21 July when they were married by a registrar and immediately left Scotland the early afternoon of her wedding day. How boring for the morbid loungers who filled the public gallery of the Divorce Court craving titillation. Instead, they heard a tedious parsing of the arcane intricacies of Scottish marriage law. Prior to 1856, the Borders village of Gretna Green was the storied destination for "fugitive marriages," romantic elopements in high-life and low. To at least complicate such "irregular" nuptials, Parliament passed "Lord Brougham's Law," requiring a 21-day residence in Scotland (officially worded "for the 21 days next preceding such marriage.") In 1870, our runaway couple thought they complied with the new law by residing in Edinburgh for 21 consecutive days. Seven years later, counsel for "Mrs. Davies" made a novel claim: Amy and John had only resided in Scotland for "half the day they arrived, then nineteen days, and half the day they were married before returning to England." This was not, they demanded, 21 *full* days. At least her husband co-operated. From India, Capt. Davies (he had been promoted in 1876), did not stir himself to save his marriage. Did they both want out? In the Divorce Court, collusion between the parties was an "absolute bar" to any action. Davies did not reply to the nullity petition.

This was a new tactic. How does one define a day? The presiding judge, Sir James Hannen, adjourned to consult with experts in Scotland. The following February, Hannen ruled. A day, by common understanding, runs from midnight to midnight. The law in Scotland required 21 days residency. Therefore, using the "rule of computation," Miss Lawford and Lt. Davies had only been in Scotland for 19 full days plus two partial days. Their marriage was not lawful and, therefore, void. The ruling was "much to Miss Lawford's delight." By law, she could resume using her maiden name. The process seemed rather a tortuous path to reach an end. Whatever the calendar calculations, Amy and Davies left Edinburgh in 1870 believing they had been legally married. They lived as husband and wife; they had a child together. She went out to India with her husband when his regiment was posted thither. They had lived together for as long as six years. Did no one ask why, once these missing half-days were discovered, the couple did not go back and get re-married legally? Clearly, she (they?) wanted a divorce. Since 1857, divorce was more readily available but, as with many things, made more difficult for women. A husband had only to prove his wife's adultery; a wife need two grounds. Adultery and some aggravating circumstance. The process was costly and, for a woman, left an indelible mark. A clever loophole allowed Amy to escape that stigma. Remember, she came from a family of lawyers; her father was a judge. Her annulment filing was handled by Lawford & Waterhouse, prominent London solicitors. Hannen's ruling meant the marriage never happened. Amy gained her freedom from Davies. Had she found a new gentleman? If there was a "person of interest" waiting in Amy's world in 1877, he remains unknown.

The story hastens next to 1883. Five years had passed from "Miss Lawford's" annulment. The same half-decade had passed since the death of Lord Coleridge's wife. We know almost everything about his lordship's life, personal and professional, over that five-year period. We know almost nothing about Miss Lawford, where she was living or how she occupied her time. They found themselves together, traveling alone, on the *Britannic*. There were reports she met him during his lordship's American tour, perhaps in Chicago, and then accompanied him for the remainder of his stay, giving rise to comment as her position in the entourage was not clear. It was later claimed Mrs. Lawford arranged it all; she and Amy were supposedly in America at the time. Mother Lawford, relying on her purported Eton connections, contrived a meeting and asked his Lordship to look after Amy on the return crossing as she was traveling to England alone. This cannot be confirmed. It is odd that a young woman, even a widow, would be travelling alone. Still, it is important to remember fact-checking was rarely done and free-lance "journalists" learned quickly the better the story the better the sale. The most curious claim appeared in *Life*, a gossip weekly in November 1886:

> I have been interested to learn, on very good authority that Lady Coleridge, prior to her marriage, had performed the onerous and responsible duties of stewardess on a large ocean steamer, a position demanding tact and temper. It was, I believe, whilst acting in that capacity that she first attracted the learned and alluring peer, and it is whispered that her mother deemed his Lordship's attentions too marked to hear of their being interpreted as a mere steamship flirtation.

The article appeared (much later) in many English papers

without contradiction.[7] Efforts to trace a Lawford, Baring-Lawford, or Davies in the employment records of White Star or Cunard have been unsuccessful. While the Coleridge papers have been clearly scrubbed, Bernard and Stephen, neither of whom had any regard for their stepmother, ever made the slightest allusion to suggest any of this was true.

Sparing the reader further rhapsodies about the romantic powers of a sea cruise, it can be confidently stated that, by the time the steamer reached Liverpool, despite their 33-year age gap, his Lordship and Miss Lawford were in love, and possibly, were lovers. It might even be said he had "engaged himself" to her. The latter, if true, would have sounded familiar to Charles Warren Adams.

---

1  Tracing the Lawford and Davies families has been done through the UK census records, National Archives, Kew, and FamilySearch.com (U.S.) Henry Baring-Lawford's Raj career can be traced in the annual India List: Civil & Military.

2  The ages of Morse Davies and Amy were not an issue. The law in Scotland (and the UK) required the groom to be at least 14, the bride just 12. Scotland did not require parental consent.

3  Slough was transferred from Bucks to Berks in the 1974 local government reorganization.

4  Meteoric Theory: Would it amaze anyone to know the full text of Capt. Davies' 1871 work is available in Google Books?

5  Baby Davies: Birth announced London Daily News, 5 September 1871; death announced Bucks Herald, 28 October 1871.

6  Lawford (Otherwise Davies v Davies: *The Law Times* Volume XXXIX, 111. The case was widely reported and discussed in legal circles. See Sir William Nevill Montgomerie Geary, *The Law of Marriage and Family Relations* (1892) 535.

7  The gossip was reprinted in three dozen newspapers, most prominently the Sheffield Telegraph and the South Wales Echo. British Newspaper Archive.

# 11. YOUR AFFECTIONATE BROTHER

LORD COLERIDGE, SANS his mysterious female companion, stepped out of the train from Liverpool at Euston Station on the evening of 5 November 1883, greeted by a "large number of legal gentlemen." Two days later, he was back on the bench. On 9 November, delighted to appear again in his full regalia, he took part in the pageantry of the Lord Mayor's Day. The papers thought he looked quite fit.[1] They could not know either of his pre-existing domestic trouble at home or the new complication of his relationship with Miss Lawford.

Mildred, of course, had been waiting for her father at home. As she remembered it, and this is based upon her affidavits, she hoped the emotions of the homecoming might have some effect. "I did the utmost I could to impress upon my father that I had not the least desire to leave him, but only wished to occupy my then position as long as he lived." But Lord Coleridge had returned with no change of heart; rather, he "plainly expressed his intention of adopting precisely the same attitude as before." Mildred was "thoroughly broken." She couldn't endure another winter of censure at Sussex Square, complicated by her continuing hostility with "the Stephens." It was useless to continue the struggle, she and Adams concluded. "We were not at all inclined to give up our friendship, which had naturally grown all the closer, and therefore decided to marry."

There was never any chance she and Adams might marry and share quarters in her father's home. Father and son-in-law passing the port after dinner wasn't in the cards. On Saturday, 11 November, Adams came to Sussex Square at Mildred's request for the two of them to renew their appeals to her father. All she requested was that he sanction their marriage and agree to "the provision, and not a farthing more than he had always promised." The figure of £17,000 was mentioned which set Lord Coleridge reeling and he rejected "on the spot." They must not expect any such amount, he said. Still, if they wished to marry, he would not interfere. He asked for one day to prepare a marriage settlement. The next day, a Sunday morning, Mildred recalled her father arose in good spirits. That afternoon, he went to his club, the Athenaeum. Seated at one of the "abundantly provided writing tables" in the first-floor library, he drafted, in his frequently illegible hand, the so-called "Athenaeum Memorandum." [Emphases the author's]

Mr. Adams desires to marry my daughter, but he informs me --- at least so I understand him - that he has absolutely no income of his own, nor any present or speedy prospect of obtaining any, even the smallest. As far as I am aware, this has been the case for at least a year, during which he has been carrying on an intercourse with my daughter of a character which any experience of life must have shown him would probably end in the present state of things. *He has been constantly in my daughter's company in my house and elsewhere, but as far as I am aware has made no efforts to obtain permanent employment or secure a regular income. He engaged himself to my daughter, not only without my sanction, but without even asking for it.* He is no longer young, and he has changed his course of life, if not often, then certainly oftener than is common, without as yet having acquired any competent maintenance or the means of gaining one. He has also a daughter of his own, whose claims upon him for maintenance I have no doubt he fully recognizes.

It could answer no good end to go into a history of the

past, not even to discuss whether my extreme distaste to the conduct of Mr. Adams be well or ill founded. His conduct has at least been in defiance of all ordinary rules, and seems to me wholly indefensible, and it is enough for my present purpose that I feel this very strongly. Under these circumstances, *I am in fact asked to provide the whole maintenance of Mr. Adams and my daughter; to help forward a marriage I dislike and disapprove of;* in truth, to permit him to take advantage of conduct, which as a man certainly full of intelligence and knowledge of mankind, he never, in my opinion, ought to have permitted himself to indulge in. No less than this is asked of me; for two people cannot marry without an income, and the proposed husband frankly avows that he has none at present, and it must depend upon uncertain contingencies when, if ever, he will have and what it will be. If Mr. Adams were a young man; if although at present without means, he had every prospect of obtaining them; or *if, without such prospect, he were a man whom personally I loved and admired, the matter would be different; but as it is, what is asked appears to me altogether unusual and unreasonable, and I must decline to do it.* But I remember that my daughter has set her heart on this connection, and I am very desirous of acting, if I can, justly and liberally.

So far as any discomforts at home have affected my daughter, they are in the process of removal, according to my promise, and they must very soon disappear. I will add this - that my statements may not be indefinite as to time. I hope both from my daughter and Mr. Adams a real endeavour to act fairly by me - he by honestly trying for some definite employment, she by doing her best to be cheerful and reasonable. *I don't think June 1884 too long to test the reality of the efforts I have referred to. But if then or sooner the reasonable conditions (as they seem to me) which I have mentioned are, I will not say satisfied, but if any real earnest of satisfying them is given me, I will at once settle £300 a year on my daughter for life.* Nay, more, I will remake at once my will to that extent, as I am well aware of the more than common risks which attend my life. This I will undertake to do. I do not say this is all I will do, but this at least I will. *If this paper is not accepted by the parties in the faith and spirit in which I write it, they, of course, are free to take what course they please, but they must not expect me to help them.*

The document was sealed and dispatched by messenger to Adams. His lordship returned home, arriving, according to Mildred, "in a great state of satisfaction." He showed her his draft copy of the memorandum. Mildred knew her man and predicted Adams would be furious. Amid the memo's verbosity were pointed blows. He accused Adams of presuming Lord Coleridge would bankroll the "whole maintenance" of his marriage. Even this his lordship might have considered doing if Adams "were a man whom personally I loved and admired." Clearly, he did not. Mildred later swore, but her father denied, that he verbally promised to ask Prime Minister Gladstone to find a government job for Adams. Mildred thought Adams would never accept any such handout. Coleridge wondered how one man could be so "absurdly sensitive." And that was that.

The following day, Adams returned the memorandum to Lord Coleridge marked PERUSED C.W.A. 13-11-83. Of course, he included a letter (Emphases the author's):

Lord Coleridge's memo, to which I have appended my initials in token of perusal, and of which I retain a certified copy, is herewith returned as requested. It appears to me to admit of but one reply. Into its representations of past events or present position I do not think it necessary to enter, save by a plain assertion that they are altogether inaccurate and unjust. Nor, though quite prepared to do so on a fitting occasion, do I find called upon to enter here on any justification of my own conduct. I will simply deal with the two or three leading points in the memo, which render any further discussion useless and at once impossible. And first as to its general tenor, and to *the plain insinuation which pervades it throughout, that for the twelve months I have been, instead of attempting to provide for myself, simply scheming to extort, by marriage, with his daughter, an ignominious pension from Lord Coleridge.* I cannot but think in making such an insinuation against my father's son, the Lord Chief Justice must have forgotten, if nothing else, at least those immunities of age and office to which he has at other times appealed, and which, according at all events to the old-fashioned code under which I was brought up, should forbid the offering of wanton insult by those whom they protect from any fitting reply. Bearing them myself in mind, I am content with simply stating that in respect alike of my action and of my motive, the insinuation itself is as untrue as the manner of it is unworthy. The position into which Lord Coleridge's daughter and myself have been 'forced' is wholly and solely of his Lordship's own making. It has been pointed out to him over and over again that the line he has persisted in pursuing not only was unjust to us both, and singularly cruel to her, but must inevitably end, as it has now ended; and over and over again he has been implored, not only by ourselves, but by friends and close relations of his own with whom he has one by one quarrelled solely on that ground, to adopt a wiser course. So strong have been my own representations on the subject, and so earnest my efforts to ward off, for the very sake of my regards for one I esteemed so highly as his daughter, an issue which in a worldly sense needs be so undesirable for her, that I now find them to have been actually used by Lord Coleridge as ground for taunting her with my backwardness. Into the circumstances of more than that one kind to which Lord Coleridge refers, which made her position, outwardly so prosperous, really very painfully lonely and void of anything like comfort or sympathy, I do not wish, unless by his desire to enter. They are already known to him, as to myself and others. Three years ago, circumstances for which Lord Coleridge was himself directly responsible threw us into very intimate relations, and she found in me a friend thoroughly sympathising in thought and feeling, and both able and willing to afford her loyal help and counsel on many points with regard to which she was in sore need of both. Above all a friend in whom she could trust, as absolutely free from *arriere pensee* of any kind. *Our friendship was a pure and loyal friendship; so at our age friendship may surely be, even between man and woman, without thought of anything further. The mere idea of anything more was for different reasons most repugnant to us both,* and would so have remained, had it not been forced upon us with a persistence which in time familiarised us with it, and rendered it at length the only peaceful issue. Unfortunately, Lord Coleridge was unable to realise such a relationship. A long life passed at Nisi Prius and in the Divorce Court may, no doubt, not unnaturally result in a somewhat cynical view of human nature. But *his Lordship was unable to conceive of any man as actuated by views other than sordid, or any woman by feelings other than sexual.* Unfortunately, too, he appears to have fallen into the yet more fatal error of supposing that the means by which a man of the world succeed in pushing his way to fortune - the kicking down of the ladder by which you have climbed, and slamming the door in face of the friend whose services are no longer needed - would equally commend themselves to the mind of a loyal-hearted woman. It is no fault of mine if this double mistake has led to its inevitable result. Lord Coleridge states that he is asked to provide the whole maintenance of us both. So far as I at all events am concerned, this statement is, in plain words, untrue. I have never asked, or hinted at asking, of him a single sixpence present or future. Only last Saturday he himself complained angrily of my "want of common sense" in refusing to do so. Nay, it is a plain reverse of truth. Nearly six months ago, at our very first interview, he commenced by a statement that he had altered his will in some way not stated, but impliedly to the exclusion of his daughter. I replied that personally I was relieved to hear what happily freed me from a 'hampering scruple.' Thereupon he changed his ground, assuring me with much becoming indignation that I was quite mistaken in him, that he was not at all the sort of man to make any difference in his daughter's provision on such grounds, and that, 'however she might marry, she would in any case have £17,000.' This plain assurance I accepted and acted upon in simple good faith. I referred to it in my letter to Lord Coleridge on his departure to the U.S. as the consideration which chiefly tied my hands, and it is only now that I learn the true state of the case, and how my own disinterested scruples have been made the means of tampering and thwarting us both. So much for any share of mine in the asserted requests. For his daughter's part, she has, it seems to me, not unnaturally expressed in such terms as a daughter may, her sense of the injustice which after promising her all her life a fitting and independent provision, suddenly leaves her at the age of 36, and without a shadow of fault on her part, wholly dependent, even for bare existence, upon a younger brother. But I know that so far from begging for money, she at once, helplessly weak and ill as she is, set herself to find some means of self-support. *I am at this moment engaged, by her request, in business negotiations, with a view, should she recover, of turning her musical talent to account,* until such time, I trust not distant, as I shall be able to welcome her into my own keeping. Of Lord Coleridge's present proposition I need say but few words. *Knowing what we both know - for it has been urged upon her by every medical man through whose hands she has passed - of the more than critical condition of his daughter's health and the deadly injury the present state of things is inflicting upon her, one is almost tempted to ask if the suggestions of its prolongation to June next be not, if serious, dictated by the conviction that by that time she will be beyond the need of earthly provision.* If other than serious, I can only say that the jest appears to me, under the circumstances, a singularly heartless one. Of the other details of the proposition I have only to observe in passing that they are from first to last in flat discrepancy with the statements and pledges voluntarily proffered by Lord Coleridge on Saturday last. But there is no need to enter upon them. The form and tone of his Lordship's proposition render its conditions, be they what they may, simply of no importance. *I reject it unhesitatingly without discussion and without reserve. And, so rejecting, I cast upon Lord Coleridge himself the entire responsibility of whatever untoward consequence may ensue.* He will clearly understand that I am not relinquishing one tittle of the relationship with which his daughter has honoured me, and which at the earliest possible moment I shall without further hesitation or scruple, ask her to exchange for one yet closer. But *in his house I will never willingly set foot again.* He has made any attempt at accommodation impossible - not by the mere withholding of money, which, as I have long since proved, would be a matter of absolute indifference, but by the wanton outrage with which it has been accompanied. That it should be so I regret more deeply than I can say, but regret is all that is now left in my power. C.W.A.

To give the man his credit, Adams' ability – common perhaps in a journalist – to dash off a politely furious 1500-word reply in a single afternoon's time was most impressive. He returned in kind the frosty third-person formality of the memorandum. His suggestion that "Lord Coleridge" actually hoped, during this six-month waiting period, that his sickly daughter might die before the agreement need be acted upon, was brilliantly cold. Mrs. Bishop once told Adams that Lord Coleridge believed "any man of ordinary feeling would rather see his daughter dead than marry such a man." The real issue between the two men, of course, was Mildred's money. In the will written after his wife died in 1878, Coleridge made the provision that, *at his death,* he would leave Mildred £17,000, providing her until then with a very suitable £800 per year. In the memorandum, however, he agreed to provide her - on her marriage - the more modest sum of £300 per year. Adams cleverly and repeatedly protested his indifference to Mildred's fortune, his "disinterested scruples." The cliché is - when anyone insists it is not about the money, hold firmly to your purse or wallet. Adams proclaimed his disinterest in Lord Coleridge's money. However, as Mildred's portion had been reduced (from £800 to £300 p/a) on his account, he bore the responsibility, as her defender, to demand Mildred be restored to her "*status quo ante* Adams." Mildred was also confused and hurt by what she saw as a sharp reduction in her expectations. "Never up to that moment [had her father] given me the slightest idea of any intention to make a diminution in it." When she protested, he told her, "I made an offer and will not go beyond it."

Lord Coleridge might have been advised to let Adams' bitter riposte go unacknowledged but that would have been out of character. He was unable to avoid making a "few but necessary" comments. Adams' reply was "like every other letter he has ever written to me, full of inaccuracies and 'swelling language.'" How could it be a "wanton insult" to believe the man who would marry his daughter should have a plan or desire to make an income? Adams "had none and the prospect of none. If a husband and wife live together and the husband has no income, I must think that the person who finds an income for the wife finds it for the husband. Nevertheless, the moment I see him striving after an income I will do my best to bring about the marriage." Coleridge again rejected any notion Mildred could have expected £17,000. The offer stands: Mildred will get £300 a year if her father dies, and, "the moment Mr. Adams has any solid ground of income, Lord Coleridge will sanction the marriage and secure at once to her £300 a year." He thanked Adams for his concern for Mildred's health, but she was doing fine, citing a recent examination by Sir James Paget, the top doctor of the day.[2] Adams, temporarily, surrendered. "Mr. Adams has only to request that the correspondence may be allowed to cease."[3]

Thorough readers may have noticed in the *Athenaeum* memorandum Lord Coleridge's comment: "So far as any discomforts at home have affected my daughter, they are in the process of removal." Stephen, his pregnant wife, and 2-year-old Johnny, found a new home, well across the Park, in Knightsbridge. The irony is Lord Coleridge undoubtedly underwrote the move to Ovington Gardens although Stephen, like Adams, had no steady income. Stephen did have a new plan, his venture at the moment was selling "bin end" wines on commission.[4] Be that as it may, Mildred saw the imminent space and quiet at Sussex Square as an opportunity for her new venture. If an income was required, her father could not object if she took in select pupils for language study or pianoforte instruction. He seemed to give his assent and Mildred immediately sent out her "prospectus."

Miss Mildred M. Coleridge is desirous of receiving pupils for four courses of lectures extending from July to December (inclusive), with the exception of Christmas, Holy Week, and Whitsun Week. Terms for each course, 14 guineas, payable in advance. Pianoforte lessons, 10s, 6d. and £1 1s. ADDRESS: The Hon. Mildred Coleridge. 1 Sussex Square, Hyde Park, W.

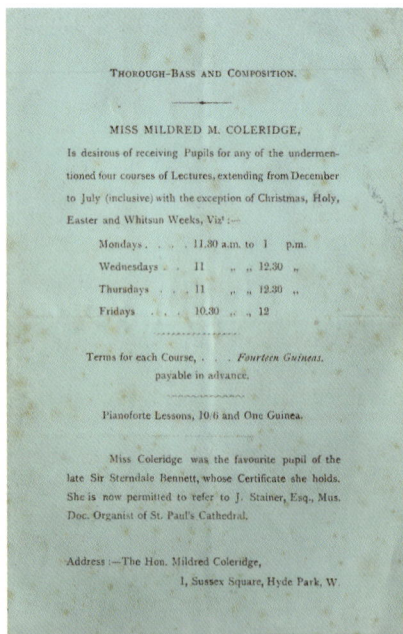

A copy of the "card" announcing Mildred's intentions to give music lessons in her father's home, 1 Sussex Square. The charge was 14 guineas, payable in advance. She first circulated this proposal among her father's network of friends and colleagues.

She planned first to circulate her card among her network of friends, the better part of that number were her father's friends.[5] Lord Coleridge had written privately to several of them explaining (*his version*) of what was going on at Sussex Square. He received supportive notes in return which he showed to Mildred, "Here's what your friends have to say." Mildred was furious and sent notes of her own to Ladies Iddesleigh, Hobhouse, Brett, etc and Mr. Butterfield. "Out of fairness," she wanted them to know *her side* of the story. Her father was threatening to cut her (and Adams) off with a "pittance" thus she intended to raise money for their future. There are no copies of these notes but their tone can be suggested by Butterfield's reply:

> If you are content and happy in the course you are taking and in the state of mind you are indulging, and the language you use about your father, your conscience must, in my opinion, be asleep. All of my sense of propriety and duty is shocked in the most painful way by your last two letters. I feel that you are not in a state to be reasoned with, and that this should be so makes me very sad. I am, my dear Mildred, W.T. Butterfield[6]

Butterfield's reaction was not unique. Her letter, obviously Adams' creation, was meant as a studied insult to her father. According to Mildred, her father announced he would not permit her to give any lessons at Sussex Square. "He was violently angry with me and threatened to order the servants not to post my letters." This rebuke was done in the presence of Stephen and his wife. To be humiliated in front of them was too much for Mildred. "I now asked and received [her father's] sanction to my going to visit an old friend of my mother's until they left, which was to be in the course of ten days or a fortnight." In other words, and this would be important, Mildred was always planning to return. She never did; Mildred insisted her father "peremptorily forbade" her to come home.

On 8 December, Aunt Maymie's diary recorded, "Millie went to Marian Blachford."[7] The Blachfords were Devon gentry and longtime friends of the family. Word of the Coleridge "calamity" quickly circulated among their intimates. Charlotte Yonge, the former Mother Goose to Mildred's Gosling, heard the news from

Aunt Maymie who wrote to her "in despair." Mildred mailed her "circulars" far and wide, accusing her father of "persecution," forcing her to seek her own income. Lady Eastlake defended Lord Coleridge – what was a man to do when "his only daughter [was] set upon a miserable marriage?"[8]

Bernard Coleridge returns after some little absence to make the greatest impact of all. Mildred's eldest brother had been preoccupied for much of 1883. He thought he'd achieved his dream of standing for the House of Commons. It was not to be; first in Exeter, then in Bristol, his Liberal party chose another man.[9] Thus, Bernard was quite cross when he came home to London in December. He arrived to hear his father's anguished recapitulation of the Mildred saga. Bernard thought this had gone on long enough. He walked the short distance to his home in Bayswater where he wrote a remarkable letter he little knew would someday be published in newspapers around the world. Let his father dance about the issues. Bernard would tell Mildred the straight truth. (Emphases the author's):

> PRIVATE 11 Westbourne Street, 11th December 1883
> My dear Mildred, *I write to you not only as your brother, but chiefly as my father's son,* because I feel it to be my duty. I write in order that when misery and unhappiness come upon you - as come they will - you may not have it to say that you were not fully warned, and that matters were concealed from you. *Are you aware of the character of the man to whom you are about to give yourself up? His family, one and all, will have nothing to do with him.* Is this all without reason? Do you know he has failed throughout his life? Why is this, for he is a man of undoubted ability? It is because of his utter want of character and principle. Do you know anything of his past history? Do you know of his behaviour on his voyage to the Cape? Do you

know he ran away with a girl under age? Do you know that
so strong was the indignation at his conduct that the Bishop
of Cape Town ordered his clergy to refuse to marry him, and
that consequently he, with his High Church professions, was
married by a Presbyterian? Do you know of the life he led that
unhappy girl after she became his wife, and how she lived to
rue bitterly the day when she consented to do what you are
contemplating - a marriage in defiance of the wishes of her
friends and relations? Do you know what sort of person his
daughter is? Under such circumstances, and with such a father,
it should be a wonder were she otherwise: but do you know that
she has an irreconcilable temper, and that she is boarded out of
charity by her relations to rescue her from her father? Have you
considered that as soon as his home becomes yours they will be
glad of the opportunity of ridding themselves of the burden
that is cast upon them, and will send her back to her father?
Are you prepared to live with her? Do you know that Mr.
Adams has a violent temper? Can you disguise from yourself
in your vanity that it is money and position, not you, that he is
scheming to obtain? *Do you know he has admitted that in his
eyes you are devoid of personal attractiveness- that you would
not make him a good wife, and that you would be to him a
white elephant?*

[But you told one girl at any rate with an indelicacy
which has shocked and astounded her parents that you do not
contemplate living with Mr. Adams as his wife. This is a subject
which, unless you had previously broached it, I should forbear
to touch. But are you so ignorant as not to know that misery
almost always accompanies such unnatural unions? And do you
not see the transparent reasons for Mr. Adams' views on the

subject? I do not know which astonishes me most in this matter, your ignorance or your folly.]

This bracketed paragraph from Bernard's letter did not appear in any of the detailed newspaper reports on the trial. It was found only in the official trial papers at the National Archives at Kew.[10] Clearly, the inference to their future marital relations and to "unnatural unions" had been "flagged" as inappropriate for the public prints. Bernard's letter continued, unexpurgated to its conclusion.

What would you think in another case of a man who, while never tired of proclaiming that the instincts of a gentleman were absolute, makes himself at home and accepts hospitalities in a house in the absence of the master, when he knows that master refuses to see him? You declare to the world that you are ill-treated at home by my father. Never was there so glaring an instance of the danger of allowing a person to have no want, wish or whim ungratified. Whatever may be my father's faults to you, he has been uniformly indulgent beyond anything I have ever seen in any other instance. Indeed, it is we brothers who have had cause, if anybody, to complain. You have always been held up by him as a model for our imitation. You were believed in by him long after others had ceased to believe in you. You say that your health has not been attended to; on the contrary, you have always been treated as though you were exceptionally precious. The frequent visits of the doctor, and the consternation at the most familiar and trifling ailments, have always excited good-natured amusement. Alas, the love that has been lavished on you has, indeed, been ill-requited. With respect to my father, you may say that I laid myself open to retort. Under the circumstances of the case, however, I mean to speak out. *Your conduct all through this matter, including the base devise of scattering circulars broadcast for the sole purpose of insulting him, and, finally, your peevish flight from home, has excited from the world at large, which knows nothing of the rest of the facts, laughter and ridicule at your expense;* in the minds of those that know you and your surroundings, and have no inclination to laugh, sorrow and indignation. Now that you have left your home, we hear of things that you say or write which make people say not only that your control over your temper is gone, but also that you display an absolute indifference to the truth. And, further, that you discover a malignity of nature only possessed by one whose heart is black. The facts to which I have alluded I had from those who have every opportunity of knowing them to be true. They are communicated in confidence. *Don't put Mr. Adams upon me. I care not a fig for all his bluster.* I have no appetite for it and shall answer no letters. There are sometimes things which have to be said, and I have felt it to be my duty to say them. I take no pleasure in writing thus. I write solemnly and with a full sense of responsibility, to warn you from allowing yourself to fall a victim to such a man. Be warned in time.

Your affectionate brother - Bernard Coleridge.

1  "Lord Coleridge is looking very well after his weeks of travel." Western Times, 10 November 1883, 2.

2  Sir James Paget (1814-99) remained friends with Lord Coleridge although they disagreed on vivisection.

3  It was a four-day exchange. The memorandum was written on 12 November 1883. Adams replied on the following day. Lord Coleridge volleyed back on 14 November. Adams begged off any further correspondence on 15 November.

4  Stephen's wine auction: Morning Post, 11 December 1883. The sale of Champagne, Hock, etc, including dozens to be sold without reserve by direction of the Hon. Stephen J. Coleridge; 120 dozen, all without reserve. A portion of the wines are lying in cellars in the City, where they may be inspected the day prior to the sale, and the remainder are lying at 54, Pall-Mall.

5  Mildred sent her card to several of her father's friends: The Lord Chancellor (Selborne). As a young man, he broke his engagement with Aunt Maymie during a religious crisis in his life. He later married another and Mildred was very close with his daughters. Charles Baron Bowen, a judge probably best known today for his creation of the trope: "the man on the Clapham omnibus," the ordinary, reasonable man. Not to overlook Bowen's brilliant umbrella poem, "The rain it raineth on the just ..."; William Brett, Baron Esher, conservative judge, married to a woman whispered to be Napoleon's illegitimate daughter; Arthur Baron Hobhouse, judge, strong advocate of women's property rights but he fully backed Lord Coleridge on this matter; and Stafford Northcote, 1st Earl of Iddesleigh, leading Tory figure but lifelong friend of Coleridge. His sister, Cecilia, was the Mrs. Bishop who was Mildred's leading advocate. Iddesleigh apologised to Coleridge for that, "I cannot account for Cecilia's strange conduct." CFP Add MS 86200.

6  Butterfield's reply dated 30 November 1883. The letter featured in the second Adams v Coleridge trial.

7  "Milly went to Marian Blachford:" CFP Add MS 86078 (8 December 1883).

8  Lady Eastlake to A.H. Layard, 10 December 1883, Sheldon ed., *Letters of Elizabeth Rigby, Lady Eastlake* (2009).

9  Bernard's disappointments: The Bristol Mercury: "Mr. Coleridge may be a good man, but let some other constituency have him."

10  National Archives, Kew. Adams v Coleridge J54/393.

# 12. YOUR AFFECTIONATE FATHER

BERNARD'S LETTER, EVENTUALLY put in print, literally, around the world, was a stunner. He "ran amuck like a literary Malay at his elder sister," was one reading. It was filled with "heartless rhetoric and particularly bad English," wrote another. *Vanity Fair* thought it more resembled the work of a hysterical jealous woman.[1]

In his defense, Bernard would have said the same things to Mildred across the breakfast table if she'd remained at home. He believed he had, as her brother, the right (in law, the privilege) to privately address a sister about to marry an unsuitable man. But he took a risk writing it down. Being a lawyer, he thoughtfully marked the letter with the word PRIVATE in block letters, though he should have known merely labeling a letter private is not sufficient.[2]

Bernard was well and truly pleased with his brutal letter. It brought a quick response. Mildred replied the next day:

Dear Bernard - That part of your letter which relates to myself I will say nothing about. I hardly know whether I am more grieved or ashamed that a brother of mine should have so written. I will not lower myself by any further reference to it. With regard to your statements with respect to Mr. Adams, his marriage, married life, family and relations, &c., I not only know, but I am in a position to prove that, with the solitary exception of the mistake committed by the Bishop in Cape Town, they are every one of them absolutely false. Now, I am determined, cost what it may, that this backbiting and slander shall be brought to an end. You, no doubt, have not invented these miserable falsehoods, but you have made yourself responsible for them. I have this moment returned from the Temple, where I have been to take advice on this point. Unless by tomorrow evening I receive from you either the fullest retraction of everything, or such information as to the persons from whom they originated as will enable me to bring them to account, I will, on Friday morning, place your letter in Mr. Adams's hands. I shall request him, as a personal kindness to myself, to take such steps as may be necessary to protect us both from such annoyance in the future. Now, one word more with reference to your suggestion as to Mr. Adams's motives. I think when you reflect that he is prepared to marry me without a farthing, and that you are the person who will profit by the money which would have been mine, had not my father been set against me, you will feel some shame in having made me so unworthy an insinuation, or, at least, will perceive the unwisdom of it as coming from you.

Bernard must have known his sister would share the letter with Adams. If not, he was a fool. Most contemporary observers thought Mildred would act "as girls are apt to act under such circumstances."[3] She would give the letter to Adams. Knowing Adams as they did, Lord Coleridge and Bernard feared it would lead to litigation. Lord Coleridge immediately warned her not to do it:

Mildred: My dear child. Your brother showed me [*NB how the Coleridges delighted in passing their letters around!*] on the way here a letter of yours to him, in which you threaten to what, in your sober serious mind, you cannot think of ever doing. But if you should bring our whole family into the position which you threaten, it will be simply due to them and myself to break off at once all communication between us. Your affectionate father, Coleridge.

The Coleridge men were already too late. Mildred's reply to Bernard, with its threatening language, "unless by tomorrow evening," we are prepared "to take such steps as may be necessary," etc., was not in Mildred's style. By 15 December, however, the Coleridges knew Adams possessed Bernard's letter. Mildred later swore that she never "disobeyed a single injunction" of her father's yet she had defied his warning. Lord Coleridge ended all personal relations with his "dear child":

My Dear Mildred: As you have done what I warned you not to do [i.e. share the letter with Adams], the consequence must follow which I stated in my last letter, to which I refer you, and by which I must stand. But as, whatever happens, you must now be enabled to live separately from me, my solicitor will be instructed to communicate with you as to the settlement which I shall make upon you; and any matter of business between us will for the future be transacted through him. Your affectionate father, Coleridge[4]

He was as good as his word. Mildred later swore she made repeated efforts to contact her father without success. Notes from Harrison, the family solicitor, were the only reply. Lord Coleridge "peremptorily forbade her" from returning to her home in Sussex Square. If she turned for help to others in the family, on her father's instructions, they "systematically cut her."

Thackeray gets the credit for the expression "skeleton in the closet."[5] Every house has one, the author believed; his most certainly did. Up to this point, the rupture among the Coleridges was known only within the family and their intimates. They were hardly the first family to fall out over a questionable suitor. Similar contretemps occurred in families in every station of life and, sadly, many were irreparable. Still, no one would want to make a public case out of it.

The first public indication of ripples on the Coleridge's placid lake came on 18 December 1883 when an advertisement appeared in the personals column of *The Morning Post*:

> Home wanted immediately by a single lady; London or neighbourhood; private sitting-room; terms must be very moderate. Address, the Hon. Mildred Coleridge, care of the Rev. H. Seymour, Nettlecombe Rectory, Taunton.

There it was – Mildred's name – in a paper taken by most of London society. It would embarrass her father, certainly, but Mildred did need a place to live. Marian (Legge?) Blachford had asked her to leave. Mildred and Adams apparently traduced Lord Coleridge before the old lady who reported it all:

> Dear Lord Coleridge, Your own daughter, cruel and wicked as it is, has accused you to me of unfaithfulness and [not decipherable] to your dear wife. I could not believe it. It shocked and almost stunned me. It grieves me to accuse your own daughter of such slander of her own father and how she has tried to poison my mind against you.[6]

A question must be asked. Was Mildred's reference to

"unfaithfulness" on her father's part connected in any way to the reports of his recently acquired "lady companion?" Adams, it can be safely presumed, would have hunted down all he could find out about those rumours. The truth – if he could discover it – would have been a powerful card to play against Lord Coleridge. Regardless, the aged Blachford wanted no further part in this increasingly venomous family dispute. Mildred could not remain under her roof.

Mildred's lodging choices were narrowing. On the Coleridge side of the family, no one dared challenge the Lord Chief. The most painful result was an end to Mildred's friendship with her cousin Mary Coleridge, her former pupil and travel companion. Mary was now 21 and a fledgling poet; still living in South Kensington, with her family. In Bernard's letter, he mentioned Mildred had discussed her coming marriage with "one girl," which, it seems certain, was Mary Coleridge. Mildred admitted to Mary that she did not "contemplate living with Mr. Adams as his wife." This revelation "shocked and astounded" Mary's parents. Mary's father, Arthur Duke Coleridge, had known Mildred for many years and sincerely wished to mediate for her but found Lord Coleridge adamant.[7] Arthur was told Mildred left Sussex Square voluntarily; she chose Adams over her family and a public scandal now appeared unavoidable. Hence, no Coleridge doors should be open to her. Arthur was not the man to challenge the family's acknowledged leader. Reluctantly, he informed Mildred he could not give her shelter. Mary was also instructed to end all communication with her cousin. Mildred was crushed by this and let Arthur know she would never speak to him or "Aunt Minnie" (Mrs. Arthur) ever again. Mildred and Mary's friendship died that day. Twenty years later, Arthur Coleridge repented his actions, calling Lord Coleridge's edict "a hard measure." But Mildred, like father like daughter, would also keep her word.

As no Coleridges would take her in, Mildred turned to a maternal uncle, the Rev. Henry Fortescue Seymour.[8] He and his family were staying near Hyde Park Square and gave Mildred a room until they returned to Somerset. Lord Coleridge wrote to acknowledge Mildred's presence with the Seymours which he accepted. But if the Seymours permitted Adams to be in their home, "I have not a word to say." Rev. Seymour replied that Mildred was always welcome in his home and denied Adams had ever been his guest. "I will reply to no further communications thereon, and I decline to hear or to read any letters or correspondence belonging thereto. I do not wish to be mixed up in this matter in any way."[9]

Open hostilities had commenced. Lord Coleridge, as promised, communicated through his solicitor. Adams received the following from Mr. Harrison of Bedford Row:

> You are aware of Lord Coleridge's strong disapproval of any marriage taking place between you and his daughter. He wishes you to understand distinctly that should any marriage take place between his daughter and yourself, under no circumstances, either during his life or at his death, will he make any pecuniary allowance or provision. Should you insist on the marriage taking place, and forcing the lady to occupy and live in a totally different position to that which she has been accustomed, it is our duty to point out that your wife will have to be supported by you out of your own means, or at all events not by or out of those of Lord Coleridge or any of his family, one and all of whom are as strongly opposed to the marriage as Lord Coleridge himself.[10]

This was a new threat to cut Mildred off completely. Adams

replied, describing Coleridge's vindictiveness as "plainly insane." By the most "transparently flimsy pretext," he has turned his daughter out in to the world with almost nothing. As for himself, Adams admitted he was "somewhat foolishly indifferent to money." Portents of poverty meant nothing to him:

> Be good enough to inform [Lord Coleridge] that in disinheriting and deserting his daughter he has removed two of the principal barriers between us, and that if she will so far honour me as to entrust her happiness to my care, it is now my intention to marry her at the earliest possible moment.

1  "Malay," Sheffield Daily Telegraph, 25 November, 1884, 5; "Jealous woman," Vanity Fair, Vol 32 (1883) 343.
2  Picton v Jackman (1830) Merely labelling a letter "Private and confidential," or merely stating "I speak in confidence," will not make a communication confidential in the legal sense of that term.
3  "As girls are apt to act," The American Law Review, January-February 1885.
4  The Coleridge letters were released to the press by Adams in January 1885. (q.v.)
5  "What skeleton was there in the closet?" Thackeray, Adventures of Philip on his Way through the World (1862).
6  The Blachford letter is dated 31 December 1883. I have some uncertainty about the writer. The first Lord Blachford (Frederick Rogers) was an Oxford & Devon friend of Lord Coleridge. He was married but childless. He had a sister, Marian, married to a clergyman named Legge in Lewisham. It is possible that Marian Blachford may be Marian Legge. She was 69 in 1883.
7  Arthur Duke Coleridge (1820-1913): Clerk of the Assize for the Midland Circuit from 1876-d. In private life, he was an amateur musician and tenor, associated with Jenny Lind, Gilbert & Sullivan. Founded the London Bach choir. He had taken the lead in Mildred's musical education.
8  Rev H.F. Seymour, 1827-1900, was Jane's next youngest brother. He was rector of Nettlecombe, in Exmoor, for the last thirty years of his life.
9  Coleridge to Rev Seymour, 31 December 1883, replies 4 & 7 January 1884. CFP Add MS 85979.
10  Harrison's letter to Adams: 22 December 1883. Adams reply is undated.

# 13. SHE IS NOT AS OTHERS

"She had never married. Why not? He wondered. Sacrificed to the family, he supposed."
*The Years*, Virginia Woolf (1937)

FOR THE FIRST time in anyone's memory, Lord Coleridge and his family remained in London for Christmas. Reporters were beginning to scent a story. A columnist in *The Exeter & Plymouth Gazette* wrote:

> One hears the query: Why hasn't Lord Coleridge spent his Christmas at Heath's Court this year? No one appears to know exactly why; but rumours say that he prefers to remain in London with his daughter, who, the papers state, is engaged to a Commoner. It is said that the engagement is disapproved of.

Disapproval was an understatement. For sheer pettiness, there was the kerfuffle over Mildred's pianoforte. She had found lodgings, a bed and sitting room, in the home of a respectable lady in Abingdon Road, Kensington. It wasn't the West End but within her budget. "Milly's harmony lessons" were planned for the new year. Going through Harrison, the solicitor, Mildred asked that her Broadwood pianoforte be delivered to her new address. Harrison informed her that Lord Coleridge's position was, if she wanted a pianoforte, rent one and he would pay for it. The pianoforte in his home, though only Mildred really ever played it, was his lordship's property and would not be moved.[1]

Meanwhile, Mildred's plan to generate some income found its way into the "news."

> What is this strange story I hear of the daughter of another lord who has determined to put her great abilities to use? I suppose Miss Coleridge, who has learned music, may teach it. I suppose there is no reason why the daughter of a peer should not give lessons to pupils, and, if she gives them, there is no reason why she should give them for nothing.

The Coleridges believed Adams was planting these stories to embarrass the family. To Lord Coleridge and his sons, the idea Mildred would turn her back on her family was inexplicable. Her brothers believed she "had the life." She ran the house. Still, she didn't sweep the area steps or tip the bin-men. She had her own suite in two magnificent homes, servants, a carriage, etc. "Her word was law," supposedly. For her fragile health, the finest doctors were consulted. Her father included her in everything he could. She was beloved by his friends whose homes were always open to her. Financially, she wanted nothing. "All" that was asked in return was she continue to do what she seemingly loved to do, tend to the needs of her busy, ageing, frequently unwell, father. She was meant to provide the "Sunbeams that make everything glad."[2] That was her duty, in the eyes of many. Butterfield chastened Mildred for conduct that shocked his "sense of propriety and *duty*." Lady Eastlake thought Mildred's behavior was "so much at variance with her own interests as with her *duty*." From Oxford, Jowett wrote Lord Coleridge to commiserate, suggesting that Mildred was "a poor deluded creature who has lost for a time her sense of *duty*." And Lord Iddesleigh opined there was no greater sorrow for a parent than the "*undutiful* conduct of a child."

It is striking so many people who knew Mildred referred to her as a "child." Again, Mildred turned 36 a few days after leaving Sussex Square. Lord Coleridge – forgivably perhaps – might address her as his "dear child." Aunt Maymie, too, described her at this point as a "blissful besotted child." Maymie, of course, was in despair over Mildred. "*She is not as others.*" What did she mean exactly, "not as others?" Mildred was very intelligent, accomplished in languages and music. In her correspondence, to and from, there was no baby-talk; everything was mature and well-written. The problem lay elsewhere. To recap, Mildred was 36, tall but not graceful, and plain. Her health was ever feeble. She was socially backward and painfully shy. She was, what Charlotte Bronte once described, one of those "unmarried and never-to-be-married women." Miss Bronte, alone in her father's vicarage, wrote, "There is no more respectable character on this earth who makes her own way through life, without support of a husband ... retains in her possession a well-regulated mind, a disposition to enjoy simple pleasures, [and] fortitude to support inevitable pain."[3]

In her mid-thirties, Mildred found herself alone; spinsterhood "marked her as one of society's unfortunates, cast aside from the common lot of her sex."[4] Her solitary fate wasn't inevitable. The men she knew were mostly her father's older friends from Devon, the bar and politics. Certainly, many had unmarried sons. There is no record of Mildred ever being courted. No matchmakers were employed in hopes of luring a more suitable soul from the numerous curates, solicitors, or third sons of some 5th lord. She'd been around such men for years without interest. She was hardly known for being part of the rising "anti-man" cadre regularly scorned in the (male) press. Hence, the Coleridges had decided she was just not going to be married. And, for a woman in Mildred's position, counted upon as caregiver for the aged, "no one would actually stand in the way of her marrying but they were very glad when she did not."⁵ A bookish, retiring woman like Mildred was destined to be "naturally single."

When Adams walked into Mildred's life, he carried nothing to recommend him. He was – in one marvelous description – "an egregiously combative misfit."⁶ He ticked no boxes with the Coleridges. A free-lance partisan journalist, even worse, a "Tory-for-hire," he dared to crash into a home full of Coleridge Liberals. He was previously wed and widowed, which was forgivable, but his first marriage, although sadly short, had not been without problems. What about his mysteriously troubled daughter? He couldn't even support her. Why couldn't Mildred see what all her family saw – the man was a fortune hunter. Was he the first suitor to face such an objection? Of course not. Countess Blessington, a source for such things, advised, "a lover of a persevering spirit may effect much in removing apprehension on that score, by cheerfully submitting to a reasonable time of probation, in the hope of amelioration in his worldly circumstances. Happiness delayed will be none the less precious."

None of that worked with this odious man. How had he got such influence over Mildred? Flattery, in great part. He fawned over her "research," her translations; he convinced her they were "the only two" who could get the vital work done at the VSS. He was unctuous to her father, "our Noble Vice President." Clearly, he coveted her money. His lordship must have been non-plussed to hear specifics from his will - and Mildred's expectations in it - coming out of the mouth of a stranger. Adams could only have heard of that £17000 from Mildred. The man's mercenary intentions were so obvious. £17,000 - put in the consols, you know, "safe as 'ouses," could provide Adams (and his wife) an income he could never have dreamed of and, the best of it all, he wouldn't have to work for it. He'd be a man of independent means. But when told he could have Mildred at £300 a year, like it or not, he baulked and blustered and postured about London as her knight errant. £300 was simply not enough to marry his "white elephant."

Adams blithely admitted he didn't *love* Mildred. Lord Coleridge, according to Adams, was "unable to conceive of any man as actuated by views other than sordid, or any woman by feelings other than sexual." Mildred's unsolicited but quite specific comment that she and Adams did not propose to live as husband and wife plainly stunned the family. Where did that come from, they gasped? A woman of Mildred's age and station was presumed to have "a lack of sexual interest, if not complete revulsion." As early as the 1880s, a small group of "advanced thinkers" were suggesting celibate marriages, the parties vowing a mutually agreed upon refusal of sexual intercourse. Adams was never an advanced thinker in such matters. More likely he and Mildred were planning what would be later called a companionate marriage: "a conjugal utopia of mutual forbearance and respect." (Hamerton). Lesley Hall suggests the marriage of George Bernard Shaw and Charlotte Payne Townshend was, albeit a decade later, "a union of companionship and friendship between two individuals who shared numerous interests in political and social reform."[7] Either way, in his letter to Mildred, Bernard expressed his outrage. "Are you so ignorant as not to know that misery almost always accompanies such unnatural unions?" Adams, they fully expected, would seek his release elsewhere, either in infidelity or with prostitutes. Maymie, again, spoke for all of the Coleridges. "Think what it would be for her to be the wife of that man. To prevent a marriage if it can be done must be the best for her."

Weeks passed after Bernard's letter to Mildred. Early in 1884, Adams wrote to the Coleridge solicitors demanding a retraction and apology for the letter of 11 December 1883 which contained charges "entirely without foundation." Adams was ready to refute every imputation and eager for an opportunity in a court of law. But he would give Bernard a chance to apologise: "He has no desire whatsoever to annoy Mr. Coleridge, and if these imputations are removed his object will be accomplished and the action might drop." The letter from Adams was marked as received. There was no reply. Bernard was to have excellent representation. Lord Coleridge arranged Sir Henry James to handle the case; James was the present Attorney-General in Gladstone's cabinet, and a leading criminal lawyer. Lord Coleridge warned Sir Henry, it was a "painful affair arising out of the strange misconduct of my daughter who, after engaging herself to a familiar blackguard behind my back & without my sanction, has left my house."[8]

Mildred and Adams were excited about the battle ahead. Adams was keeping score on the wounds he traced to Coleridge influence. A job offer was mysteriously withdrawn. A longtime acquaintance, Sir Walter Riddell, flatly refused his handshake in the street. The cuts were hurtful, but as Adams said, "I go so little into society." Aunt Maymie, for the moment, remained in occasional contact with her one-time beloved niece and reported, "Milly thinks the trial will be heard by Easter." Mildred was confident of victory and she and Adams would be married by summer. Charlotte Yonge heard Mildred was counting upon a marriage as early as St. George's Day (April 23). Adams dampened talk of marriage until resolution of Mildred's financial settlement. Meanwhile, Maymie's spies reported Adams was storming about London charging Mildred was thrown out "friendless upon the world." Except for him, of course.

While Mildred's exact financial expectations remained in dispute, Adams decided they were sizeable enough to insure her life. He would be the beneficiary. They could use that policy as security and borrow against it for their expenses. Adams, of course, had been claiming

Mildred's health had been ruined by her father's harshness. Would any insurance company even write her a policy? He sent Mildred to her primary physician, Sir James Paget, who wrote up a rather lukewarm appraisal: other than her troubling vision, he found her in "her usual health." Patient confidentiality aside, Paget shared it all with Lord Coleridge, "Although I wrote that she is in as good health as usual, I said also that her usual health was rather feeble."[9]

However feeble, Mildred was strong enough to begin advertising for pupils. Presumably her hired piano was tuned and in place. Learning some basic pianoforte for the drawing-room was thought essential for young girls, the "light-headed husband hunters," from better families. But Mildred's "prospectus" broadened her syllabus beyond music instruction. Her newest advertisement appeared in the *Times* and *Morning Post*:

> Daily Governess. The Hon. Mildred Coleridge, 83 Abingdon Road, Kensington, gives instruction in music (theory and practice), German, Italian and French, and rudimentary Greek and Latin. Literature class on Wednesday afternoons.[10]

To have children dropped off every day for their instruction seemed *infra dig* for a woman of Mildred's standing. The timing was also bad - London was "sadly overstocked" with governesses at that moment. Perhaps she could find employment in Whitehall; female clerks were becoming more common in government offices. According to one report, the pay was good and the independence would suit a "high-spirited maiden." Everyone had an idea. Beatrix Potter quipped to a friend, "Miss Coleridge, by way of revenge, is advertising to take in washing!"[11]

Busy-bodies read those personal columns carefully. What were they to think of Mildred's ad? "There was a screw loose somewhere in the Coleridge *entourage*."[12]

Little did they know the whole of it.

It had been some time since Lord Coleridge and Mrs. Davies parted in Liverpool. Henceforward, she will be known as Miss Amy Lawford. The use of her married name on the *Britannic* passenger list, Mrs. A.M. Davies, was apparently the last ever public reference to her former husband. Meantime, once back in London, the Lord Chief Justice had no time to be an ardent lover. Professionally, he was an extremely important and busy man. Privately, the infuriating Adams and his own smitten daughter continued to vex him and consumed much of his time when not on the bench. Moreover, "the formalities that vanish on shipboard quickly reappear on land." His lordship would have fewer opportunities to "dance attendance" upon Miss Lawford. It would excite comment should the Lord Chief Justice be seen giving the young lady – any young lady - carriage rides in "the Row" or sharing a candlelit table at the Cafe Royal, where, it was said, "those who are known" might dine discreetly.

Amy, meanwhile, had moved in with her mother, Mrs. Baring Lawford, who rented a comfortable house, south of the Park, at 42 Victoria Road, South Kensington, a respectable address. Amy's sister (Flo) and brother (Egerton) also resided there. Mrs. Lawford was later cast by the press for the role of scheming plotter on behalf of her eldest daughter. There were some reports she was actually lurking about on the *Britannic* and stage-managed the entire affair but her name does not appear on the passenger list. What seems clear is Mrs. Lawford had got all the details from her daughter about what happened on the *Britannic*. Amy had given herself to Lord Coleridge and, her mother surely believed, her lover had made certain promises.

Meanwhile, on the north side of the park, in Paddington, when did his sons become aware of their father's romantic entanglement and how did they react? Did he just confess it? Did he admit to being an old fool, enraptured by a pretty young woman, for whom he had developed great affection. He had done things and said things that could not now be undone or unsaid. Would he have hoped his sons would welcome their father's late life chance for happiness and companionship? If he didn't just come out with the news, perhaps the younger Coleridges gleaned some West End gossip, overheard a chatty servant, or, why not, perused the contents of a carelessly laid letter. In late January 1884, Gilbert, the youngest son, who had remained in America, touring about with his banjo and tennis racket, was suddenly and urgently summoned from New York by cablegram.[13] The timing is, at the very least, suggestive. It was all Gilbert's fault, wasn't it? Bernard and Stephen were quite justified to think if their little brother hadn't opted to stay in America but had accompanied/chaperoned his father home on the *Britannic*, none of this would have happened.

Of course, that role had been Mildred's since her mother's death. She had shielded her father – at his wish – as his hostess at home and escort at dinner parties. Nonetheless, the prospect of Lord Coleridge's remarriage in his mid-60s could not have been a total surprise. The drawing rooms and galleries of London were well stocked with widows, peeresses and women left well provided for by their late husbands in the respectable trades: the church, law, banking, and their comfortable ilk. Lord Coleridge, handsome, wealthy, and celebrated, need not be alone. He might easily have found a "suitable" woman from his class and standing. Yet Miss Lawford and her family, however distinguished they might have been in Bengal, were unknown in Belgravia. A thumb through the *Handbook to the Upper Ten Thousand* (which actually numbered Twenty Thousand) would find no mention of the Baring Lawfords. Who was this woman, then, the widow who styles herself Miss Lawford? That alone was worth employing one of the private enquiry agents in the *Times* personals, offering "thorough investigations, evidence procured, discretion guaranteed." How long, not very, before they retrieved the remarkable *Otherwise Davies* files? She had testified under oath that, when aged 17, past the age of consent, she willingly participated in a clandestine marriage. She had lived with her husband for as long as six years and they had a child together. Then, for her own reasons, she won an annulment based upon some slippery reading of a Scottish clock.

Had her age been mentioned? The husband was generally expected to be older than his wife; three to seven years seemed to be acceptable.[14] When did his lordship reveal the Lawford woman was half his age? She was two years younger than Bernard, his oldest son. Such marriages in the peerage always drew comment. Lord Malmesbury, a spry 73-year-old, had recently married the 26-year-old daughter of a fine West Country family. The reactions ranged from "some little surprise" to "angry indignation" but the young lady became a Countess nonetheless. Malmesbury was an "amiable but not very brilliant peer," Lord Coleridge was rather the opposite.

Why should his sons object to a step-baroness reigning in Sussex Square if their beloved father had found happiness? Topping the list, to be sure, was the obvious fact that "the remarriage of old men of fortune and position is seldom pleasing to their children."[15] Lord Coleridge, as we have seen, never shied from explaining to his children what they could expect from his estate in the natural order of things. That natural order, his sons presumed, did not include the prospect of a new step-mother of child-bearing age. His lordship's siblings were equally astonished. Father Coleridge was staggered to hear his brother describe how he "petted" this woman on the steamer. Petting at the time, fortunately, meant comforting and not physical contact. Lord Coleridge insisted she had related the full story of her first marriage. Father Henry was unimpressed; he held the strong position of his Catholic faith, refusing to accept the authority of "the vile divorce court." He dearly loved his brother but wrote to their sister, Maymie, "I can never recognise her or enter his home when she is there as his wife."[16] Mildred, of course, was not included in any of these discussions. God forbid Adams should get hold of such intelligence. Had he already? Adams and Mildred were already out there in London banging on doors spreading their litany of calumnies against the family. This couldn't be happening, could it?

Lord Coleridge was accustomed to get his way; he often told his children, "My mother taught me your father's opinions are always right." On this occasion, his family eventually prevailed. Outnumbered, and with reluctance at some level, he accepted the view that a marriage to Miss Lawford was ill-advised. Exactly who handled the delicate negotiations with the young woman and her protective mother cannot be said. The family position was that Lord Coleridge had been delighted to meet Miss Lawford aboard the ship, he was taken by her youth and beauty, and formed a great regard for her. But to be clear: he never talked to her of marriage, he never proposed to her or gave her any reason to believe an engagement was forthcoming. Any litigation would be costly and hurtful to all parties, a suggestion that Miss Lawford's past would be of some relevance.

According to Stephen Coleridge, an agreement was reached: "She (Miss Lawford) was eventually pensioned off for £500 a year."[17] Many relationships were "sorted" in like fashion. "By far the greater number of cases are settled privately," a supposed expert fixer claimed, especially when a gentleman is "anxious to prevent exposure."[18] The legal term for this pension was *solatium*, "a payment made to a victim as compensation for injured feelings or emotional pain and suffering."

It must be said there is only Stephen's word on this, but he was there. He provided no details; none will be found in the Coleridge business papers. In 1884, £500 a year was a substantial sum (about £75,000 in 2023.) Notably, it was £200 more a year than his lordship planned to provide for his discontented daughter.

At about this time, very few people probably noticed a brief item in the legal press. The Lord Chief Justice was soon to preside at the Surrey Assizes. He would be assisted by a "Judge's Marshal," an ancient post by then a sinecure. It paid two guineas a day, plus expenses. Would it surprise you to know that the post was quietly given to a young lawyer, just out of the Inner Temple, Egerton Charles Baring Lawford, B.A., Amy's younger brother? Such temporary appointments provided "valuable experience" for young men-at-the-bar and it was to be hoped that all the Lawfords would most appreciate the condescension of the Lord Chief Justice who would keep the Lawford interests very much in mind.

The Lord Chief Justice could return to the complexities of the Whalley will appeal and the interminable Belt libel case. What a shock it must have been, then, to learn that a London newspaper was quite near to breaking the story of his lordship's romantic entanglement. On 26 March 1884, the *Pall Mall Gazette* reported: "A great sensation has been created in fashionable society by the report that a distinguished Judge, who stands almost at the head of the Bench, has proposed." The blind reference would never fool the *cognoscenti* who quickly figured out the judge in question. But Mr. Stead's irrepressible paper had the right judge but the wrong lady. The *Gazette* reported that the unnamed jurist had offered his hand to Miss Mary Anderson, an American actress and singer in the middle of a sensational run in *Pygmalion* in the West End at the *Lyceum* in the Strand. *The Gazette* was delighted to reveal "the suit of the noble and learned Lord has not prospered," he'd been rejected. "The story, however, has got noised abroad, and is exciting the greatest interest, not unmixed with amusement, in society."

The amusement was to be had at the Gazette's expense; the paper had fallen for Miss Anderson's agents who worked diligently to keep their lady's name before the public. If the Archbishop of Canterbury hadn't been a married man, he'd have been in the frame. Notwithstanding the obvious stunt, Lord Coleridge felt the need to send an immediate reply to the *Gazette*:

> It would be an affectation to doubt that the paragraph headed, "The Judge and the Actress" in your paper this evening refers to me. I desire, in the fewest possible words, to state that I never had the pleasure of seeing Miss Anderson in my life, either in public or private, and that I never wrote a line to her. The whole matter is an absolute and impudent falsification. Coleridge

Why did he feel the need to refute this silly item? "It is generally thought that Lord Coleridge would have done better had he remained silent under the imputation." He was a vain man. Why should the mere mention of his re-marriage prompt such "amusement?" Of course, there was the age gap, always good for a laugh. Miss Mary Anderson was just 25. His Lordship no doubt was mindful that Miss Amy Lawford had just turned 31. It is more likely the Lord Chief promptly shot down the Anderson rumour to assure Mrs. Lawford that his heart had not been not proffered elsewhere. The Anderson gossip item was a close call and Coleridge knew it foreshadowed the likely reaction when and if the world discovered his relationship with this young woman of "graceful carriage." The scare also rekindled his loathing for the "Society" papers.

Edmund Yates was editor of *The World*, with its influential gossip column "What the *World* Says." A few weeks after the Miss Anderson twaddle, by coincidence, Yates found himself in the Lord Chief Justice's courtroom.[19] One of *The World's* published titbits had proved false; Yates was sued for criminal libel and lost. At sentencing, the Lord Chief in his "sternest, solemnest voice," seized his opportunity:

Edmond Yates is credited (?) as the father of the gossip column. From 1874, Yates edited The World, known for the tidbits to be found among "What The World Says." The photo appears in Yates' memoir, Memories & Recollections, Vol 2.

> Public men, in England at least, must submit to public comment as one of the necessary incidents of their career. But private men, indeed all men, whether public or private, in their private relations, are entitled to have their privacy respected. Why should we have our lives pried into, our movements watched, our dress recorded, our company catalogued, our most private relations dragged into the light of day — not for any conceivable good to the great English people, but only to gratify the foolish vanity or the abject curiosity of a small minority of a privileged class?[20]

Yates received a shocking four months in jail. "That's a snorter," he exclaimed. It was certainly surprising and, many thought, excessive. "English editors, however much they deserve it, are rarely sent to gaol." Lord Randolph Churchill thought Coleridge made an "ass of himself." While throwing Yates in the clink may have been something of a catharsis for the Lord Chief Justice, he picked a bad time to start making too many enemies in Fleet Street. Yates, for one, would have his innings (q.v.)

Another attack of lumbago, almost certainly stress-related, forced Lord Coleridge from the bench even before the long summer vacation. He was rarely seen in society. He declined a dinner invitation from Prime Minister Gladstone, "You may or may not have chanced to hear that I am in much trouble at home and I cannot go into society at present." To an American friend, he explained, "I know it is wrong to be morose, and I shall try all I can to bear my lot, if sadly, yet bravely and simply." Coleridge had corresponded with Ellis Yarnall of Philadelphia for thirty years and wrote to him about Mildred. Yarnall replied, "You have sons who love you, and the dead are near ... Do not, my dear friend, allow yourself to despond. Live for those who love you, and be sure that the years will bring you peace." But Coleridge was not to be consoled:

> My heart is lonely. The love of children, except in rare cases—my father was one—is not that devoted, sympathetic love which the love of a wife, and even of a dear, and tried, and life-long friend, often is. I am gradually awakening to the fact that all the real hope and joy of my life is gone without return. I know it is wrong to be morose, and I shall try all I can to bear my lot, if sadly, yet bravely and simply.[21]

The tone of the previous letter indicates by the summer of 1884, Lord Coleridge had acceded to his family's opposition to a second marriage. The matter of Miss Lawford settled, for the moment, the focus can return to Mildred and Adams. Reports of an approaching scandal were now in the air. "The circumstances of this case are somewhat peculiar." In September, the *Western Times* in Exeter reported the partisans of Mr. Charles Warren Adams were prepared to portray Lord Coleridge as the "flinty hearted father in a domestic drama."[22] It was said Mr. Adams was seeking staggering damages of £10,000. "British society expect a delicious morsel." The case was on the trial list for November; on the 19th, Lord Coleridge wrote his nephew, "This hateful case of Bernard's comes on tomorrow."

1   A new pianoforte would have cost well over 50 guineas. They could be purchased on the "three-year system" with quarterly payments. One could be hired for 12s a month. With risk, "It is dangerous to meddle with a hired pianoforte." Musical Times, 1 May 1889, 272.
2   Sunbeams/quoted by Deborah Gorham in *The Victorian Girl and the Feminine Ideal* (1982)
3   Charlotte Bronte, Shirley, "And what does it signify whether unmarried and never-to-be married women are unattractive and inelegant or not?" (171).
4   Unfortunates: Phillipa Levine, "So Few Prizes and so Many Blanks," quoted in JA Mohammed, F Jacob, eds. *Marriage Discourses* (2021).
5   Bridget Hill, Women Alone: Spinsters in England, 1660-1850 (2001) 69.
6   "Egregiously combative misfit:" Julia Courtney, Charlotte Mary Yonge: A Novelist and her Readers, unpublished dissertation, University of London (1990).
7   Martha Vicinus, "Celibate Marriages," Victorian Review, Vol. 39, No. 2. Hamerton quoted in *Courtship and Marriage in Victorian England*, Jennifer Phegley (2011). Lesley Hall email to author, 19 November 2020.
8   Lord Coleridge to Sir Henry James, 17 Dec 1883, Coleridge Family Papers. Business papers of John Duke Coleridge; Family and Property, including records of the Adams-Coleridge libel trial. Add MS 86211.
9   Paget reported that he had told Adams he saw "no reason to believe that [Mildred] has any organic disease, or, with the exception of slight inflammation of the eyes, was in any way, less healthy than usual." Paget to Lord Coleridge: CFP Add MS 86304.
10   "Daily Governess," Morning Post, 6 May 1884, 8.
11   Potter: *The Journal of Beatrix Potter*, 1881-1897 16 May 1884.
12   This alludes to Derwent Coleridge's famous comment about his father, Samuel, the poet: "There was always some defect – some screw loose in the marvelous and on the whole admirable machine."
13   Gilbert's cablegram: Montreal Star, 13 February 1884.
14   Age gap: Pat Jalland, *Women, Marriage & Politics* 1860-1914 (1986).

15  Remarriage of old men of fortune, American Law Review, Vol 19, (1885) 764.

16  Father Coleridge: CFP Add MS 85936 and "The Gospel Law as to Divorce," H.J. Coleridge, The Life of Our Life: The Sermon on the Mount (1883) 118-133. "A man who marries a wife put away by her husband is an adulterer." He also believed "the virginal purity of woman is the fairest creation on earth."

17  Stephen Coleridge's handwritten note, Sir Paul Coleridge's papers.

18  Quoting an unnamed London solicitor, "A defendant who is anxious to prevent exposure will often cheerfully pay a sum equal to two or three times the damages that a jury would have awarded. There are girls who make quite a business of this kind of thing." 4 December 1897, Newcastle (Australia) Herald (newspaper.com)

19  What The World said about Lady Stratheden's elopement with Lord Lonsdale was found to be false. The notorious Lonsdale sued for libel. Yates hadn't written the item but as publisher he was responsible when Lonsdale sued. Yates glibly explained occasionally informants get things wrong. He regretted the error and he made full amends to Lady Stratheden. After a fruitless appeal, Yates went to Holloway as a first-class misdemeanant, allowed his own meals and unlimited visitors. He served 53 days; released 10 March 1885, "in deference to medical reports."

20  "Mr. Yates Sentenced," Manchester Guardian, 3 April 1884, 8.

21  27 July 1884, Coleridge to Ellis Yarnall, Forty Years of Friendship (1913) 218.

22  "Flinty hearted father," Western Times, 22 September 1884, 2; "Somewhat peculiar," Morning Post, 29 October 1884, 6.

# 14. TRIAL 1: MR. MANISTY MAKES A MUDDLE

THE LEGAL RECORD of *Adams v Coleridge* must be one of the most voluminous in Victorian law.[1] Over two years, from the first filing to the final settlement, there were two trials, one appeal, an accepted settlement, two failed mediations, and, as we shall see, two marriages, albeit with less paperwork and press coverage. The major papers routinely printed thousands of words, giving fascinated readers a daily verbatim transcript, including unabridged letters, many more than have already been seen in full or partial form.

We open late on the afternoon of 20 November 1884. Who could not sympathise with the burden laid upon Mr. Justice Manisty? It was Sir Henry Manisty's fate to be assigned to hear the case of *Adams v. Coleridge*. Manisty was 76 and, other than being "thoroughly old fashioned," he had little in common with the Lord Chief Justice. Manisty was from Northumberland, retaining "a strong North Country accent." Not favoured by family name or political connections, he did not reach the bench until he was 68.[2] He and Lord Coleridge were not social companions. In fact, when Manisty and Coleridge were recently together on the bench, some thought the Lord Chief Justice overdid it when he upbraided Manisty for his "uncalled-for and unnecessary remarks."

The earlier portion of Manisty's day involved a sensational breach of promise action brought by an actress against the Viscount Garmoyle. A last-minute settlement ended the case and Manisty might well have hoped that spirit would be contagious. *Adams v Coleridge* was not called until very late in the day, and the judge entreated the two parties to take advantage of one more evening's opportunity to find compromise. "I earnestly suggest you consider whether this is necessary." Adams said he would not discuss any settlement that did not completely vindicate his character. Neither side would blink.

Thus, despite an unseasonably early snowfall, the public gallery was filled on Friday morning with those eager to hear "The Extraordinary Libel Case." Aunt Maymie and "several Coleridges" were given special seats. Most of the gallery was taken up with junior members of the bar. From above, rear, the gallery overlooked Adams seated alone at a table in the well of the court. He was handling his own case; legally, he was termed the "party in person." Mildred, who was on his witness list, could not be present until her evidence was required. Across the gangway, the defendant, the Hon. Bernard Coleridge, supported by Sir Henry James, by repute, the handsomest lawyer in Britain. His private life was irregular; he resided discreetly with his mistress in Belgravia. Lord Chief Justice Coleridge was nowhere to be seen. To be sure, he had no reason to be in court; he was not the Coleridge on trial. Still, he was very much "the man who wasn't there." Adams went in to the fray the underdog but much the people's favourite. "Lord Coleridge is disliked by most people who know him, and by many who do not."

Shortly before eleven, Mr. Justice Manisty invited Adams to state his case. It has been established the plaintiff was a tall man; perhaps as much as 6-foot-5. A man of "stalwart frame and imposing appearance," he was middle aged with iron grey hair and a beard. Points off, however, for being over-dressed. Too flashy with a heavy watch chain outside his frock coat, a protruding white silk handkerchief from a breast pocket and numerous rings on the fingers of his left hand.[3] What mattered more, of course, was his readiness for the task at hand.

He was prepared for this hour. Years earlier, in another of his forgotten books, Adams had advice for amateurs who wished to try their hand on the stage. "The first point in all amateur performances is that the actors should be thoroughly perfect in the words of their parts. An amateur has rarely the stage tact and self-possession necessary." This was his moment.[4]

He spoke in what was called a "good cultivated manner." He spoke and he spoke. His opening statement filled the day. Manisty reminded Adams that while "Every man his own lawyer" is a right under English common law, there were rules. He must not try the court's tolerance. As predicted, there were frequent interruptions from the bench as well as the defendant's counsel. Repeatedly, Manisty cautioned Adams not to mention Lord Coleridge.

> Manisty: Lord Coleridge does not signify in this matter.
> The defendant is Mr. Bernard Coleridge.
> Adams: My lord, I will prove that Bernard Coleridge is
> merely a cat's paw for his father.
> Manisty: That fact is absolutely irrelevant. I cannot allow it.

Adams began by telling the jurymen how difficult it had been to find a lawyer who would dare take on the Lord Chief Justice. (Objection!) But he decided since Bernard Coleridge's letter was directed at him, who better than he to make the case. He then read Bernard's letter in its entirety. It was quite a performance. Adams was clearly pleased to be the subject of such a furious attack. It was a dramatic reading, with pauses, gestures and frequent turns to fix his stare at the defendant. During the passages featuring Bernard's more heated prose, Adams' tone drew laughter from the gallery, promptly suppressed. His rendition concluded, Adams insisted he, above all men, had no interest in a public airing of this family dispute. It gave him no pleasure to read a letter in open court filled with lies and misinformation about his character. He had come prepared to call witnesses to answer every charge Bernard made. For months, he tried to reach Bernard, seeking merely an apology. Hear me out, he pleaded; listen to my evidence, and spare your family and the sister for whom you supposedly cared so much. 'Twas a pity but Bernard Coleridge never replied to those appeals. Gesturing to the defendant, Adams sneered, Bernard "lacked either the candour to withdraw the letter or the courage to maintain it."

In the letter, Bernard suggested Adams schemed to use Mildred to ingratiate himself into the "money and position" of a prominent family like the Coleridges. Adams pointed with pride to his own family, the Adams of Ansty Hall, historic superiors to the Coleridges, who held nothing more than a "mushroom peerage."[5] Why would he aspire to join the family of Lord Coleridge? "I certainly do not covet the position of being Bernard Coleridge's brother-in-law." It was a good line but, once again, laughter was discouraged. Adams, moreover, denied any wish to gain the friendship of Stephen Coleridge, a man frequently in debt, who "ekes out a precarious existence by selling cheap wines on commission." It wasn't necessary to mention Stephen Coleridge, but Adams surely enjoyed doing it.

There was only one member of the Coleridge family with whom Adams wished to associate - the Hon. Mildred Coleridge. "There is no woman living on this earth whose feelings are more sensitive to this action." Miss Coleridge would take the stand to describe how the "screw has been most mercilessly applied" by her family to crush her wishes. He assured the jury Mildred supported him fully. The hour had grown late; the new incandescent lamps in the Law Courts were a disappointment. Manisty had heard enough. "Mr. Adams, I really must ask you to stop; this case will go on for an eternity." He told

Adams: "Be ready in the morning with your witnesses."

The trial, ironically, was being held in Courtroom IV, also known as the Lord Chief Justice's court, the largest in the building. It was "a lofty but gloomy apartment," forty by forty square feet but slightly more in height. The lower walls were wainscoted in oak, above were bare walls of brown stone. For the appearance of warmth, blood-red flowered tapestries were hung. There was a large windowed cupola in the roof which wasn't much help in November. The public came early on Saturday morning to capture the limited seats. The galley was reached by a dark, spiral staircase of 70 steps. Grim-faced ushers limited admission, some dared to engage in the "reprehensible practice" of demanding tips. Interest in the trial had been piqued, "so full it is with painful details." Everyone was finally in place.

Adams called his first witness, himself. As viewed by the bar and the public, the witness box was to the right of Justice Manisty; the jury sat left of the bench, with a direct view of the witness opposite.[6] The plaintiff's height was enhanced as he stood in the witness box six feet above the floor. He began by telling the jury of his sickly youth. Some scoffs were heard and Adams barked back, "I grew very rapidly."[7] Manisty would allow no interruptions. Adams remembered how his heart-broken parents sent him to Somerset far from London's dirt and cold. His schooling, his early career efforts in the Army and the Ordinance Office – were all forestalled by ill-health and not from indolence or any question of his character. Such vicissitudes were not uncommon in the lives of men who must struggle to make their way. He had worked hard in publishing and journalism, much more volatile careers than the law; he was – as a result – not a rich man. Indicating Bernard Coleridge seated opposite, Adams reminded the jury of all that man's privileges. He had followed his father to Eton, to Oxford, and was now heir to a peerage. This was the man who had attacked his good name.

Adams wanted to rebut all the slanders surrounding his prior marriage to the mysterious first Mrs. Adams. In Bernard's letter, he asked Mildred, "Do you know of [Adams'] behaviour on his voyage to the Cape?" Adams explained he was going out to Cape Town for a new life when he met Miss Georgianna Polson and her family aboard ship. The voyage was storm-tossed and the occasionally terrified souls aboard were naturally drawn closer. By the time they arrived, Adams told the Rev. Mr. Polson he wished to marry his daughter. For reasons Adams never quite understood, Rev. Polson did not like him and made a knowingly false claim that Adams was already married. As such, the Bishop of Cape Town refused to marry the young couple. Georgianna was very unhappy and became unwell as a result. At the Cape, the Polsons were staying with Lady Duff Gordon, who'd also been on the ship out and befriended the young people. She urged Georgianna to marry Adams even in a Presbyterian Church, which happened in October 1861. Rev. Polson ultimately admitted he had been wrong and accepted the marriage, even arranging for the bishop to remarry the couple. His former father-in-law was now dead and Adams told the jury he had no enemies in the Polson family.

His stay at the Cape was not long as Mrs. Adams could not abide the African climate. They returned to England. Their daughter was born in October 1862. With his mother's help, Adams bought control of a small publishing house where he struggled for six years. In the end, he was swindled, lost everything, and began life anew at 35. He supported himself and his family with occasional literary work about England ever since; a hard life but honourable. His wife, who suffered from "religious depression," was never strong. Her last years were blighted by cancer. As a result, his daughter, whom he dearly loved, lived with relations. Mrs. Adams died in 1880. He paused, eyes red and voice quavering. "My loss is too heavy and too recent to speak of."

Recovering, he defiantly looked at the jury, declaring that, despite the misfortune of finances and health, his married life had been "absolutely cloudless and our domestic happiness never disturbed by a single tiff."

Adams stepped down from the box and called witnesses to support his testimony. The Rev. James Longridge of Hammersmith, described Adams as a "prominent member" of his congregation for four years. The clergyman frequently visited Mrs. Adams in her last illness. He saw no foundation for any charge the Adams' led an unhappy life. The two aged McKenzie sisters were neighbours; they thought the Adams were quite happy. Sir Henry James asked Louisa McKenzie if she'd ever seen any Polsons in the Adams' home? No, Louisa said. The witness was aware Mr. Adams' daughter lived with a relation elsewhere. Had Adams' daughter ever been in his home? Louisa never met her.

Resuming his testimony, Adams insisted he never failed financially to support his daughter. He was delighted when he got the job at the VSS. He was well-paid and deservingly so. It was there, of course, he met Miss Coleridge, the defendant's sister. His first impression was she was a "lady of about thirty-seven years of age, of weak health, and impaired eye-sight, but of remarkable learning." They were "much thrown together" and he came to rely upon her. Beyond vivisection, they talked of many things including his daughter and religion. Mildred's church views were more in line with Adams, a high Anglican churchman. A sincere affection developed but Adams joked, "I had no more desire to marry her than marry the Pope." Adams glossed over his departure from the VSS, blaming "certain disagreements." He and Miss Coleridge wished only to remain friends, a desire the united Coleridge family conspired to prevent. They were spied upon and harassed. His character was attacked by cowardly accusers who never came forward. He and Mildred proposed a nominal engagement but the "persecution" continued. As Adams explained it: "We had become thoroughly attached to one another as people do get under such circumstances and we decided to marry and have done with it."

Yes, Adams conceded, he had called Mildred a "white elephant." It was a fact – he couldn't afford a wife of Mildred's standing and unfortunate health. He made that remark in a private conversation with Lord Coleridge who, in the "grossest breach of confidence," shared it with his son. Manisty again insisted Lord Coleridge not be mentioned. Returning to Bernard's letter, Adams had been accused of "making himself at home and accepting the hospitalities of the house in the absence of the master." Adams assured the jury that, but for one occasion, his visits to Sussex Square had been at his lordship's invitation. The exception took place while Lord Coleridge was in America. Adams agreed to assist Miss Coleridge with her errands. Returning to Sussex Square, she invited him for supper. He refused. She was insistent, "Oh, don't worry. We're all on board wages." Nervous laughter and muttering ran through the gallery. Adams agreed to go inside and the two ate a meagre meal in the darkened library; she enjoyed a small piece of fried sole. "She begged me to take something so I had a little piece of bread and butter."

With the lingering image of that spartan repast, Adams called the Hon. Mildred Coleridge. The reams of newsprint dedicated to *Adams v Coleridge* contain very few descriptive accounts. As Mildred entered the courtroom, we can thank an observant pressman for a rare description of the now famous Miss Coleridge. "A lady of tall, slender, and somewhat stooping figure entered the court, and made her way towards the witness stand. She was dressed entirely in black silk, relieved by a thick gold watch chain, and wore gold eyeglasses. Her features were spare, and somewhat aquiline, and her hair brown."

There were no photographs in the daily papers. Few people had ever seen Mildred; she was never a "celebrity," one of those "professional beauties" who smiled out of their frames in shop windows around the West End. Mildred was no beauty; bluntly, she was "not a particularly attractive lady." She carried herself with a "cultured and refined" air. Her jacket was of a "masculine cut." She was a blue-stocking: "a woman of the kind one is accustomed to meet at Social Science Congresses."[8]

Mildred "dashed" into the courtroom, "an old maid with a sharp countenance." In a shrill voice, she announced, "Here I am." But Sir Henry James was already up to say Bernard did not wish to subject his sister to the ordeal of the witness box. They would have no questions for her. Bernard's letter was a privileged communication between brother and sister and Miss Coleridge was no party to this action. Mildred lingered awkwardly while Adams, Sir Henry and Justice Manisty debated. Sir Henry carried the point. Adams turned to Mildred to say, "Well, it appears we won't be needing your testimony." To which, Mildred, replied, "Oh, won't you?" With a respectful bow and "pleasant smile" to Mr. Justice Manisty, a man she knew very well, she exited the stage once again. Having been called as a witness, she could remain in court, seated near Adams. Whenever he referred to Mildred, Adams would gesture a bejeweled hand in her direction. She "seemed on the whole to be rather enjoying" herself.

The final witness was Miss Effie Rose Bishop, Mrs. Bishop's daughter, and a VSS member. She knew Adams and Mildred well and never saw anything "in the least resembling love-making." The expression - at that time – meant merely flirting, courting.[9] Miss Bishop never understood the fuss. Adams rested his case.

For the defence, Sir Henry James said he would call no witnesses. In fact, he argued there was no case. The law of privilege protected letters between a brother and a sister, absent malice, which Mr. Adams failed to call any witnesses to show. James cited the leading case, "an intimate friend of a person about to marry is entitled to give warning against the proposed marriage."[10] He called upon Manisty to dismiss the action. Justice Manisty agreed Sir Henry's privilege argument was compelling. Nevertheless, he thought it was best to get a jury verdict in this case and the two sides began their final statements.

From the floor, Adams could look up to the gawping faces staring down. Looking directly at Mildred, he wanted all in court to know, regardless of the outcome, "I will marry Miss Coleridge without a farthing." This was never about her money. In fact, he suggested Bernard was the man driven by money. Bernard's scheme was to drive Mildred from the family and have her disinherited, knowing his portion would thereby be enlarged. As Adams spoke, Bernard seemed to make an effort to stand but Sir Henry placed a calming hand on his shoulder. Adams noticed the exchange and chided Bernard. "Oh, now he wants to speak! He missed his chance." Bernard had refused to enter the witness box and explain himself to a jury of Londoners. Adams concluded, "I have given up everything and worked nearly a full year to be ready for this opportunity to clear my name. Yet, Bernard Coleridge sat mute, lacking the courage to even answer a few questions."

Bernard, appearing quite miserable, remained seated, head down. He had accepted his counsel's advice; it was too late to change. Sir Henry believed putting Bernard on the stand would have been dangerous. Adams was not a "proper" barrister, who knew what he might throw at Bernard. and the impact that could have on the jury? In closing, Sir Henry adhered to his brief and restated the law of privilege. The jurymen might not grasp such legal niceties so he appealed to them as fathers and brothers. Consider if Mildred were your daughter or sister. Bernard Coleridge was aghast his only sister was accepting a man without income, fortune, or prospects. In romantic books, such marriages did take place but they usually involved couples with great affection for one another. Yet, Adams espoused "peculiar feelings" for Miss Coleridge, he called her a white elephant and professed no affection for her at all. As for the plaintiff's bizarre theory that Bernard was scheming for Mildred's share, it was nonsense. It would have been in Bernard's interest for her to go off with Adams. Let her walk away. Why write a letter pleading with her to return to share her father's favour and fortune? "You men of common sense," Sir Henry asked the jury, "do you really believe that was Bernard Coleridge's motive for writing this letter?"

Instructing the jury, Justice Manisty appeared to do all he could on Bernard's behalf. He explained the established precedent in such cases: letters from intimate relations involving such a major life step as marriage were protected by privilege, "even if every one of the allegations was false." Bernard was under no legal obligation to prove anything he wrote. The only question for the jury was to decide whether Bernard wrote the letter maliciously, knowing the charges were false.

Taking Bernard's original letter with them, the jury retired in the late afternoon. They returned in forty minutes. It was later reported that ten were for Adams straightaway, the other two required a little convincing. The foreman rose. They found for the plaintiff, Mr. Adams. Manisty struggled to restore silence in the room; there were no gavels to bang in English courts. The foreman was permitted to continue:

> We think that Mr. Coleridge, having not retracted when he was offered the opportunity, there must have been some vindictiveness in his mind, and that having the opportunity once offered to him again he did not accept it. We found there was vindictiveness.

Q: Manisty: And did you find malice?
A: Yes, malice.

Manisty sent the jury out again to compute their damage figure. Taking very little time, the jurymen returned and the foreman declared Adams was due the sum of £3000. It was a huge figure, amounting to over half Bernard's annual income. Amid the tumult, Sir Henry clamoured to be heard from the defence table. He insisted there was "no evidence to warrant such a verdict." Justice Manisty, obviously discomfited by the turn of events, declared, "Sir Henry, I must agree. I am of the opinion there was no evidence on which such a verdict could be given, and I, therefore, direct judgment for the defendant." In her diary, Maymie wrote: "Judgement for B." Bernard could finally lift his head.[11]

This baffling reversal was stunning. The Daily Chronicle felt "absolute amazement must be produced throughout the length and breadth of the land." What had just happened?

1  Adams v Coleridge J54/393 (Kew). For this trial and the second in 1886, there are no official transcripts; for the speeches and conduct of the proceedings, the leading London dailies have been relied on: The Times, Daily News, The Standard, Morning Post and Pall Mall Gazette.
2  Mr. Justice Manisty's entry in *The Dictionary of National Biography*, Vol 12 (1909).
3  Adams: "Elaborate chains, pins, rings, and lockets on men are not 'good form.'"
L. J. Ransone, "*Good Form*" in England (1888). 6.
4  "Amateur performances," C. Warren Adams, *Drawing Room Charades for Acting*, (1856).
5  Mushroom Peerage: Lord Coleridge had only held a peerage since 1872. Essentially, a 'mushroom peer' is a person suddenly come into wealth and a title, an upstart, an allusion to the fungus that starts up in the night. theesotericcuriosa.blogspot.com. See Lawrence James, *Aristocrats: Power, Grace, and Decadence: Britain's Great Ruling Classes* (2010), 200.
6  Court IV: Coleridge wanted the witness box placed between the bench and the jury, so the witness could be better heard. The designers disapproved as it upset their "symmetry."
7  Poor health: he claimed it was "consequent on his attaining the abnormal altitude of six feet four inches at sixteen years of age."
8  Mildred's physical description seems only to have appeared in provincial papers, e.g. Bicester Herald, 28 November 1884, 4. The blue-stocking reference: Sheffield Independent, 29 November 1884, 6. A "blue-stocking" referred to a "learned, pedantic, woman." *The Imperial Dictionary of the English Language* (1885).
9  A Brief History of Making Love see DGardner.substack.com
10  Leading case: *Todd v. Hawkins* (1834) A relation or intimate friend may confidentially advise a lady not to marry a particular suitor, and assign reasons; and the statements he makes will be privileged. For more, enjoy William Blake Odgers, *A Digest of the Law of Libel and Slander: And of Actions on the Case for Words Causing Damages, etc.* (1905).
11  "Judgement for B," Maymie diary (1884) CFP Add MS 86079.

# 15. THE IDOL HAS BEEN SMASHED

AROUND THE LAW COURTS, they said Mr. Justice Manisty was sustained by a "good conscience and sound port." In the uproar following his ruling, he surely sent for a bottle of his best. "Nothing can be more unsatisfactory than the termination of *Adams v Coleridge*," declared the mighty *Times*. The trial had been followed across the country with "breathless interest." On the morning after the inexplicable verdict, Charles Warren Adams, like Byron, "awoke to find himself one of the best-known men in England." Manisty, meantime, found himself "the best abused man in England," according to the *Western Times*. "In his over-anxiety to avoid a scandal he created a greater one." He must resign, many thought. Clearly, the great British public decided Adams had been robbed of his well-earned verdict, not to mention £3000. "Adams made a favourable impression upon all his hearers, lawyers and laymen alike, by his eloquence, his manliness and his patience under the frequent sneering interruptions of Manisty." *The Spectator*, while conceding Manisty may have been right on the legal point, his ruling, snatching victory away at the last moment, would lead the public to believe "when a judge is concerned no judge will do impartial justice." It took a bold man to face this powerful clique of lawyers and "they will try to ruin him if they can." In the House of Commons, an Irish MP demanded an inquiry into Manisty's ruling which turned the verdict of a jury into "a mockery, a delusion, and a snare." Mr. Callan, member for County Louth, sat down to rousing cheers from the backbenches.

It was extremely uncommon for a judge to explain himself to the press but Manisty felt the need.[1] Before the start of business on Monday morning, he addressed the remarkable conclusion of "The Coleridge Libel Case." If he had wanted to, he could have, at any time, directed a verdict citing the law of privileged communications. Had he done that, Adams would undoubtedly have appealed. If Adams won that appeal, as well he might, then he faced the expense of another trial. Thus, Manisty felt by permitting the case to go to the jury, and getting a verdict on the record, he'd actually done Adams a favour, skipping a step. He hoped to clear the way for *Adams v. Coleridge* to go directly to the Court of Appeal. The legal press generally endorsed Manisty's actions. "Society is gravely injured when the naturalness and unrestraint of family intercourse is restricted." Privilege was worthy of protection.

As popular as Adams had become in defeat, Bernard and the Coleridges emerged friendless in victory. Like his father, Bernard had carried himself with an air of irreproachability and it had cost him. The jury plainly disliked Bernard, whether he was poorly advised or not. He'd shown a "general insolence of demeanour." Like father, like son. Credit Adams for those sentiments. While Lord Coleridge had not been the one on trial, Adams landed enough punches to leave his Lordship's halo askew. *The New York Times* held the elder Coleridge responsible for everything; he had displayed "cruelty and injustice entirely incompatible with an affectionate parent, a just Judge, and a high-minded gentleman."

New salt was added to the wounded Coleridge clan with a letter from Mildred's steadfast friend, Mrs. Bishop, published in the *Daily Telegraph* a few days after the trial. Mrs. Bishop regretted her dicky heart kept her from being a witness on Adams' behalf. The public needed to know the truth about Mildred:

I speak with knowledge, for I am one of her mother's (the late Lady Coleridge) oldest friends, and have been fully cognizant of all the details of this unhappy business from the first. So far as being "a woman of property," Miss Coleridge has not, in possession or prospect, one solitary sixpence beyond the few pounds she has economised during the last 10 months out of the cheques sent her at irregular intervals by her father and her own earnings as a music mistress. For six years, since her mother's death, she managed her father's establishment, not only as the lady of the house, but as working housekeeper, and with a personal allowance of £80 a year. For the last 11 months she has been living in a small lodging house in Kensington, giving music lessons. From the time she quitted her father's house in December last to the present moment she has had no regular allowance whatever, receiving only occasional cheques, upon which she has no ground whatever for relying, even while she remains single.[2]

*The Telegraph* suggested the letter made clear that Mildred had been her father's "chief drudge." Life behind the doors of "a household which had been deemed a special dwelling of celestial peace," had been revealed for all to read. It was the society journals that Lord Coleridge so savagely denounced just months before that took greatest delight. Edmund Yates of *The World*, still free while appealing his sentence, had been waiting for just such an opportunity. He'd vowed, that given the chance, "in a perfectly dignified & decorous manner, [Coleridge] must be flayed alive." The Adams trial gift-wrapped it. *The World's* column deserves to be quoted at length (emphasis the author's):

Miss Coleridge was driven to become a daily governess, living in a small house or lodging in a cheap suburb, because her home, the home from which her mother had six years ago been removed by death, and which was controlled by the father who was therefore morally charged with the responsibilities of both parents, had ceased to be for her a habitable place. This deplorable and humiliating condition of things may have been brought about by her ill-starred engagement. But to admit this is only to compel us to go back one stage further. It is inconceivable that any young woman of ordinary self-respect, brought up with the notions of delicacy and breeding which one is bound to believe that, at least during the life time of her mother, Miss Coleridge had an opportunity of acquiring, would have accepted an offer of marriage as cold, conventional, and one might almost say as compulsory as, according to Mr. Adams, was that which he was constrained to make. The inference which all sensible, all humane parents, all daughters who have any knowledge of decent homes, will draw is that *Miss Coleridge deliberately preferred a frigid and joyless marriage to the domestic misery she has endured for years.* And this young woman was matured in an atmosphere where from her infancy she must have listened to the pious precepts and devotional platitudes of a smug religionism...Lord Coleridge is more than a mere judge. He is far above the weakness of any of his predecessors, and poses in all respects as the ethical superior of the late Sir Alexander Cockburn. Yet so beneficent was the influence which he had exercised in his own household, so eminently adapted was he to be taken as model for the father of a family, that *while he was sitting in judgement posing as an invisible embodiment of civil and divine authority, his daughter was being driven out of doors and compelled to play the trade of a daily governess.* Seldom, even on the threadbare

155

level of shabby-genteel existence, never certainly in such a social
position as that of Lord Coleridge, has the curtain been lifted
upon a domestic interior so graceless and so squalid. Mr. Adams
appears to have acted with wisdom in not allowing himself
to partake of the greatly grudged hospitality of the Coleridge
family. He appears also to have very correctly understood the
whole family position. When, therefore, the small sole and the
bread and butter made an appearance, the affianced husband
of the lady declined to partake of the proffered refreshments,
except so far as to consume a fragment of bread and butter, and
this only in order not to wound the feelings of his hostess. Even
thus he would not have been prevailed upon, without hearing
that Miss Coleridge like the servants in the establishment was on
board wages. *What a picture! The only and motherless daughter
of that eloquent and upright judge to whose lips the finest and
holiest of sentiments are always springing from a guileless and
chivalrous heart, treated in her father's house upon exactly
the same footing as a scullery wench!* But there is no need to
dwell upon all the details of this distressing tale of parsimony,
meanness, and cruelty in the household of a judge. The Lord
Chief Justice owes it entirely to himself and the wrong-headed
and discourteous obstinacy of his son, who entirely ignored
Mr. Adams' offer to disprove the charges brought against him
to Mr. Bernard Coleridge's satisfaction in private, that the
public is now acquainted with the shocking and sickening
story. Months ago, on the 9th of April, when Lord Coleridge
denounced this journal for prying into the private doings of
others, chronicling their lives and generally pandering to an
unhealthy appetite, all the facts on which this action was based,
and which have been dragged into the light of day were known

to us. We were fully and particularly informed as to the quality and the amount of dirty linen which has now been washed in public. Had we stooped to the cheap sensation-mongering with which we were then charged we could not have wished for more attractive material. But not the slightest mention of or allusion to the matter was made in these columns. The silence which we maintained then would not have been broken now unless *one of the most despicable scandals ever enacted in an English household* had not become public property. The Coleridge family alone are responsible for having published to the world these details of their private relations which in deference to their feelings we suppressed.[3]

It was a savage attack. "Seldom in recent times have more scathing and merciless sentences been written about a public man." Women's publications, typically supportive of his Liberal lordship, turned. *The Englishwoman's Review*: "When we consider what would have been the money-cost to the father for all these "services rendered," had anyone but a daughter under taken them, we feel that £80 was a very small acknowledgment, and our sympathies are with Miss Coleridge."[4] *The Freeman's Journal* in Ireland insisted Lord Coleridge stood unmasked as a "humbug." In distant Auckland, "A Lady's Letter from London," carried word, "The idol has been smashed and only very common clay remains."[5] The society observer Archibald Forbes predicted "the Coleridge family will never recover."

For all the ink spilled in denunciation of the Lord Chief Justice, a scant drop or two was spent defending the man. The *Law Times*, for instance, argued "Lord Coleridge is entitled to disapprove of a son-in-law none the less because he happens to be Lord Chief Justice, and to enforce this disapproval by the only means in the power of a father towards an adult daughter—namely, by omitting her name from his will." He let her leave his home with his clear message: "You may go with Adams but you shall have less." Harrison, the family solicitor, wrote to the *Telegraph* to assure the public Lord Coleridge continued to send his daughter's allotment, the first of every month. All the cheques were promptly cashed. There was that, then.

Lord Coleridge kept silent under the hailstorm of attacks. His work continued; he showed no signs of pre-occupation as he presided over one of his most famous trials, the sensational "Boy-Eating Case."[6] Friends remained supportive, including Jowett, who wrote, "Do not suppose your friends are unmoved spectators of anything which affects you so deeply or that they have no feeling about it but unmixed pain. It is intensely disagreeable...No father was ever kinder to his children."[7]

Meanwhile, Adams and Mildred enjoyed something like celebrity status. Their story was thought fit for a musical comedy: the high-spirited daughter, a "recalcitrant maid of many summers," versus her indignant father. In the West End, the *Gaiety* was staging a bit of burlesque, *A Very Little Hamlet*, by William Yardley, known for sprinkling his plays with topical references. Of course, he sneaked in a line mentioning Mr. Adams. The quip "provoked quite a startling demonstration of the popularity of the plaintiff in a recent libel suit." Another humour paper, *The Owl*, offered a clever little trifle:

> There was Miss Coleridge eating fried fish,
> And looking too utterly utter,
> With Mr. Adams, as meek as you'd wish,
> Delighting in nice bread and butter![8]

In early December, several papers falsely reported that England's most famous lovers, Charles Adams and Mildred Coleridge, had gotten married in "quite a private ceremony." The supposed date was 8 December; Mildred's wedding dress was described as pink satin with a low neck. If that wasn't suspect detail enough, Adams quickly fired off a complete denial. How could they possibly marry without the £3000 Judge Manisty made disappear before their eyes? As a result, a short-lived newspaper appeal was undertaken for public contributions for poor Mildred's trousseau.

Deprived of his forensic triumph and financial reward, Adams was certain to file an appeal. Was a private settlement still possible? Sir Farrer Herschell (a future Lord Chancellor) approached Adams with a "magnanimous" offer from Lord Coleridge. Bernard would withdraw his now famous letter, issue a public apology, and Adams would get £500 in reparations. Mildred's allowance would be doubled to £600 per year. Lord Coleridge wasn't hopeful; "Manisty's incredible muddle," as he called it, left Adams and Mildred with the sense £3000 had been snatched from their grasp and maybe another jury could give them more. Still, the settlement offered money in hand for Adams, more for Mildred, and avoided the costs of an appeal.

Any hopes along that line were crushed by a second intervention on the part of Mrs. Bishop. She turned over to Adams her correspondence with Lord Coleridge in the days following the "darkened room" affair. Included was the letter in which Coleridge basically accused Adams of chasing off the clerks and lying in wait in Victoria Street, hoping to entrap and seduce poor motherless Mildred. Only Miss Cobbe's interruption had saved Mildred from a terrible fate. Mrs. Bishop handed Adams the letter, telling him. "Do with it what you will." Adams knew well what the letter meant: no more could Lord Coleridge send Bernard out to fight his battles. The stakes had been raised.

When he learned Adams' held that letter, Coleridge tried a private apology, writing to Adams:

My impressions of 1882 have been removed by occurrences since. Such being the case, I am willing to say so. I am willing to have no false pride or shame in this matter. I am willing to admit I had formed a wrong impression at the time.

Adams needed more; it would have to be a public apology and there would have to be financial reparations. Otherwise, and though he had no wish, certainly, to do it, Adams was prepared to bring a new libel action, this time naming the Lord Chief Justice of England. Coleridge was not easily cowed, instructing Herschell to end the settlement discussion. "A happier Christmas to you, my dear Herschell, and to those around you, than I shall enjoy."[9]

Another Christmas correspondent was Sir Charles Bowen, Lord Justice of Appeal, who had been at Coleridge's side in the Tichborne trial. He warned his Chief, "You have now before you the prospect of a bitter personal assault by determined enemies." Adams "means war to the knife."[10]

Bowen was correct. There would be war; he could not know that it would be fought on two fronts. Who better than an old war correspondent like Archibald Forbes to lust for combat? During the mostly peaceable 1880s, Forbes turned to writing bi-monthly gossip columns, "London Jottings," for overseas English-language papers. He informed his readers about the Adams' trial, of course, but Lord Coleridge's "cup of unpleasantness" would soon be running over: "It is reported with considerable circumstance that his lordship will ere long occupy the humiliating position of defendant in a suit for breach of promise of marriage." Forbes claimed that "financial offers of a very lavish kind" had been made but "the lady" rejected them. "I should imagine that this Christmas Day the Lord Chief Justice of England is the reverse of a happy man."[11]

1  "Statement of Mr. Justice Manisty," Pall Mall Gazette, 24 November 1884. Meanwhile, the Telegraph published several letters from disgruntled jurymen. 24 November 1884.

2  Mrs. Bishop's letter, Daily Telegraph, 26 November 1884, 5.

3  The World, 25 November 1884.

4  Englishwoman's Review, 14 February 1885.

5  24 January 1885, "From the Auckland Star's London Correspondent," the commentary was dated 4 December 1884.

6  "The Boy-Eating case:" Two yachtsmen adrift in a lifeboat in the south Atlantic killed and ate their dying cabin boy. In a "beautifully written opinion," Coleridge found the men guilty of murder, "A man ought to die rather than kill an innocent person." Sentenced to hang with a strong recommendation for mercy, the convicted men served six months. See A.W. Bryan Simpson, Cannibalism and the Common Law (1984).

7  Jowett: CFP Add MS 86286.

8  "Very Little Hamlet," Evening Standard, 1 December 1884, 2. The Owl (Birmingham) 5 December 1884.

9  Herschel CFP Add MS 86285.

10  "War to the knife," Bowen CFP Add MS 86253.

11  "London Jottings:" Forbes' column was dated Christmas day but it took six weeks by ship to reach the readers of the South Australian Weekly Chronicle (Adelaide, SA) published 7 February 1885, 6 (trove.nla.gov.au).

# 16. A FELICITOUS TERMINATION

ON ITS CHRISTMAS wish list, one of the humour papers hoped for harmony 'round the hearth in the Coleridge home: "I should like to see Mr. Adams and Miss Mildred Coleridge with their feet under the Lord Chief Justice's mahogany, and the Hon. Bernard drinking a bumper to the young couple's health."[1] A Merry Christmas to us all, my dears. God bless us, everyone. Would it surprise you to know that neither Mildred not Adams were anywhere near the sombre holiday table at Heath's Court?

Also missing were Stephen Coleridge and his wife who had sailed for America that December, travelling with a theatrical company headlined by the leading English stage figures Henry Irving and (Stephen's muse) Ellen Terry. On arrival, however, the American scribes were most interested in Stephen, a "fine-looking man and entertaining talker" who gave a series of chatty interviews about the recently concluded trial in London. Mildred "was entirely at the head of my father's house," Stephen reported. All she wanted, she had. She could do whatever she desired with her time. "She is very well-educated, can speak several languages fluently, and is a skilled musician" and no one in the family opposed her giving lessons. Adams was the problem. To Stephen, he was "a man without a shilling," "aimless and unsteady," and "unable to earn a bare livelihood." Given his lack of income and position, the family "very naturally endeavoured to put a stop to the intimacy." Mildred was never turned out of doors, she left purely "in a feeling of pique." Stephen reminded readers that Adams, at trial, vowed to marry Mildred without a farthing. "Why has he not fulfilled his engagement if his designs are not mercenary?" Stephen was asked, where is your sister now? "In lodgings, I fancy," said Stephen "with a little shrug of the shoulders."[2]

Stephen was quite pleased with his spin control chats. The *Pittsburgh Daily Press* declared Stephen "puts quite a different and more agreeable light on the affair than the one given by the sensation mongers in London." On New Year's Day, the *Cleveland Lea*der headlined, "A Wise Father Opposing the Suit of an Impecunious Adventurer." Stephen sent several of the cuttings home, boasting, "I found my father's face black as ink in America and left it white, which is something to say."

Stephen's merry tour continued, while, at home, despair was everywhere amongst the Coleridges. Bernard was forced to withdraw his name from consideration at the Athenaeum, where his father, of course, was one of the club's most prominent members. It was that or be black-balled.[3] Lord Coleridge was assured it had more to do with Bernard's politics than the Adams trial. Still, it was another blow to Coleridge pride. Matthew Arnold came to Sussex Square and found his old friend "sorely troubled. Things are so bad they cannot possibly be made worse."[4]

Steady the Buffs, worse was to come. *The New York Times* declared the Adams-Coleridge matter far from over. Adams was now threatening to reveal the real reason Mildred left her father's home, i.e., "a scandal of which the public has as yet heard nothing."[5] What could that possibly refer to? Moreover, Archie Forbes' little jotting in that Australian newspaper had sailed halfway round the world and been picked up in an English paper or two. "Lawmen say that an action for breach of promise to marry has been laid against an eminent Englishman by an American lady."[6] They dared not identify the gentleman by name but suggested that if the report was true, it promised to be the greatest sensation for many, many a year.

The pension arrangement with Amy Lawford earlier mentioned was supposed to preclude this possibility. But, according to Stephen, "Subsequently, she recovered her influence over him" - the Lord Chief - by threatening to file a breach of promise action.[7] By law, the exchange of mutual promises to marry created "an actionable contract, an enforceable obligation." In reality, "breach" cases were frequently uproarious affairs, a staple of the music halls with jilted damsels and ageing, wealthy, lotharios. The public loved the spectacle: "a reg'lar good day for a breach o'promise trial," quoting Sam Weller from *The Pickwick Papers*.[8] Reformers hoped to end the breach of promise action. Some at the bar defended it. Lord Coleridge had presided over many such trials. "Would it surprise you to know" that only recently, he'd expressed his belief that women often deserved "protection against the misconduct of men." There were some breaches, he argued, worth "substantial damages."[9] His lordship had to know some "flaming women's advocate" employed by the Lawfords would throw that back in his face. Any suit on Miss Lawford's part, however, would have been undercut if she had, in fact, previously agreed to accept money for her wounded feelings. No "lady of delicacy" would put a cash figure on her affections. All true, and Lord Coleridge would probably hold the higher ground in court. But he was not the common defendant in such affairs, an amorous curate or a solicitor in the shires. He was the highest jurist in the Empire. He would sooner have resigned. "Lord Coleridge in an Embarrassing Dilemma," headlined the *New York Times*. The more the Coleridges pushed, the more determined Mrs. Lawford (Amy's mother) was to enforce the Lord Chief's promises, if necessary, in court. Does any of this, in the very least, sound familiar? In the words of Father Coleridge, "This puts poor Milly out of sight altogether."[10]

In the midst of everything, "poor Milly" reappeared in the gossip columns with reports that she and Adams had finally done it: they were married. The nuptial news was quickly shot down again by *The World*. "The Hon. Mildred Coleridge requests me to contradict a report which is, it seems, in circulation to the effect that her marriage with Mr. Adams is already an accomplished fact. The report is false. 'When my marriage does take place,' says Miss Coleridge, 'it will be publicly announced in the ordinary manner.'"

Friends of the Coleridge family could only watch and read this steady drip of nettling publicity with concern. The papers reported: "The Adams and Coleridge Case, it is stated, is not yet done with, and a still more sensational development is imminent." Charlotte Yonge wrote to a friend, "It is altogether the most extraordinary and miserable business I ever heard of, and my poor Mary (Maymie) is quite heartbroken about it."[11] Another friend of long-standing, Cardinal Newman, wrote to Lord Coleridge, offering a few prayers. Coleridge was grateful, but not hopeful. "I wish I had anything pleasant to tell you about myself, but my troubles seem to thicken. However, they will come to a head, and an end, of some sort, before very long."[12]

By troubles, his lordship would not have included some disappointing news from America where he was well-remembered from his recent visit. A horse named "Lord Coleridge" was entered in the May 1885 Kentucky Derby. Alas, the gallant colt finished last in a field of ten.

Adams' appeal of Mr. Justice Manisty's controversial ruling opened on 4 June 1885. At the appellate level, there were no witnesses. Each side made a statement and the three judges (Baggallay, Lindley & Brett) would withdraw, review the record, and decide whether the matter should be sent back for a new trial. Adams argued he had not been given a fair chance by Justice Manisty who refused to allow any mention of Lord Coleridge. Hadn't Bernard plainly stated in his letter that he wrote as "*my father's son*?" Adams also accused Manisty of too many interruptions; the press described it as the judge's "running fire." Adams cited the judge's several prejudicial remarks. "He told the jury I lived by my wits." In Adams's view, that could be said of every learned man. Manisty also told the jury Adams had no home to offer Miss Coleridge. Untrue, Adams explained. "Thank God, I have a happy home; no home as gorgeous as the one from which Miss Coleridge has been expelled but I trust my home will be equally happy for Miss Mildred, a woman I revere and esteem before all women living." As Adams whinged on, Justice Brett made an excellent point. "Mr. Adams, you say Justice Manisty treated you unfairly, but the jury gave you a verdict." They surely did, at least until Manisty took it away.

Sir Henry James returned to speak for Bernard. He reviewed the laws of privilege which "a sentimental jury of laymen" simply failed to understand. Bernard had written a "sacred communication" to his sister. Sir Henry was reminded from the bench that privilege does not protect "the reckless venting of ungovernable rage." Justice Lindley wondered why Bernard had not given evidence. "That is not a point in his favour." Sir Henry said his client (Bernard) most certainly wished to testify but - on the advice of counsel - he did not. If there was any censure, let it fall on him, begged Sir Henry.

This is a much-abridged account of the hearing which lasted into a second day.[13] The judges adjourned without setting a date for their ruling. As the room cleared, Sir Henry approached Adams for a conversation. The two men left together. A weekend intervened. On 9 June 1885, the press was informed that a "felicitous termination" of *Adams v Coleridge* had been reached. In the formal statement that followed, the Hon. Bernard Coleridge, "unreservedly" withdrew the charges he had made in his letter to Mildred. Mr. Adams, in return, formally acknowledged Bernard's statement and expressed his happiness. Since it was the Coleridge family's wish to address all matters at once, Lord Coleridge also withdrew his remarks in the so-called Bishop letter:

> Lord Coleridge desires, and has long desired, to say that whatever construction may have been placed upon anything he has written or said, he thinks it due to Mr. Adams to withdraw any language which might be construed as casting imputations upon his character or motives. Lord Coleridge cannot regard it as being necessary to say that he has never intended to cast any reflection upon the conduct of his daughter.

The settlement meant more money for Mildred. Lord Coleridge agreed that his daughter "shall be replaced in the same pecuniary position as she would have been in if these misunderstandings had not arisen." He was "perfectly willing to make the suitable provision of £600 per annum" for his daughter. If she predeceased "her husband," the gentleman would receive £480 a year. Adams expressed his satisfaction with these new terms and assured the appeal judges, "I have no thought of bringing any further actions in connection with these matters." He may have meant it at the time.

Hoorah for that, everyone could agree. Lord Coleridge wrote to Gladstone, "I am relieved to a great extent from the cloud which has so long overshadowed me."[14] There was still the matter of the compensation due Adams from the Coleridges, *pere et fils*. An arbitrator, acceptable to all parties, was chosen: Sir Robert Collier, a veteran lawyer, with no close ties to the Coleridge family.[15] Everyone was allowed to wish this "unpleasant business" was over. Even Yates at *The World* relented: "The dirty linen of the Coleridge family has, after a preliminary damping and soaping, been withdrawn from the public wash-tub." Those doughty romantic heroes, Mildred and Charles, were ascendant, he with his good name restored. "Mr. Adams and Miss Coleridge have come unscathed out of the furnace of affliction. They are now justified in concluding their love must be true since its course has not run smoothly."

As for the proud Coleridge men, to publicly grovel before the loathsome Adams was "a damn tough bullet to chew." Adams had driven a hard bargain. When told Mildred would be getting £400 a year, he scoffed, "I can't take her for 400 a year." What kind of man would say something like that? Lord Coleridge found some hope in the actuarial tables. The reprehensible Adams was not young and did not look healthy. Perhaps, he wouldn't have many years to enjoy "the fruits of his evil-doing." Bernard was bitter over his forced apology. Sir Henry's statement was too conciliatory. His father urged him to keep a stiff upper lip. "Don't go about saying we were defeated. James will say what he has to say."[16]

In the end, thoughtful observers conceded there had been "some loss of dignity" in the Coleridge world. In the privacy of Sussex Square, Lord Coleridge confided to Bernard, "I am now a very sad unhappy man." It is unlikely his spirits were lifted in any way by the receipt of a note from Mildred. It was "an affectionate letter begging him (her words)" to come to her wedding.

1  "Christmas Wish List:" Referee, December 1884.
2  Stephen Coleridge in US: 25 Dec 84, Chicago Tribune (Special from the Philadelphia News).
3  Butterfield, a fellow member of the club, urged Lord Coleridge to let the matter drop. Add MS 86259. Bernard eventually became a member, albeit a quarter-century later, in 1909
4  Arnold wrote to a mutual friend (Grant Duff), "I am going to make a desperate effort to get Mildred to agree to a reconciliation and settlement." He failed. Lang, Arnold letters, 4 March 1885.
5  "Scandal": New York Times, 30 Nov 1884, 1.
6  "Eminent Englishman and an American lady:" Sporting Gazette, 21 February 1885.
7  Stephen Coleridge, the papers of Sir Paul Coleridge.
8  For "Breach of Promise," see especially, Ginger S. Frost, *Promises Broken: Courtship, Class, and Gender in Victorian England* (1995).
9  Lord Coleridge's opinion, quoted in Steinbach, *Promises, Promises: Not Marrying in England*, 1780-1920, 286.
10  "Poor Milly," CFP Add MS 85936.
11  5 April 1885, Letters of CM Yonge, newcastle.edu.au 5 April 1885.
12  8 April 1885, CFP Add MS 86195.
13  Appeal details: "The Coleridge Libel Case," details from The Standard 5 Jun 1885, 3; 6-2, 9-3.
14  "Cloud" letter to Gladstone, Coleridge papers CFP Add MS 44138.
15  Collier/Monkswell, (1817-1886) Long legal career; specialising in railways and mining. He held numerous government appointments. His pastime was painting Alpine glacial scenes. His son, John Collier, became a prominent portraitist.
16  Letters from John Duke Coleridge to his son Bernard, afterwards 2nd Baron Coleridge. CFP Add MS.

# 17. TWO QUIET WEDDINGS & AN EX-HUSBAND

A WOMAN CONSIDERING what day of the week to be married might do worse than consult the old rhyme, "Monday is for wealth; Tuesday is for health [but] Wednesday is the best day of all."[1] Thus, it was a Wednesday, 24 June 1885, when Mildred Coleridge left her new lodgings at 24 Kempsford Gardens to walk the very short distance to Earls Court Square and the Church of St. Matthias.

The wedding of Mildred Coleridge and Charles Adams was intended to be strictly private. A special license was purchased eliminating the need for posted banns or other advance publicity which reduced the risk of "wedding crashers," crowds of unwanted onlookers who gathered outside the church, often subjecting the couple to "cruel teasing." If privacy was desired, St. Matthias was well-chosen. It was a relatively new parish and not overly fashionable. The entrance doors were around to one side of the church so only those "in the know" could find them. The red brick building had recently been "cleaned, ventilated and redecorated." For special events, there were seats for 1200 people; not this Wednesday.

Private or not, the marriage traditions would be observed. The father of the bride was expected to pay for the wedding; which Lord Coleridge did, indirectly. It was a modest event afforded only by the bride's monthly paternal stipend. The typical father of the bride would have been delighted to bring his daughter to the altar, "Who giveth this woman to be married to this man?" Lord Coleridge declined that honour despite what Mildred called her "affectionate" letter asking that he simply attend the service. The Lord Chief had no court conflicts on that day, according to the law calendar. Perhaps, there were other calls upon his time. "In consequence of his refusal, no other members of Lord Coleridge's family were invited." Bernard was travelling. Stephen was busy. Aunt Maymie chose that day to accompany Gilbert to a Handel festival at the Crystal Palace. In her diary, Maymie tersely recorded the wedding of her dearest niece, "Poor Milly was married to Mr. Adams. Alas."

Despite the lack of Coleridges, "there was a sufficiently large attendance to satisfy all the parties concerned." A numerous Seymour contingent was present; Mildred's loyal uncle, the Rev. Henry Seymour from Nettlecombe would marry them. Mrs. Bishop wouldn't miss it, of course, with her daughter Effie. And Mrs. Barry Procter made an appearance. Nearly ninety, she was a friend of the greatest Coleridge of them all, the poet, and came out of respect for her long departed old friend. Mr. Adams was waiting at the church along with his two brothers. The mathematician, Walter Marsham Adams signed the registry as a witness. The Rev. Coker Adams, every bit as cussed as his now famous brother, came down from his parish in Norfolk to assist Rev. Seymour in the ceremony.[2]

As Mildred had wished, all went off quietly. The afternoon papers printed a brief announcement issued by the Press Association: "The marriage of Mr. Charles Warren Adams and the Hon. Mildred Coleridge took place this morning at St Matthias, Earls Court, the ceremony being performed by Miss Coleridge's maternal uncle." There was no discussion of the bride's attire, the flowers, the vows, the ring, the wedding breakfast, etc. Readers did learn "the ceremony was concluded with a grand choral celebration of the Holy Communion." The juiciest detail was the lack of Coleridges in attendance; the bride's father having "refused to attend." No matter, the *Liverpool Mercury* wrote, "Lord Coleridge's absence damped nobody's happiness and everybody was ready to wish the successful suitor (in two senses) a happy honeymoon."

Thus, the most talked about couple in London were wed. Mocked once as an "elderly rolling stone," Adams had achieved the dream of thousands of young (and not so young) men of uncertain fortune, he'd married a peer's daughter. It was out of a storybook. "The ending has been of the usual type - namely marriage - only instead of a white elephant he marries an heiress with £600 a year." Congratulations to the groom, who "played his part with dignity." And Mildred had also won out against great odds. "It may console parents with refractory sons and daughters, who insist on falling in love with the wrong people, to know that the Lord Chief Justice of England has been as powerless maintaining home rule as people less highly gifted and favoured by fortune." But let this be an end to it. "The curtain has fallen upon what we may be permitted to hope is the last act of the Coleridge-Adams comedy."

Officially, they were now Mr. Adams and the Honourable Mrs. Adams. Charles remained a commoner while Mildred retained her honorific prefix, if barely. In censorious drawing rooms, "a lady of high rank does not raise her husband to the same positions as she formerly occupied; but sinks down to his standard."[3] In the meantime, they honeymooned. They took their wedding trip in the Southwest of England. In late July, while spending a fortnight in Sidmouth, the newlyweds took the train up from the coast, a pleasant thirty minutes to the red brick station at Ottery. Mildred showed her husband where Coleridges had resided for generations. There was a must-do candlelit walk to the Pixie's Parlour, the cavern where the poet's initials (S.T.C.) were still seen carved in the sandstone.[4] In town, it was a Thursday, market day, and the streets of Ottery were crowded; Mildred was recognised by many of the locals. Heath's Court was off limits, beyond its walled surround. The Exeter papers reported "the notorious" Mr. and Mrs. Adams ended their visit with evening services at the church. Mildred "reverently" laid flowers at her mother's memorial in the south transept while Adams stood at a respectful distance. Naturally, the couple's visit was soon "the general talk of the town."

The effrontery of Mildred to bring Adams to Ottery infuriated Bernard who wrote a grumbly note to his father. Lord Coleridge replied: "My dear Boy, this is disgusting about Mildred & Adams but it is like them, so what would you have?" Bernard must have actually expressed a wish to employ physical violence of some nature against Adams and it is remarkable to read that the Lord Chief Justice of England didn't exactly rule it out. "I agree in your last statement. 50 years ago, her three brothers would have called him out long ago & have cut short his [life?]. We are better in the main for the abolition of dueling." A comforting thought in 1885.[5]

Mildred's wedding did not go unnoticed. One of the sporting papers quipped, "When the Ancient Mariner marries again the event may attract more attention." Updating that fitful romance, almost two full years had passed since Lord Coleridge's homeward crossing, delighting in the pleasant company of Miss Lawford. The Coleridge family remained solidly united in opposition to any marriage. In his last conversation with his father on this subject, Bernard ("My dear boy," indeed) had been assured there would be no marriage. The Lawfords were, presumably, disappointed but in receipt of some compensation. Perhaps it was Mildred's wedding, following as it did the (apparent) settlement of *Adams v Coleridge,* that prompted the Lawfords to rethink their decision. His lordship had no more excuses or distractions. The pressure was renewed and, quite clearly, word of this stalemate had got out.

The Lord Chief Justice's romantic caper and his family's pushback were kept out of the British papers. There were libel laws.[6] He was a public figure. The press might comment upon his rulings, his hauteur, who came to his dinner parties, etc. Stay out of his private life. English-language papers in America, the Antipodes, from Tennessee to Tasmania, were under no such cloud and, quoting "Our London Correspondent," could publish just about anything. Bolder stories about the Coleridge-Lawford affair began appearing in early August 1885. American and Canadian newspapers carried a report – datelined London – that Lord Coleridge would soon be marrying an American woman "though he would rather not." Other than Amy's nationality, the story was correct. They had met aboard ship, formed an ardent attachment, but since returning to London, his ardour had cooled. Emboldened by her defiant mother, the young lady would not be discarded. The Lord Chief Justice must decide: marriage or be sued for breach-of-promise. He had been snared in "the matrimonial meshes of a Yankee girl's net." In the wake of the Mildred saga, many felt the great man was due "a dose of the injustice he was lately disposed to dispense to his daughter." The drama was all the talk among "the loungers at the clubs." London was "convulsed" with excitement. For Lord Coleridge, meanwhile, it was "Too Dreadfully Dreadful."[7]

Indeed, it would be. A breach of promise action would have been a reputation-crushing and likely career-ending scandal. For Amy Lawford, too, it was character suicide. She would be forever known as the old man's mistress, discarded, and paid off. Still, the Lawfords had the stronger hand, by far. They had little to lose and would have expected weighty damages from any jury informed of the conduct of their Lord Chief Justice. Victorian judges and juries (all men, of course) had always shown a leaning to be over generous to the teary-eyed female plaintiffs. Only months earlier, an actress was awarded

On his return from America.

The story of Lord Coleridge's romantic crossing aboard the *Britannic* was said to be the talk of the law courts. This remarkable sketch was done by Frank Lockwood QC, a popular barrister known as much for his wit and his skill with pen and ink. The drawing is undated. Presumably, Lockwood shared it with very few people during his lordship's lifetime.

£10,000 after being jilted by the Viscount Garmoyle. He was described as a "chinless booby." How much more would a jury demand from the exalted Lord Coleridge?[8]

Exactly when Lord Coleridge decided to go forward with the marriage may never be known. The Coleridge papers and letters were culled of any reference to Miss Lawford and the possibility of a breach action. On 4 August 1885, through his solicitor, an application was made for a special marriage license, the exclusive purview of the Archbishop of Canterbury.

In brief, he requested the "solemnization of a true, pure, and lawful matrimony ... with all the speed that may be." The license freed the applicant from the public posting of the banns in the parish churches of the groom and bride. Few people still paid any notice to banns but the name Coleridge might draw unwanted attention. The license also permitted the ceremony to take place in any church or chapel, *or other "meet and convenient place"* by a minister of the Church of England. Lastly, the ceremony could take place outside the canonical hours - which were between 8am and noon.[9] This explained why, even at 30 guineas (fees and stamps), the licenses were quite popular, "a fact to some extent accounted for by the late hours of the upper classes."

The details and merits of all requests were personally reviewed by the archbishop, but there would be no problem. For Lord Coleridge, it was just paperwork but at what physical cost. On the 4th, presiding in Court IV, he appeared unwell. The following day, a bulletin was issued: "Lord Chief Justice Coleridge was confined to his house by an attack of lumbago." The stress was intense; the public was told overwork was the reason for his lordship's "continued indisposition." At Sussex Square, he no longer had Mildred to apply the poultices and hush the house. It was finally announced his Lordship would not return to the bench until after the approaching Long Vacation (three months) which he would spend resting at his home in Devon.

The special license was good for 30 days but still Lord Coleridge hesitated. His ardour for Amy Lawford may have gone off the boil but it never completely cooled down. He truly cared for the young woman and was concerned for her reputation. Did she want to go through with the marriage? He warned her mother that his enemies would be merciless. If they found anything suspect in Amy's background, they would come at him but, by extension, destroy the Lawfords in the process. The leading "enemy" was still Yates of *The World*, smarting from his stretch in the nick, and who freely bashed the L.C.J. in the columns of his weekly ever since. In a letter to Bernard, Lord Coleridge said he had taken the advice of two legal friends. "Roupell and Bowen agreed, *I should go to Yates*. Not to ask a favour but a question."[10] What did Yates know and what would he print? If Yates was going to publish, then his Lordship would have "broken off all plans to marry." The difficulty was that he wasn't yet strong enough to "go to Yates." Here again, overseas readers were given some fascinating detail.

> There is a very pretty story going about, with a lovely moral and a charming bit of poetic justice thrown in, as to the means by which the editor of *The World* was induced to forgive -

well, perhaps, not to forgive, for that is not Mr. Yates' way -
but at least to forget his old enemy in his time of trouble, and
to say nothing about the mysterious marriage.[11]

The "pretty story" reported that lumbago prevented Lord
Coleridge from going to the editor's office in Covent Garden.
Supposedly, Mrs. Lawford, accompanied by her other daughter, Flora,
called upon Yates instead. The editor told them Lord Coleridge's
"confidential butler" had called twice but he would never deign to see
a manservant. Mother did all the talking. She demanded to know if
Yates planned to publish any stories relating to "some passages in the
private and domestic life of Lord Coleridge, the effect of which might
be to prevent his marriage?" Yates was straightforward. "Madam, pray
restrain yourself. It would give me no pain to see Lord Coleridge hung
from the highest bough in England but I am incapable of printing any
item likely to inflict pain and distress upon an unoffending woman."
Go ahead with your marriage plans, he assured his visitors. "I certainly
shall do nothing to interfere."

What did Yates know, if anything? Obviously, Amy's
annulment. Had he also learned of the earlier financial arrangement.
Such mercenary negotiations would have been thought vulgar, at
the least. Of great interest, had Yates learned a most amazing detail,
i.e. that "Miss" Lawford's first husband was very much alive? As for
the discarded Capt. Davies, if anyone thought the young officer died
out in India, Miss Lawford would not contradict them. When did
the Coleridges discover, however, that he wasn't dead? The captain's
army career was wrecked in 1880 by a Kiplingesque regimental scandal
in Secunderabad. Davies was charged with writing letters slanderous
to the surgeon-major's wife and her sister. An apology wasn't good
enough; Davies put in his papers and returned home in 1881. This

was reported in the Anglo-Indian press but not in England.[12] The fact of the matter was Davies wasn't only alive, but he was residing in England. Not just somewhere on the island but in the county of Devon. Not discreetly among the quiet watering places and verdant fields of that lovely shire, but comfortably in Exeter, just 12 miles, an hour's canter, from Heath's Court.

To explain, on Davies' return to London, he met a woman named Mary Colston, a young dressmaker from Lincolnshire who worked for a Mayfair *modiste*. They were soon living together in Exeter with their first child, a baby girl. Miss Colston was now "Madame Ezcurra," and running a grand dressmaking shop in the cathedral city under that name. A second child was born in 1884, the father was registered as "Auguste Ezcurra." (Augustus was one of Davies' many given names.) Who would have known? There was no genealogical data base a click or two away in late Victorian Britain[13]. Was he even married to Madame? The locals presumed they'd been married in France. It was a curious relationship. Capt. Davies' official address was in nearby Topsham, where he lived with his mother. He sold strawberries and raised game birds and exotic poultry.

The ex-captain's private life was no one's business but the fact of his existence would preclude his former wife from styling herself a widow. A widow is a woman whose lawful husband was dead and who had not remarried. It's tangled because her marriage to Davies had been annulled; in the eyes of the law, she never had a lawful husband. She couldn't be a widow. Bernard believed his father lied to him. His lordship admitted it, "I thought she was (a widow.)" This was a serious matter. It's fashionable now to assert the Victorians were really not all that strict but we're talking about the Coleridge household. The Chief's brother, Father Coleridge S.J., held fast to the Bible (Romans 7:2-3) A married woman is bound to her husband as long as he is alive. If she has sexual relations with another man while her husband is still alive, she is an adulteress. By inference, that other man (his lordship) would be equally guilty. To be clear, whether Capt. Davies was alive or not would not affect the legality of Lord Coleridge's second marriage. Still, the fact that "Miss Lawford" had a living ex-husband would have given rise to discussions Lord Coleridge would not have wished to hear. The public would eagerly seek news about the woman so little known in Society who would soon become the 2nd Baroness Coleridge.

Whatever Yates knew, he had assured the Lawford ladies of his silence. The women reported back to Sussex Square and, that evening, 8 August 1885, a letter was delivered to Yates with the Coleridge seal. His Lordship knew Yates had been visited by "the mother and sister of the lady whom I am about to marry." He had hoped to speak with Yates first but "they anticipated me." Lord Coleridge claimed he'd received threats, from "those who used your name" [Yates.] He would not go ahead with his marriage unless he could be assured Miss Lawford's reputation would not be harmed. He knew of the editor's promise to the ladies. "Although I do not know how you may receive them, I cannot forbear sending to you my hearty thanks." (signed) COLERIDGE. Yates considered the note to be an insult and an outrage. He had it framed and was delighted to show it to friends.

A wonderful story but unverifiable. Some of the details were not revealed until Yates and Coleridge had died, both men passed away in 1894. It also gives Yates credit for a good deal more influence than he likely had. The man delighted in his many sources in society but it was not as if he had that gossip mongering corner of Fleet Street to himself. There were other much more scurrilous journals in London to fear.

The wedding plans could go forward. If one hoped for a London wedding to go unnoticed, the middle of August was ideal. The annual flight from the capital was underway: the clubs had emptied, the great drawing rooms were under sheets, and the "high life" set stormed the grouse moors or clustered in the country "somewhere nice." Lord Coleridge's "dear boys" were busy out of town. Bernard was wrapping up his work on the western circuit before joining Gilbert at Heath's Court to ready it for their ailing father's expected arrival. Stephen had gone somewhere to write a play.

The Long Vacation began on 12 August. The next morning, Lord Coleridge rose from his bed and took a carriage from Paddington across Hyde Park to a specific "meet and convenient place" - the Lawford's "unpretentious" home at 42 Victoria Road.[14] It was still a felony in those days to be married in a private home although the practice had become "tolerably common." His Lordship, of course, carried his special license in the pocket of his formal frock coat. The more casual morning suit had become the preferred wedding attire, for some. His lordship would have needed no reminder that his waistcoat and trousers "should on no account be too gay." The marriage was performed in the Lawford conservatory, rather a grand name for a room 9-feet square with a makeshift altar. Therein, the 65-year-old John Duke Baron Coleridge was married to Amy Lawford by the Rev J.T. Richardson Fussell, a friend of the bride's family, who was assisted by a curate from the nearest parish church of Kensington who registered the marriage.[15] The ceremony was followed by a brief wedding breakfast; more a wedding tea, given the hour. The cake was cut. Her brother, Egerton, stood in for the bride's deceased father to offer a first, brief toast. The groom would be expected to respond. His lordship's "liquid tones" were heard by one of the smallest audiences he ever addressed. The only guests were Lawfords: Egerton, Flora, and the redoubtable Mrs. Lawford. In the press, a brief but frosty mention was made that "Lord Coleridge's children were not present and sent no gifts."

That Thursday afternoon, the Hon. Bernard Coleridge, who had reached Heath's Court, received a telegram apprising him of the event. The news had created an (under-stated) "flutter of excitement" in the family circle. Father Coleridge said his brother's last comment to him was to marry this woman would be both foolish and wrong.[16] All were astounded. The old boy had crossed them up. The next morning, and - for the second time in as many months - word of a Coleridge marriage came from a press agency. "The Central News office announces the marriage of Lord Chief Justice Coleridge with Miss Amy Lawford, by special license, yesterday." At Heath's Court, the doors were closed to all inquiries. All was "silence, mystery [but] no denial." Word quickly spread, "Hush! Lord Coleridge is married? If a thunderbolt had fallen into the innocent and peaceful streets of Ottery St. Mary ... there would hardly have been more awe and mystery."[17] It must have greatly stung the family to read of his Lordship's marriage to a "Miss Lawford—of whom, by the way, nothing much is known in society." A thought, please, for miserable Aunt Maymie. She'd suffered another heartbreak, two weddings missed, first Millie and now her beloved brother. In her diary, her words were few: "John was married. Alas. Alas."[18]

Coleridge's decision to marry privately made great sense. Post Mildred, "public feeling [was] very much against him and an ordinary wedding in an open church might have led to an indecorous if not regrettable incident." The surprising news "created a tremendous social sensation and every detail of the affair is eagerly sought for and retold." Details of the romance, with many inaccuracies, were rushed into print. The new Lady Coleridge was blond. She was brunette. She was an American. She placed first in her class at Havard (sic) law school.[19] Lord Coleridge was the biggest catch yet for those American mothers feared for their "skill and energy in connubial management on behalf of their daughters." It was *The World*, of all papers, that sorted the new baroness' birthplace, reporting "on the very best authority," she was not an American. Beyond that, the paper helpfully provided some details of the bride's costume, "Lady Coleridge was married in a traveling dress of gray cloth, trimmed with white frieze velvet and silver braid. [For Amy, a (purported) widow, her dress would be expected to be cream or gray.] She carried a bouquet of stephanotis and white roses [no orange-blossoms, a prerogative of the maiden bride].[20] Her ornaments consisted of a large opal and diamond pendant, "the gift of the bridegroom." No chaff of any sort. Yates kept his word.

Reporters converged on the Lawford home, finding a "snug little villa" hidden in shrubbery. The neighborhood was good, the house was small, and neatly furnished in excellent taste. Mother Lawford graciously invited one or two inside, showing the wee conservatory where the marriage took place, still displaying flowers, while, in the kitchen, the remaining wedding cake was unboxed for more evidence. She confirmed her daughter was from a good English family. Mrs. Lawford's late husband, Amy's father, had been a senior judge in the Indian Civil Service. She was delighted with her daughter's marriage and willingly complied with Lord Coleridge's request for privacy. He had hoped news of the nuptials might be delayed for at least one week. That was a non-starter: "Had the Lord Chief Justice been married at Westminster Abbey by the Prelate himself the matter could not have been more talked of than it has."

For days, the papers sifted the "various rumours." The *Britannic* romance fascinated everyone. His attentions to this "fair but somewhat mysterious stranger ... attracted the attention of the other passengers." On his arrival in Liverpool, he was "accompanied by a lady whose position was not very clearly understood at the time, and whose presence caused much gossip." There was unanimity on one thing – (regardless of her hair colour), the new peeress was pretty and extremely vivacious. A decided brunette, she was about 30 years old, with "graceful carriage, a slender though perfectly molded figure and aquiline features." Her complexion was fair with soft eyes, a pretty mouth and slightly *retroussé* nose. She was petite, 5 foot 4; her feet were very small. That seemed to cover everything. Foreign readers were told Mother Lawford was her daughter's stalwart, "unwilling to see such a prize slip through her daughter's fingers." She knew about the "fervour" of love-making while at sea. "She reminded his lordship of the tender and love-laden sentences addressed by him to her daughter, brought back to his recollection verbatim, together with many other circumstances connected with the brief wooing which might have a certain degree of influence upon a jury." The home papers steered clear of the breach of promise question, although privately "it had been the talk of the Law Courts for a month or two." That it hadn't happened was for the best, of course. The Coleridge name had already been heard too much in the Law Courts. Lord Coleridge could not bear to face any new litigation, hence, he swallowed hard and, to use the sporting phrase, "the old boy came up to scratch."

The honeymoon couple, by the way, left London on the 15:30 train from Waterloo. Their destination was Petersfield, a pleasant little market town in Hampshire on "the Sailor's Road" from London to Portsmouth. The jolly tars must have given it a pass because it had a reputation for dullness. "Petersfield is one of those towns in which one always feels that it is time to go to bed." They spent the first few nights of their marriage at *The Dolphin*, an old coaching inn on the High Street. "After a day or so," Mrs. Lawford joined them and there were three in the "honeymoon party" from thereon. The papers were still filled with speculation surrounding his lordship's "sly" marriage. Even on his honeymoon, Lord Coleridge would not let it pass without notice. In the Olympian third-person word was sent to London: "The Lord Chief Justice cannot see why the details of his private life should interest the public." Really, m'Lord? The absorbing romance of the Lord Chief Justice of England slipping away to marry a little-known woman half his age in a private house in a London suburb on a street once named Love Lane, would be quite enough on its own. But coming on the heels of the scandalous Adams affair it was simply too much to be believed. It was like an 800-page Trollope novel ending with multiple marriages. Just when it seemed the Coleridge family might again assume their dignified seclusion, their domestic arrangements were under renewed public speculation.

The stop in Petersfield had been mentioned in a few of the papers and the town was soon besieged with "busybodies." Before making a quiet departure for Bath, from Petersfield, Lord Coleridge sent Bernard a birthday telegram, "I wish you many happy returns of the day tomorrow & I bless God who gave me such a son. So, if you will take it, your father's blessing from my heart. My love & best wishes to Min & to the children." The peace offering was not well-received. In fact, Bernard replied so coldly, his father quickly scolded him. His words and tone were "quite unnecessary" and not fit for a son to use to his father.[21] What better time to visit the "New" Royal Baths in Bath. His lordship enjoyed the waters, he was happy to sign the guestbook: "I have great pleasure bearing witness to the excellence and comfort of these baths and the unfailing civility of the attendant. The hot douche I have found most useful and effective. Coleridge."[22] They moved on for a week in the Malvern Hills, next to Gloucester, and why not Chepstow.

This wandering honeymoon indicated to some that his lordship was in no rush to bring Lady Coleridge home to Heath's Court. Not without reason. Devon was a long way from London but the story of her ladyship's first marriage – several years wed to her first cousin - had reached many ears. Peter Orlando Hutchinson of Sidmouth kept a chatty diary of great interest.

> Many sinister stories are being freely circulated about the neighbourhood in respect to the second wife, some of them impugning her moral character... People are perplexed to know how she will be received in society. Some are inclined to be lenient - some are afraid to be otherwise - some are going to wait "to see what others do" - and some declare they look upon her as another man's wife.

Was Capt. Davies going to be a problem in Exeter? He could not have missed the sensational news of the Lord Chief Justice's wedding to an unknown Miss Amy Lawford. Not unknown to him. One can easily see the value of Davies' information. Details of their Scottish marriage and that "Romantic Tale of the Divorce Court" might find an eager buyer. Yet Capt. Davies remained in Exeter – in plain sight, as it were – for nearly thirty years (he died in 1916.) He seems to have kept his secrets, at least, publicly. Perhaps, underlined, he was also pensioned off?[23]

It wasn't until 10 October 1885, in "changeful" weather and more than eight weeks after his wedding, Lord Coleridge and the new baroness arrived at Heath's Court. Bernard and his family were not there to welcome them. His exchange of letters with his father hadn't ended well. "Lady Coleridge is my wife; she seems to me every day I live more worthy of my utmost love and respect. I am her husband and bound not to permit any language (hurtful?) to her by anyone." Bernard had gone off to Sheffield, chasing the latest elusive parliamentary opportunity. Leaving behind at most a frosty note, "Apologies, Father. Must dash," Bernard scurried off to Yorkshire. A potentially painful reunion had been avoided, for the time being.

Thus, it was an empty house, but for staff, to welcome Lord Coleridge home. As the carriage arrived, there was none of the usual fanfaronade. No early tar-barrels were lit to enliven their homecoming. No cheering villagers un-harnessed the horses and pulled the carriage up the sweeping drive, past the landscaped gardens, and into the cobbled courtyard. In fact, the reception from Ottery's townsfolk and country gentry was decidedly lukewarm. "The arrival of the happy pair has not evoked any manifestations of sympathy or of kindly feeling, and the county families have not rushed to offer their congratulations. This is somewhat mortifying."[24]

1  Celtic Folk Rhyme: "Monday for wealth, Tuesday for health, Wednesday the best day of all, Thursday for losses, Friday for crosses, and Saturday no luck at all."
2  The Adams brothers were every bit as unconventional as Charles: Walter Marsham Adams was a mathematician ("The Shilling Manual of Trigonometry,") but more known as an Egyptologist. His "esoteric" books survived him: *The House of the Hidden Places* and *The Book of the Master.* The Rev Coker Adams, rector of Saham Toney, Norfolk, excommunicated an 82-year-old farmer. The Daily Telegraph suggested Rev Adams "be petrified and preserved as a specimen of the medieval clergy."
3  "Hon. Mrs. Adams," *Mrs. Humphry's Etiquette for Every Day* (1904), 196.
4  The parlour is still there (Grid Ref 0959 9444) though recent visitors report the poet's initials are well-worn and surrounded by "more recent scratched graffiti." jsbookreader.blogspot.com.
5  Letters from John Duke Coleridge to his son Bernard. CFP Add MS.
6  Libel: fair criticism was allowed upon the public life of public men ... provided such criticism did not touch upon their private lives, even if the assertion was true. Fair criticism did not include anything tending to injure the reputation of another or expose that other person to public ridicule. Arthur Underhill, *A Summary of the Law of Torts, Or, Wrongs Independent of Contract* (1878).
7  First US reports: 3 August 1885, Page 1 in American papers from the New York Times to the San Francisco Examiner (newspapers.com).
8  Garmoyle details: The Standard, 21 November 1884, 3.
9  Canonical hours: Less than a year later, Parliament extended the hours until four o'clock in the afternoon. The quoted price was "irrespective of what fees may be given to the clergyman." For more on the special licenses, see Phegley, 112.

10   Roupell letter dated 3 September, two weeks after the wedding.

11   The first appearance of the "pretty story" was "Lord Coleridge's Forced Marriage; Edmund Yates" Revenge," The Evening Star (Washington DC), 27 Aug 1885, 1, quoting "a reliable source." In England, on 29 August 85, Sporting Gazette reported much the same. Yates and Coleridge died three weeks apart in 1894, Yates first. The supposed details of the "pretty story" appeared in the American press soon after the LCJ's death, see: 1 July 94, The Sun (NY.)

12   Davies: "Curious Affair at Secunderabad," The Englishman's Overland Mail (Bengal) 19 January 1881, 18.

13   The credit for the genealogical digging into the Davies/Ezcurra menage must go to unidentified researchers at RootsChat.com, specifically, Topic878779: John Augustus Seymour Morse Davies & Madame Ezcurra.

14   Victoria Road: Pevsner, the architecture critic of record, thought it was a street of ordinary suburban stucco homes. In 2022, 42 Victoria Road was on the market at £10,000,000!

15   The marriage certificate was filled out and signed by Rev. Fussell. The bride was identified as a 37-year-old "spinster." The common meaning of the term at that time was a woman of marriageable age who had never been married before. Amy Lawford was within her legal rights to claim spinsterhood as her previous marriage had been legally annulled, or voided.

16   Foolish: Henry Coleridge letters, CFP Add MS 85936.

17   "Thunderbolt," Western Times, 17 August 1885, 2.

18   Maymie diary (1885) CFP Add MS 86080.

19   The Havard (Harvard) clanger can be found in The Irish Law Times, 22 August 1885. Amy had supposedly topped her law school class. During "shop talk" on the voyage home, her knowledge "simply astonished" the Lord Chief Justice. Remarkable stuff.

20   Phegley, *Courtship and Marriage*, op. cit, 129.

21   CFP, Letters from John Duke Coleridge to his son Bernard 1885-1894. Two volumes.

22   Douche: 24 September 1885, Bath Chronicle & Weekly Gazette, 7.

23   Capt. Davies remained in the Exeter area until his death in 1916. "Madame Ezcurra" survived him; at her death in 1938, she was described as the widow of Capt. Seymour Morse Davies.

24   Ottery gossip: Peter Orlando Hutchinson's *Travels in Victorian Devon*, compiled and edited by Jeremy Butler. POH-Diary-Transcripts-Full.pdf.

# 18. A GRIEVOUS BLUNDER

BY 1885, "THE art of letter-writing [was] considered dead," killed by the speed of advancing civilization, the penny post, the telegraph, and soon the telephone. Lord Coleridge, as in many areas, was resistant to change and was a great sender and saver of letters, (albeit in his execrable handwriting). In the British Library, a bulging file holds the correspondence and condolences at the time of Jane, Lady Coleridge's illness and death. Yet in the numerous boxes at St. Pancras, there isn't a single letter offering congratulations to the Lord Chief upon his second marriage. Not one. Perhaps there were none. In such a case, why not self-congratulate? Coleridge wrote to the historian Goldwyn Smith, an Oxford friend who had moved to Canada. "My dear Smith:"

> I do not like you to know of my re-marriage only from the papers. I have done what Robert Southey said was either the wisest or the most foolish thing a man can do - re-marry at sixty-three. I hope the former of the two alternatives may prove true to me. Now I have a sweet and good woman who has undertaken to try to cheer the few years which remain of a life which cannot, in the nature of things, last many more years.[1]

Lord Coleridge's second marriage, however cheering personally, would greatly complicate his family's pre-existing legal challenges. Lord Coleridge and his son Bernard were hardly speaking but they remained yoked in the still festering matter of *Adams v Coleridge*. As

1885 dragged on, (the distraction of two weddings notwithstanding) Adams began whining about the original settlement agreement, worked out in June, but which remained unsigned. Nor had the Coleridge papers been sent to the arbitrator, as required. Sir Robert Collier, by the way, the accepted arbitrator, received a peerage that summer and henceforth will be referred to as Lord Monkswell. In November, Adams could wait no more. He sublimely appealed to the courts, "I hope you will not think me cantankerous," he said. He was tired of "kicking his heels around London" waiting on the Coleridges. Mildred came in to court with her husband; the newspapers reported Mrs. Adams was "dressed with exceptional taste but there was nothing about her costume to indicate she was a bride." According to fashion historians, a married woman was expected to wear her hair up, covered by a hat. A married woman was permitted to display more jewellery, indicative of her husband's prosperity. Mildred, not so much, perhaps. What she did wear was "a radiant smile." Sir Henry James still held the briefs for both Coleridges and offered his deepest regrets for the delay but reminded the court the Lord Chief Justice was an extremely busy man and Bernard Coleridge was contesting a parliamentary seat in Yorkshire and unavailable. Sir Henry was finally able to herd his clients together to sign the agreement on 26 November. Bernard was in a better mood; he'd finally won a seat in the House and even accepted his father's congratulations.[2] The pertinent letters and documents could now be sent to Lord Monkswell for his review. The end was in sight, it seemed, but it was all about to go pear-shaped again.

Lord Monkswell's magnificent home was on the Thames at Milbank. His library looked out on the river slowly spilling to the east. Under the terms of the June agreement, Monkswell's task was to review the relevant documents and arrive at a figure due from each Coleridge compensating Adams for damage done to his reputation.

It was expected the review would particularly focus on three letters: 1) Bernard's "white elephant" letter to Mildred warning her not to marry Adams; 2) Lord Coleridge's letter to Mrs. Bishop believing Adams attempted to entrap Mildred in the darkened room; and 3) the Athenaeum memorandum. Monkswell would not meet with any of the principals.

In early December, a clerk from Adams' solicitor went to Milbank to be certain Monkswell had what he needed. Monkswell's clerk assured him the Coleridge papers were in house and nodded to two large boxes on a nearby table. In modern terms, it was a document dump. It had taken two clerks from Harrison's chambers to transport several hundred pages of letters, affidavits and press cuttings. After a quick riffle through the papers, Adams' man sent a wire to his client who replied quickly, "Copy Everything!"

Adams and Mildred were living in Canterbury. Adams left the cathedral city the very next morning for London and went directly to see Lord Monkswell. Adams could not believe the volume and nature of the materials left with the arbitrator by the Coleridges. Adams found several letters containing entirely new (to him) personal attacks, including one from the aged mother of his late dear wife:

> PRIVATE. I know of the event likely to take place [that is the marriage to Mildred] but if a broken-hearted mother's words are of any avail, pause. No tongue can tell the length he will not go to. The most frightful things have been imputed to him, and not without reason; whilst his antecedents would shock the most unscrupulous. The poor child [Adams' daughter] is living on charity entirely, for he will not allow her a *sou* for her support.[3]

The letter from Mrs. Polson had been mailed from her home

in Nice to Maymie Coleridge, who sent it on to her brother, with a letter of her own: "I believe what she says but unluckily everybody who knows her says you can't trust her one bit. The general view is that she really is cracked."[4] Nevertheless, Father Henry Coleridge wrote to his brother, "Let everything be done to break the continuity of the exercise of this baleful influence [over Mildred.]"

Another letter detailed a conversation with one of Adams' nieces who had been tracked down by Sophie Martyn in Torquay, who promptly reported her intelligence to Lord Coleridge:

> My dear Cousin John - Maymie was so very anxious that I should ask Miss Emily Adams about her uncle that I walked over and asked her whether she knew of her uncle Charles' engagement. She started and said – "What a blessing, as it may get rid of him." But when I told her, she said how very sorry she was for us all, for she could not believe Miss Coleridge would be happy with him.[5]

Miss Emily Adams also claimed to recall that, after the "shipwreck," Charles came to stay with her family in Devon. He joked of his plans to "make love" to Miss Polson when their voyage resumed, but he did not plan to marry her. More recently, no one in the family would have anything to do with Adams but all are united to help the man's poor daughter. She cannot live with her father, "he does make her so wretched." Her intelligence shared, Martyn closed her note to Lord Coleridge: "There is nothing to be done but to wait and pray. But I think of you so much and the utter bitterness that must await you."

The document bundles at Lord Monkswell's also included a collection of press clippings from Stephen Coleridge's series of American interviews of which the young man was so proud. One of the headlines, from a paper in Cleveland, Ohio, read: "Miss Coleridge's Cinderella Existence in the House of Her Father."

To Adams, the "pitiful indecency" of this eleventh hour dossier was obvious. The Coleridges had raked up "fresh irrelevancies" to poison the arbitrator's mind. Monkswell, who was caring for his dying wife, assured Adams he'd hardly had time to look at the material but "nothing not strictly relevant will in the slightest degree affect me." The arbitrator alerted Lord Coleridge to the paperwork gaffe and warned him Adams was furious. Coleridge called it a "grievous blunder," and put the blame on Harrison, who blamed his clerks, of course. They had carried the wrong bundle of papers to Monkswell. Coleridge was "beyond measure annoyed and distressed" by this error but still refused to communicate directly with his son-in-law. Instead, Harrison forwarded Coleridge's note to Adams: "Personally I wish him and Mrs. Adams both to be informed that neither Bernard nor I ever saw the papers which were sent to Lord Monkswell."[6] At that point, Monkswell promised all parties that his arbitration award would be announced in January, after the holidays. Lord and Lady Coleridge passed their first Christmas quietly at Heath's Court, surrounded by family. If by family, you meant Lawfords.

On the 18th of January, Lord Monkswell issued his ruling. He decided Bernard Coleridge should pay Adams £500 for the "White Elephant" letter to his sister, now Mrs. Adams. For Adams, this was far short of the £3000 a jury awarded him fifteen months earlier but *he had agreed in June* to settle with £500 from Bernard. Monkswell didn't feel any more compensation was needed. Adams' greatest hopes, all along, had rested on the letters of Lord Coleridge. There, however, he met with gutting disappointment. Monkswell thought the letter to Mrs. Bishop should be read as one written by a father on the very day he learned of the alleged "darkened room" plot against his daughter, as recounted by Miss Cobbe. Read with that in mind, Monkswell thought his lordship's angry letter was understandable. The arbitrator reminded Adams, Lord Coleridge had subsequently withdrawn that letter and publicly apologized for it. Monkswell, therefore, put the reparations owed to Mr. Adams by the Lord Chief Justice at a mere *40 shillings*. Forty bob! Two pounds or roughly a week's pay for one of Harrison's feckless clerks. Adams, with justification, was furious. "Could any man with the slightest self-respect sit down with such an award as that in the hands of his sworn enemy?"

Certainly, this wouldn't be the end of it. Adams refused to sign the final documents and raged about London denouncing Monkswell. Wasn't it curious, that a middling lawyer, a "man whose labours came little before the world," received his peerage from the Queen only after he was named arbitrator? He implied Lord Coleridge pulled strings for Monkswell to reach the House of Lords in exchange for his "co-operation." The Coleridges then "mistakenly" sent all those folders filled with "vulgar little lies" to provide Monkswell, with the cover he needed. Adams would not stand for it. The Coleridges would hide "behind the petticoats of every gossiping woman from whom [they] extracted some scrap of scandal, however false, malignant, or insane" and, their tool, Monkswell did their bidding.[7]

There was no comment from the Lord Chief Justice; with a salary of £8000 per year, he could easily come up with 40 shillings. Lord Coleridge left London on his assizes circuit in Wales, accompanied by her ladyship. She was with him in Carmarthen, in Brecon - where she was "the cynosure of all eyes," and in Chester, where the fawning local pressmen were struck by her looks. "His lordship's opinion on the matter of beauty is evidently no less entitled to respect than his acknowledged mastery of law." It became Lady Coleridge's practice to follow "the Chief" about on his legal duties, which he had always insisted be conducted in great state. He would require a formal welcome by the High Sheriff and Lord Lieutenant, in their "superfluous toggery," as Coleridge called it, although he delighted in any occasion to put it on. Lady Coleridge added welcome glamour and drew crowds of the curious eager to see the aged jurist's young new wife.[8] At Mansion House, in June, at the Lord Mayor's annual dinner for Her Majesty's Judges, Lord Coleridge was accompanied by his wife. He would speak, of course, but only briefly. One reporter feared his "splendid voice is broken." The Exeter papers suggested he intended to resign. He had considered it, writing to Yarnall, his friend in America:

> I have plenty of strength left: I think my mental powers, such as they ever were, are not impaired. But I have never liked my profession, and the practice of it, which, even with the excitement of advocacy, was barely interesting, is now positively repulsive.

But he needed the money and he wanted to please the new baroness:

> I have made too small a fortune for my wife and children. My wife is so bright and young, so fitted to adorn the society in which she moves, that to take her from it and bring her down here (i.e. Ottery) for my own delight, would be a very selfish thing to do.[9]

The circumstances of Lady Coleridge's annulled first marriage would limit the society in which she hoped to move, let alone adorn. An annulment of any kind was a highly irregular circumstance. Although a court had found her blameless, the court of Queen Victoria was quite another matter.[10] "The rule that divorced ladies may neither attend nor be presented at court is rigourously enforced" (with the recent and sole exception of the rather hapless Lady Blandford, legally freed from her notorious husband.) The Queen did not consider annulments worthy of a pass. The wife of Sir John Millais, whose first marriage to John Ruskin was annulled for non-consummation, was never presented at Court. There is no official record in the Royal Archives of the 2d Lady Coleridge being presented to Queen Victoria. Lord Coleridge, although very much a patrician, had no craving for the blessings of the royal family. In fact, he once confessed that he was "never a great admirer of the Queen." That was likely a political not a personal judgement. "I must say the Queen was always a perfect lady in her consideration for other people's feelings."[11] If not for those of the second Baroness. Nevertheless, he and her ladyship would not lack for invitations.

Meanwhile, his persistent son-in-law was still out there, filing nettling motions. In June, he sought greater access to the Coleridge papers. "I have come all the way from Cornwall," he announced to the judge who dismissed his motion. No matter, on he went. The newspapers reported Adams was preparing to sue Lord Coleridge for his refusal to allow Mildred to have various personal items from Sussex Square, including her famous pianoforte, as well as portraits, and paintings done by her mother. They were "the personal property of his wife, and on this he means to go to law." Adams had the free time to do all this as he remained unemployed. Mildred was now his wife and, as he saw it, his only employment was to do whatever possible to restore her previous position in the world. In the meantime, Charles and Mildred were still living on (Mildred's!) £300 a year, cheques for £25 arriving the first of each month which were regularly cashed. That would have been doubled to £600 per annum under the settlement agreement but Adams refused to sign it. Of course, Adams again cheerfully proclaimed this whole contest had nothing to do with money.

Mildred's plan to establish an income of her own, if ever meant seriously, with music lessons and even being a daily governess, had not been a success. Not that she could be blamed, Adams kept them on the move. Citing Mildred's health, Adams preferred to live elsewhere than London. £300 a year went further in Canterbury where they lived for some time near the cathedral. They summered at Aunt Harriete Seymour's cottage in Cornwall. They stayed with Adams' brothers in East Anglia and with Mrs. Bishop in Devon. In Torquay, Adams, with Mildred in attendance, gave an evening lecture to an anti-vivisectionist group. The event was well-attended although many came just to see the famous couple. They were married "after some litigation that will not soon be forgotten."

In October, a weary public learned "the case of *Adams v Coleridge* will again shortly be before the Courts." The Lord Chief Justice was being sorely tried. "Mr. Adams gives his papa-in-law no peace." Adams spent months readying his new action, delighted he'd finally flushed his real target from the covert – the Lord Chief Justice of England. Bernard Coleridge was still listed as co-defendant but no one was fooled, least of all, Lord Coleridge. "If my ruin is desired by my daughter and her friends, it is far better they should effect it, if they can, in a case in which I am a party and can be heard in my own defence." Adams brought a libel action against Lord Coleridge, primarily for the "darkened room" letter to Mrs. Bishop, as well as the Athenaeum Memorandum. He also accused the Coleridges, father and son, of maliciously conspiring to place irrelevant and libelous materials in front of the arbitrator (Monkswell), with the object of wrongfully influencing the ultimate award. Did anyone expect him to accept 40s? "Would it surprise Lord Coleridge to know" Adams was seeking damages of £20,000? (Approximately £2.5 million in 2020.)

Complicating the Coleridge defence was the continuing chill

within the family. Relations between father and son were unimproved. As the trial neared, peace talks were attempted. Bernard and his wife returned to Heath's Court for the first time with the second Lady Coleridge presiding. The eldest son could not fail to notice the changes that had been made. Butterfield's magnificent creation was not three years old. In many ways, the architect had created a memorial to Jane, the first Lady Coleridge. She loved Ottery but did not live to see "her house." Her portrait, her artwork, her favourite artists, hung everywhere; a small replica of her recumbent effigy was kept in a private shrine off the library. It would be natural, would it not, for the new baroness to wish, with grace, to put her touches on the place? While much was done to make the visit a success, Bernard felt like "a stranger in a home I once looked upon as mine."[12] Lawfords were everywhere. Where were the Coleridges? Even Aunt Maymie had moved away from Ottery. She could never accept the new baroness. "I left the Manor House forever," she wrote in her diary that June.[13] Maymie had gone to live in Torquay. Bernard may have dined at Heath's Court but he also stayed in Torquay.

There was little now to do but await the upcoming trial. There was a "general feeling of regret that the private relations of a family whose head is one of the most distinguished persons in the kingdom [sic] should again have become a matter of public discussion." Sir Charles Bowen, again urged his old friend to be cautious and consider settling. "Adams means to make it impossible for you not to go into the box and it his picture of the Chief Justice of England fighting his own daughter & having to answer assaults which she instigates & suggests before a jury composed of heavens knows whom." Do anything, Bowen pleaded, to "escape this horrid duel."[14] Prescient advice but there was no settlement. Lady Eastlake, 80-years-old, was for many years a close friend of the first Lady Coleridge. She could not believe how things had turned out. The Coleridges were "a family which has gone to ruin itself."[15]

1   Coleridge to Goldwyn Smith, 25 August 1885, *Life & Correspondence*, Vol. 2, 346.
2   Bernard finally won his elusive Commons seat on 25 November 1885, in the "gloomiest weather possible," scoring an easy victory (1258 vote margin) for the Liberals in the Sheffield Attercliffe constituency.
3   Mrs. Polson's letter was undated, beyond "February."
4   Cracked: she saw dead people (at least one); her case was investigated by the Society for Psychical Research.
5   "Dear Cousin John" dated 15 October 1883, while Lord Coleridge was still in America.
6   Harrison's apology to Adams, conveying his lordship's regrets as well, was dated 10 December 1885.
7   "Behind the petticoats," Adams to Monkswell, 15 December 1885.
8   Comments on the beautiful baroness on the assizes: Brecon County Times, 29 January 1886, 8; Cambria Daily Leader, 6 February 1886, 3.
9   Yarnall, Forty Years of Friendship op.cit. 239-240.
10   Annulments. "Persons presented and attending levees, drawing rooms, etc' for the years 1885 to 1894 found no entries relating to Lady Coleridge. An email dated 21 May 2021 from the Royal Archives at Windsor. As for Lady Millais: "Because of her first marriage, annulled by simple mutual consent, the Queen, having a great dislike to anything in the nature of a divorce, always refused to see her although she was on the friendliest relations with Sir John." Reportedly, in 1896, as Sir John lay dying, the Queen agreed to receive Lady Millais and the two women had a "most affecting interview." Staffordshire Advertiser, I January 1898.
11   Lord Coleridge, quoted by Malvina Harlan, *Some Memories of a Long Life* (Modern Library Edition; unpaginated.) Mrs. Harlan was the wife of U.S. Supreme Court Justice John Harlan.
12   Bernard "a stranger" in his home, 23 September 1886 CFP Add MS
13   Maymie diary CFP Add MS 86081.
14   Bowen CFP Add MS 86253
15   "Ruin itself:" Lady Eastlake's letter to A.H. Layard, 8 August 1886, Sheldon ed., Letters.

# 19. TRIAL 2, PT 1:
# A RAT IN A PIT

"THE FIRST EFFECT of [the Law Courts] upon the non-legal visitor is to awaken him to a sense of the exceeding complexity of the legal machine." The splendid entrance hall was surrounded by a faux-medieval maze of corridors and stairs. Lord Coleridge needed no directions. He arrived at the judge's entrance in Carey Street on the morning of Wednesday, 17 November 1886. Court IV was his usual courtroom; he entered from the door to his chambers. He was rarely seen publicly without his bespoke robes and sashes, but even in mufti, he was "tall, distinguished and always fully conscious of his importance." Without his usual full-bottomed wig, he couldn't hide the obvious: he was "as bald as Scipio Africanus ... his crown shines like a baby's cheek."[1] No one could miss the irony of the Lord Chief Justice being gaped at in his own courtroom although it was insisted the room was only chosen as the most commodious. Nevertheless, for a man of such renowned self-esteem, it was humbling indeed. "Never was a judge of such self-realized perfections in a like quandary."[2]

A "fashionable and distinguished crowd" settled in. *Adams v Coleridge & Another* (Bernard) was to be handled by Mr. Justice George Denman.[3] He was a good-looking man, a rarity on the bench. They were an "ugly lot," according to *Vanity Fair.* Denman was Her Majesty's "opportunity to show the world England could boast of a handsome judge.[4]" To Denman's right was a special box for important visitors; it seemed to be a small meeting of the House of Lords: Iddesleigh, Selborne, Herschell, etc. One very important peer was missing. Three weeks before the trial, Lord Monkswell, the mediator at the centre of this litigation, died in Cannes where he'd gone for his health. Lord Coleridge attended his funeral. It was all quite sad and particularly inconvenient. Adams was hugely disappointed; it would have given him "great satisfaction to put Monkswell in the box."

Seated in the well of the court, the Lord Chief Justice was surrounded by his distinguished counsel in their robes and wigs. Sir Henry James was now assisted by Sir Charles Russell. In all, there were four "silks" arrayed behind Lord Coleridge, forcing Bernard and his advocates to find space in the row reserved for junior counsel. Poor Bernard. Of course, Charles Warren Adams revelled in the moment, delighted to be seen as a man alone in this hostile space, prepared to take on all of "them." Court IV was, again, taller than it was wide. All seats were filled, many by members of the bar who had no stake in the fight but came for the spectacle. The case would be heard by a "special jury," a costly panel of Londoners who held a "certain station in society."[5] Given a nod to begin, Adams rose and looked about, and, in his own turn, was studied by all. He was "a herculean figure, erect and portly with a dark sallow face and a hard mouth." He began by admitting, "I would rather not be here like a rat in a pit." Adams was well-practiced in his tale of, what he called, "the last four dreary years." He met Miss Mildred Coleridge at the Victoria Street Society. Their shared work led to respect and a friendship, "as surely in God's name, as a woman of 36 and a man of 50 might be and think of nothing else." Miss Cobbe's foolish misapprehension one afternoon began it all. Lord Coleridge soon wrote to Mrs. Bishop accusing him of plotting "the vilest infamy that could be attributed to a man." In the Athenaeum Memorandum, Lord Coleridge painted him as "a fortune hunter of a peculiarly unscrupulous character." Mildred stood with him through it all; she would not back down in the face of her father, aunts, uncles, brothers and more - until Sussex Square became "too hot" for her any longer. As Adams put it, "Miss Coleridge was virtually thrown upon my hands and I would have been called a coward and a cur if I had not taken up her cause." Lord Coleridge was a wealthy man and Adams gave him credit for advanced views on primogeniture and a woman's right to property. Yet to punish his own daughter he was prepared to disinherit her. Gesturing to the Lord Chief Justice, who stared straight ahead, Adams quoted the proverb, "A merciful Providence fashioned us hollow, on purpose that we might our principles swallow." (Galatians 4:9)

Denman gave Adams quite a bit of leeway for his opening statement, interrupting only once or twice. Adams apologised, "I am an unpractised speaker, my lord." Denman parried, "No, you are an admirable speaker but get to the point." Adams hoped the jurymen understood his difficulty in confronting a personage of wealth and position as Lord Coleridge. It wasn't for the money, he insisted, again. (The £20,000 went unmentioned.) He came before them solely to "vindicate his character, for which he would fight to the last farthing and the last gasp." Adams took the entire morning. It was "a long and able, but discursive speech, the tedium of which he relieved by an occasional gleam of humour, or by some caustic remarks at the expense of his wife's relatives."

Adams read from letters he casually retrieved from an enormous "obelisk of paper" on his table. Letters he claimed were – by stealthy "error" - delivered to Lord Monkswell. He annotated as he read, challenging any insinuations upon his character. In Sophie Martyn's letter, for instance, the woman quoted Adams' niece, Emily Adams. It was Emily who said the Adams' family would be delighted to "get rid of him." Emily also provided much of the information about her uncle's first marriage.[6] Adams wanted the jury to know Emily was a child of eight when he married, (Actually, she was 12.) Regardless,

Adams dismissed Emily's statements as hearsay and false. In all, Adams brought 305 letters into court, a hundred-weight by estimate. He couldn't read them all. Clerks read some; Adams saved the juicier ones for himself. He delighted in the name-calling. Lord Hobhouse, for one, earnestly wished Mildred could be rescued from "that ruffian."

Adams also called witnesses. The most notable was Stephen Coleridge, now his brother-in-law. Acknowledged as the most handsome Coleridge, Stephen was 32, blue-eyed, over six feet, always well-dressed. An American writer pegged him as the "typical picture of the cultured English gentleman." Adams read from the cuttings of Stephen's interview tour of the states, the witness enjoyed the recitation immensely. Stephen had told the Americans Adams' "antecedents were far from satisfactory." He was "a man without a shilling who made no effort to find employment." Adams put it to Stephen the two were very much alike, often without employment. "Is it not true your father has been your only support for many years?" Stephen's only income at present was £500 a year as "private secretary" to his father.[7] His duties he could only describe as "various." Had he been paid by his father for his American publicity campaign? Certainly not, Stephen replied. Adams then read Stephen's letter to the family solicitor, claiming he went to America to "silence the tongues of slander." Things got testy when Adams quoted Stephen who once claimed Mildred left the Coleridge home to stay with friends, "ostensibly." Lowering his head to peer over his pince-nez, Adams wondered what Stephen meant by ostensibly? Why use a word suggesting an intention to deceive? Did he mean to imply his unmarried sister, a woman known by all for respectability and purity, might have gone into lodgings with Adams? "Certainly not," Coleridge snapped. Adams listed where Mildred had lodged (Lady Blachford, Mrs. Bishop, the Seymours, all her friends.) There was nothing ostensible about any of them, was there?

Russell objected, "He's badgering his own witness. He can't do that." Denman agreed, "You've made your point, Mr. Adams, move on."[8] Adams bowed, and with a last derisive glance at the witness, took his seat. Stephen was briefly questioned by the defence. He could not say how those newspaper cuttings wound up in Lord Monkswell's library.

Where was Mildred? In his opening statement, Adams explained to the jury, it would revolt his feelings to make his wife publicly testify against her father. He insisted, of course, that he acted solely out of concern for her health, not what she might say. Instead, he would read from her affidavit, a task that filled most of two days. Mildred swore she was very happy in her father's home where "she occupied in all respects the position commonly occupied by the married head of a house." She had no wish to leave. "I could not have obeyed him more faithfully had I been seven years old and not thirty-seven." Yet she was also very committed to her work at the VSS where, in 1881, she met "the plaintiff," Adams, of course. They became determined colleagues; she felt they were "the only two" who could do much of the work. Again, she denied anything improper took place between them in that so-called "darkened room" or anywhere else on any other occasion. Her father and family refused to accept their friendship. To end the spying and annoyance, they proposed the "nominal engagement." The longer her father resisted, the more incapacitated she became. The tensions in her home, with her father and with "the Stephens," got to the state in December 1883, that she left, with her father's permission, for a short stay with a friend. Eventually, her father "peremptorily forbade her return" to Sussex Square. Her brothers and Coleridge relations were instructed to shun her. By that point, she and Adams had "naturally grown all the closer and therefore decided to marry." Not for a moment had she regretted her decision. In one of the Monkswell letters, an observer described her as looking "sad and cowed" in Adams' company. Mildred rejected that opinion; she was completely happy.

Adams put Mildred's affidavit aside and called his wife to the witness box. Mildred entered from the witness room. There was no description of her appearance or what she was wearing. A sketch artist drew a woman with short dark hair, a large satin ribbon bow at her neck and wearing under-framed eyeglasses. From the elevated witness box, Mildred could look down upon her father seated below her. The emotions of the moment for both can be imagined. It was the first time father and daughter had seen each other in 1078 days, since 8 December 1883. Adams pushed on, holding in his hand a letter to Mildred, from William Butterfield, the architect, once her close friend. The letter had been found in Monkswell's papers. Butterfield had written: "It is beyond my power to understand your apparent pleasure in saying anything you can in disparagement of the honour of your father." Before Mildred could respond, Sir Charles Russell was in action. "Mr. Butterfield is not on trial. The truth or falsity of his letters, all the letters, does not signify." The only issue was how did this material get before the arbitrator. The contents were irrelevant. Russell carried the point again. Mildred was excused. She exited the spotlight, again.

Lord Coleridge later called the Dublin-born Russell "the advocate of the century." His reputation was that of "the greatest, most intolerant and not least conceited" lawyer in London.[9] Sir Henry James was a deft and courtly advocate for the speeches but some thought he bungled the first trial, not least by taking Adams too lightly. Lord Coleridge wanted Russell on his side; the man's skill at cross-examination was unrivalled and feared. On day four of the trial, Adams climbed to the witness box. Taking his trademark pinch of snuff, flourishing in his right hand a red bandana, Russell began.

In the Athenaeum Memorandum, Lord Coleridge regretted that Adams made no efforts to obtain permanent employment. "Are you employed today?" Russell inquired. "Only occasionally." Adams did some literary work which provided a small living but not sufficient to support "a woman of Miss Coleridge's bringing up."[10] Was he seeking more remunerative employment? "Oh, there's no chance of that while this is going on." He need concentrate on clearing his reputation and restoring his wife's fortune. What was this nominal engagement all about, Russell wondered. "Literally nothing at all," said Adams, "except a way to end the incessant persecution" they had undergone. Nothing at all? Russell suggested it be called "a sham engagement." Adams barked, "I do not call it a sham. It was a nominal engagement between two mature people who were being worried to death." Neither he nor Mildred intended to marry but were forced into it. In the memorandum, Lord Coleridge predicted he would have "to provide the whole maintenance of Mr. Adams and my daughter." Wasn't that exactly what had happened, Russell asked. Wasn't it true the Lord Chief Justice, on his own, increased Mildred's support to £600 a year per the settlement which only Adams refused to sign. In addition, Lord Coleridge had paid Adams' court costs from the first trial. "And what were they, Mr. Adams?" The witnessed guessed several hundred pounds. Yet Adams refused to sign the agreement. Adams had always contended that he sought to restore Mildred's standing in her father's will of 1879, quoting the figure of £17,000. Mildred believed it too. Russell suggested that while Adams enjoyed playing a lawyer, he knew nothing about wills. "You do know a will may be changed, don't you?" Lord Coleridge had, in fact, made many changes to his will. Under the pending agreement, his lordship had agreed Mildred, in her will, could assign a one-time sum of £5000 and an annual income of £480 to her surviving husband (and children, if any.) Russell thought this was a very good deal, "Is this not a positive advantage to you?" Adams disagreed. He had been suspicious of the settlement from the beginning. Sir Henry James once told him, Lord Coleridge's money was intended to be Mildred's alone. "You are not secured a sixpence." Adams resented the wording of the settlement; why was it written the money was intended merely for "*her husband.*" Why not state his name? That was an intentional insult, Adams argued. To any husband? Russell responded, "Surely you're not contemplating a successor, are you?" They shared a laugh before turning to the question of the Monkswell "bundles." Russell introduced numerous letters from Harrison and Lord Monkswell explaining the slip and conveying Lord Coleridge's solemn regrets. Russell thought it more than adequate, did Adams agree? "No, I do not," he expected to hear directly from his father-in-law.

It had been a contentious engagement for Adams, put on the defensive for the first time. Saturday meant the end of a long week for all parties. Throughout, Lord Coleridge had been quite attentive. During the letter-readings, he frequently turned to whisper a comment to one of his lawyers. On Monday, the defence would begin presenting its case and Lord Coleridge was expected to enter the witness box. A spectacle was expected. "Somehow or other, don't you know, the world seems to rejoice in the discomfiture of the Lord Chief Justice." Enjoy your weekend.

1  Description heard during his American visit, Solicitor's Journal, 15 December 1883.

2  "Never was a judge:" Walter Sichel, *The Sands of Time*, (1923), 144.

3  Adams v Coleridge & Another (1886) J54/485. Again, the trial description is an amalgam of several leading London dailies all of which reported on the case in great detail.

4  Right Hon. George Denman - showing the elevated interest in the trial, Vanity Fair chose the occasion to print Denman's caricature, 20 November 1886.

5  Special juries were chosen from esquires, bankers, merchants, etc., or any man whose private dwelling house was valued at not less than £100. Members of a special jury earned 1 guinea (21 shillings) per trial. Special juries were abolished in England in 1949. RM Jackson, *The Machinery of Justice in England* (1953).

6  By the time of this trial, Emily Adams was 37, living in Torquay. She was the daughter of the late John Adams, Charles' eldest half-brother. Emily claimed Adams was always in debt, borrowing money, dodging creditors. He also neglected his daughter, "she does try hard to please him, but it is impossible; he does make her so wretched." Emily was one of the unnamed sources for Bernard's letter to Mildred.

7  In December 1890, Lord Coleridge appointed Stephen Clerk of Assize on the South Wales Circuit, (salary of £500.) He had neither practical legal knowledge nor he did he speak Welsh. The appointment was denounced as "legal jobbery" but Stephen held the post for more than 30 years and was much respected.

8  Ostensible is that which may be held out as true, real, actual, or intended, but may or may not be so. Ostensibly is an action shown or pretended. A stronger word would have been specious. *The Century Dictionary* (1890).

9  Russell's most famous moment was still years off; in the Parnell inquiry, he unmasked Pigott as a forger. The man fled England and committed suicide. In Lord Coleridge's opinion, "When Russell is there, the judge isn't in it. Russell dominates everyone." Russell (later Lord Russell of Killowen) succeeded Coleridge as LCJ and, again, there was no other serious candidate.

10  At the time, Adams edited The Champion, an obscure anti-vivisection pamphlet, 1884-1887.

# 20. TRIAL 2, PT. 2: THE AUTOCRAT IN THE BOX

THROUGH THE WEEKEND, anticipation built for the Lord Chief Justice's taste of the other side of an English courtroom. It may be difficult for present day readers to appreciate the standing Lord Coleridge held in late-Victorian Britain. There were no footballers, actors, or rock stars competing for attention. "Great men" roamed the land. "There are certain men on the crowded stage of modern life who fill the public eye, whose personality has somehow a peculiar potency of attraction. Lord Coleridge was one of these."[1] Yet, there he was, descended from the elevated bench, seated in the well, stripped of his robes, being stared at by hundreds of eyes, a man on trial in his own courtroom.[2] It was a "painful" scene. It was "grossly indecent."

Monday morning, 22 November, London awoke to the thickest fog in living memory. Road and rail traffic were all but halted. The miasma outside was matched by the confusion within the Law Courts. On the worst days, there was more fog within than without. No one was more critical of the new building than Lord Coleridge who regularly scorned everything from the ventilation, the acoustics, to the lighting. The lovely pepper-pot turrets and groined archways were all very pretty, but as *The Times* declared, "the practical fitness of a building for its actual purposes can only be tested by use; and under this test the new courts stand condemned."[3] Despite all that, by 10:30, the parties found their way to Court IV. Seated in the gallery, amongst "the unemployed barristers," was the infamous Mrs. Weldon, perhaps the only more litigious figure in London than Mr. Adams. She and

Lord Coleridge had clashed many times and she seemed "deeply interested" in the prospect of seeing the tables reversed on the great Lord Chief Justice.[4] Missing was the Hon. Mrs. Adams. Mildred kept herself away on the days her father was in the witness box. It would have been far too distressing.

Sir Henry James began the new week with his opening statement. He congratulated the plaintiff, Mr. Adams, for his able presentation. Sir Henry's own task would be brief and simple: "the truth will vindicate Lord Coleridge." Then, he went on at some length. He regretted being in another courtroom when it once seemed this unfortunate affair had been settled. But then, and most unfortunately, Mrs. Bishop had "thought it right to hand over to Mr. Adams a secret but affectionate letter (from Lord Coleridge) avowedly for the purpose

Cupid in the Law Courts. A courtroom sketch in the Penny Illustrated Paper offering the best images of Mr. and Mrs. Adams, Lord Coleridge (his "bone dome head" glistening), family members, and the bar. In the top left, a veiled woman is unidentified. Almost certainly, that woman was the second Lady Coleridge. There is a definite resemblance.

of publicity and of litigation." Of her conduct, Sir Henry said, "I forbear to comment."[5] Lord Coleridge proffered generous terms to his estranged daughter and, the jury would likely agree, to her husband. Those terms await them still. Mr. Adams has always said it was never about the money yet now he demanded £20,000. Whatever the plaintiff says to the contrary, Sir Henry thought the jury might well conclude Adams acted all along "really on his own behalf and not on behalf of Miss Coleridge."

Sir Henry asked the Lord Chief Justice to enter the witness box. "Everybody present was roused to great interest" as Lord Coleridge climbed the steps. His baldness was always worth a comment: he was "a tall, willowy man with a big bone dome of a head." He took the oath: Do you swear the evidence you shall give to the Court touching the matters in question shall be the truth, the whole truth, and nothing but the truth - So help you God? "I do," came the solemn reply. "No one could produce a greater sense of solemnity with less effort" than the Lord Chief Justice. He kissed the Bible as required. The curiosity of seeing "the autocrat in the witness box" soon gave way to the routine of the case.

The libel action against Lord Coleridge centered on two letters. The first, the letter of December 1882, written to Mrs. Bishop and, secondly, the Athenaeum Memorandum of November 1883 which his lordship had shared/published with his (and Mildred's) friends. In the case of Mrs. Bishop, Coleridge described her as a longtime friend who was very close to his daughter.[6] Mrs. Bishop opened the correspondence, writing to him with concerns for Mildred after he forbade his daughter to have contact with Adams. Lord Coleridge said he had expected his reply to Mrs. Bishop would be treated as confidential. He recalled writing the letter much influenced by his meeting that same day with Miss Cobbe in the "darkened room." She was a formidable woman and very convincing and he believed her tale that Adams had laid plans, scheming to be alone with Mildred with an intent to "compromise" her. Subsequently, mostly after speaking with his daughter, Lord Coleridge told the court he had changed his mind. He now believed Miss Cobbe's fears "were the passionate and exaggerated feelings of a woman." He had already apologized to Adams and would again, under oath, stating, "I have long thought that letter was unjust and I withdraw it." Coleridge said his earlier withdrawal and ensuing apology were all part of the settlement agreement that Adams refused to sign.

Most of the remainder of the day was taken up with the reading of the lengthy Athenaeum memorandum and the equally verbose reply from Adams. Coleridge explained he had written the document after Mildred circulated her "prospectus" for music lessons among her friends, most of whom were, to be clear, Lord Coleridge's friends. In her affidavit, Mildred accused him of driving her out of the house. Not true, he testified. In the memorandum, he wrote: "I hope both from my daughter and Mr. Adams a real endeavour to act fairly by me - he by honestly trying for some definite employment, she doing her best to be cheerful and reasonable." Failing that, "they, of course, are free to take what course they please, but they must not expect me to help them." On 8 December 1883, Mildred left Sussex Square. "She was of mature age and I had no wish to be her gaoler, she left without my wish but not without my knowledge." With visible emotion, he admitted he had not seen his daughter until her brief court appearance earlier in the trial. From the day she left, her monthly allotment cheques were sent and cashed. Could he explain the figure of £17,000 that fixated his daughter and Mr. Adams? After his first wife's death, he rewrote his will and discussed it with his children, wishing them to know where they stood, "in the ordinary run of things." Mildred "might have expected" £17,000. But, in the end, it was *his* will:

> The supposition that come what might I should have no
> power to alter my will - no power over money which (and I
> say it humbly) I had made myself - was what I certainly never
> thought of putting forward to anyone, and I should have
> imagined that nobody could possibly entertain such an idea.

Coleridge once described the figure of £17,000 as an "absolute fabrication." He now conceded to the jury his language may have been too strong. He nonetheless believed the settlement awaiting Mr. and Mrs. Adams' acceptance was extremely fair.

Once more, back to the bundle of letters found at Lord Monkswell's, Coleridge insisted he had no role in that "misadventure." He was "exceedingly staggered" by the clerk's error and wrote sharply to his solicitor. He trusted Lord Monkswell, a man respected in all facets of his life, to understand the mistake and not let it affect his deliberations. Which, his lordship believed, was how it happened. Before he finished, Sir Henry noted that in some circles (e.g. Mr. Adams and his friends) it was said Lord Coleridge had arranged the Monkswell peerage. "Do you have any control over the making of peers, my lord?" With a rare smile, Coleridge replied, "I do not." Sir Henry surrendered the witness for cross-examination.

As with many things in the late Victorian world, Lord Coleridge did not always accept "the new." His law clerks still used quill pens. He also greatly disapproved of the new practice of courtroom sketch artists. As a defendant, of course, he had no control over the courtroom and Denman permitted it. The men from the illustrated papers scratched away. In the raised witness box, Coleridge towered above Adams although the two men were nearly equal in height. Charles

Warren Adams was as hirsute as Lord Coleridge was bald. Coleridge's disdain for beards has been noted but they were much in fashion; Lord Salisbury became Britain's first bearded prime minister that year. Adams went for the full bushy beard and hair, in what was thought to be the "intellectual style," à la Marx or Darwin. At 53, Adams was predominantly grey. He still tended to overdress and one unfriendly reporter described him as "flabby" and looking as if he slept in his clothes. Adams was wide awake and ready for his chance to question his father-in-law, to whom he hadn't spoken in three years.

Adams began, brandishing his copy of Lord Coleridge's letter to Mrs. Bishop, written following his visit to Victoria Street and Miss Cobbe's guided tour of the darkened room. Miss Cobbe reported finding Adams "in a darkened room where he had got Mildred alone by appointment, the other man of the establishment having been sent by him off to the City." Adams produced an affidavit from Arthur Davies, the assistant supposedly made to vanish that afternoon. The man swore that was an "absolutely baseless assertion." He left about one, his usual time, and returned to the rooms near two, he remembered. In general, it was the clerk's practice to go in and out of the secretary's room without knocking and many women visited Adams' office without incident. The defence did not challenge the clerk's statement. Bolstered by that, Adams went to work on Lord Coleridge.

> A: When you went to see Miss Cobbe, was this before or after the controversy over the visit from the editor of the *Malthusian Review*?
> C: I should say after.
> A: Might that have had considerable bearing on Miss Cobbe's immediately subsequent attack on me?
> C: That is a question on which I can only have an opinion.

A: She showed you the darkened room? C: If you wish me to say it, I will.

A: Did you ask whether the room had been meddled with?

C: Certainly not.

A: Let me ask instead, had she prepared the room for your visit?

C: I haven't the slightest idea.

A: Did she tell you how long I was in the room? C: No.

A: You did not ask? C: No.

A: You asked no questions and quite accepted her account?

C: She told me a great deal which, I will own, very unfavourably impressed my mind at the time. I had the greatest respect for her. She is a woman of warm feelings, and I think it very possible she had exaggerated what she had told me, and I ought not to have given such implicit credence to her statement as I did. My further acquaintance with you led me to think I was wrong and unjust in making that particular charge against you, and I desire always to withdraw it.

A: Oh, my Lord, I am no match for you in cross-examination!

Denman: You must not say that, Mr. Adams. Proceed.

A: After this change of mind, did you write to Mrs. Bishop?

C: I did not.

A: You did not think you should?

C: It was only one of the many reasons I objected to your conduct and sought to end your intercourse with my daughter. With your strange notions of what is right between an unmarried man and an unmarried woman, from time to time, you placed my daughter in situations which compromised her.

A: Never mind about time to time. On this occasion, when you accused me of sending the man away, did you mean to suggest I planned to entrap your daughter?

C: I did not say entrap.

A: Does it not suggest a trap?

C: You must make what you can of it.

A: Did you think I meant to outrage your daughter in a darkened room?

C: I had too much confidence in my daughter if you planned anything rough or coarse.

A: What did you mean to imply?

C: I only repeated what I had been told by a person of high integrity and character (Cobbe).

A: Did you not think your letter to Mrs. Bishop cast aspersions on your own daughter?

C: (vehemently) I never dreamed of breathing the smallest atom of aspersion of my daughter's character. Never! [The witness' face turned as scarlet as "the colour of his (usual) robes."]

Denman: This has lasted long enough. I have the power to stop it and I do stop it.

The theory is that "great lawyers are seldom good witnesses." How would Lord Coleridge react to the restless, aggressive manner of his questioner? The witness stood throughout and answered the questions, by and large, with "great urbanity." He maintained his posture, resting his hands occasionally on the brass rail of the box. With a few exceptions he also maintained his composure. Some of that outward confidence was belied by a notorious Coleridge trait - blushing. Lord Coleridge, wrote one observer, blushed "like an innocent young girl, and then turning white, and then blushing again. One is almost reminded of a lighthouse with revolving lights."

Moving to the Monkswell issue, Adams wanted to know why Lord Coleridge never sent him a personal letter of apology. Wouldn't that have quickly settled this matter? "Do not be very angry with me, Mr. Adams, if I say you will find it difficult to convince me of that." A lighter moment. Adams was intrigued that no letters reflecting favourably on himself were sent to the arbitrator. For instance, he had sent Lord Coleridge a copy of *The Coward Science* and included a note. You save all letters, don't you? "I do, from Browning, Newman and eminent men." Mildred recalled her father thought that letter was charming and stuck it in the book. Did you look for it? Coleridge replied, coldly: "I don't mean to say anything disagreeable, Mr. Adams, but I haven't looked at your book in years."

In one of the letters that turned up in the Monkswell papers, Lord Coleridge suggested Adams, the Bishops, and others, were "trading on what they suppose to be my fears."[7] That sounded almost like blackmail. "What are you afraid of?' Adams asked. Pausing for the right words, Coleridge stated, "A man in my position could only look forward with great distress" to this moment. He feared it all the more because of the "outburst of public feeling" against him and his family following the first trial. He seemed to choke up which prompted some sympathetic applause. "Silence," sounded Justice Denman sternly. "Nothing of that sort will be allowed."

Lord Coleridge had stated earlier that Mildred was always free to go with Adams, if she wished. Adams suggested that the only reason Mildred left Sussex Square was her frustration with Stephen Coleridge and his family. Coleridge conceded, "My son and his wife were to go to a house of their own in fulfillment of a promise I had made to my daughter." But after Stephen and his family left, "you still refused to let her return?" Mildred, said Adams, only intended to go away for a few days, she hardly took anything with her. She did not wish to leave Sussex Square. She was turned away by her father. Coleridge disagreed. As his lordship recalled those days, he learned

Mildred received Bernard's letter while she was staying with a friend. He asked that she not share the letter with Adams. However, defying her father, she did. Adams asked why that mattered. Through a grim smile, Coleridge answered, "Because I know you, sir." He knew that litigation would undoubtedly result – which it had. From that point forward, "I could not allow my daughter back into the house."

Adams suggested Mildred's eyes were giving her a great deal of trouble at the time she was banned from her home. Coleridge said his daughter's eyes were always a concern; they were no worse then. Adams wanted to know how many eye surgeries she had had but Sir Henry James objected. This was not cross-examination but persecution. A juryman agreed. Mr. Justice Denman concurred, there was no need for the line of questioning. Adams smiled and announced, in that case, he was finished. "Please, no," Denman insisted, "you may go on to another subject." Adams insisted; "If that is the view of judge and jury, I will not persist for a moment." The witness may stand down. It was over.

There were no newsreels or television cameras in Court IV. The eagerly awaited clash was witnessed live by no more than 150 people. Was Lady Coleridge present for any of it? She is not mentioned but *The Illustrated London News* sketch artist drew a full-page mural of the principals, Lord Coleridge, Adams, Denman, the leading counsel, etc. To one side, was an individual drawing of a young, attractive, well-dressed, woman, identified only as "an interested observer."[8] There is a resemblance; perhaps it's the *retroussé* nose? The reporters' box, opposite the jury, was filled with "solemn, unhappy men." Scrawling frantically, they could hardly keep up. Taking advantage of the usual delays and a trained memory, they prepared a reasonably detailed account. With a stylus and a firm hand, using inked papers, one reporter could have a half-dozen "flimsies" to pass to a messenger boy who raced them to the newspaper offices where they were soon clattering down the telegraph lines to typesetters at dozens of papers, city and provincial dailies and rural weeklies.[9] Paid by the line, the Coleridge trial was a good assignment, although they would have done much better down the hall at Lady Colin Campbell's salacious divorce case.

Going in to the trial, Lord Coleridge reasonably feared the press would revel in "the autocrat in the box" narrative and make rather a fool of him but instead the coverage was generally pro Coleridge. Heretofore, the narrative had been right out of the "everyone loves a lover" copybook, how doughty Adams rescued Cinderella from her wicked father. The momentum had turned. Coleridge was evolving into the sympathetic figure. He had been "badgered by an unprofessional cross-examiner," but emerged having "born the ordeal very well." Adams, who had been all burly and defiant, met his match, at last. Lord Coleridge was described as "remarkably patient and self-possessed under the cruel cross-examination to which he had been exposed."

The main attraction having closed, only a few of the onlookers returned after a brief recess to hear from Lord Coleridge's solicitor. Charles Harrison was one of the richest men in his profession, a yachting toff, and married to a sister of the Earl of Lanesborough.[10] The solicitor told the jury he wished to take full responsibility for the error, which he then deftly shifted to his junior clerks. Harrison said his office had copied all the filings, documents, letters, etc. going back to the first (Bernard's) trial. The documents were paged consecutively by "a printing machine." How modern.[11] The clerks had been instructed to remove several sections, which was done, except for pages 440-477. Owing to (a tortured phrase) "accidental inadvertence," those pages containing the very material so upsetting to Mr. Adams arrived at Lord Monkswell's library. For the clerks, young Russell Ambler took the fall. In the end, he misunderstood his assignment and was very sorry for what happened. He never had any contact with or instructions from

Lord Coleridge. The legal community was forgiving; junior clerks who work for solicitors "who have a Lord Chief Justice for a client are apt, perhaps, to be nervous."[12] And that concluded the evidence.

"My duty is singularly light," Sir Henry James said, as he began his closing argument. The evidence was plain; Lord Coleridge had withdrawn the letter to Mrs. Bishop and apologized. He wrote the Athenaeum memo in response to his daughter's proposed nominal engagement, or, as Sir Charles Russell called it a "sham." Lastly, his lordship played no role in the document mix-up. No one would have ever learned of any of those letters if Adams hadn't made them the basis of his "absurd" libel action. "Seven days were spent in the discussion of matters almost sacred in their privacy." Bernard Coleridge, by the way, was in court all along, making only the briefest cameo appearance as a witness. Bernard's lawyer followed Sir Henry, in effect, adding: "What he said."

Adams would go on longer, of course. He had a "heavy voice," according to one of those who had heard him for so many days, he talked "slowly but continuously." In his closing speech, he said he had given four years of his life for this moment. He was weary of it all; let anyone try three or four years of litigation against the Lord Chief Justice. "He has from first to last represented and treated me as an adventurer endeavouring to entrap his daughter into marriage, and as a person to be got rid of, if possible, without pecuniary sacrifice, but, failing that, to be got rid of for the smallest sum I could be induced to accept." Adams persevered to restore Mildred's fortune and his reputation. Lord Coleridge charged him with the vilest crime a man could commit against an innocent woman. Yes, his lordship apologized and agreed to arbitration. Then, irrelevant letters, which were in the control of "a man who certainly does not love me," were mysteriously sent to Lord Monkswell. "If only dirt enough be thrown, some of it will stick." Lord Coleridge proffered a second-hand apology but Adams had learned to be wary of his lordship's "cuttlefish skills of obfuscation." He said that.[13] Was his good name and honour worth nought but a letter of apology and 40 shillings? Adams reminded the jury how another panel of Londoners – just like them – had awarded him £3000. Adams was flailing now. As for the unsigned settlement, Adams was wary. Negotiating with Lord Coleridge was like gambling with the "heathen Chinee."[14] Denman cautioned him sharply. Adams one more time declared it was never about the money. With a last glance at the jury, Adams said "I have kept you too long and wearied you, I fear."

The jury *was* undoubtedly weary but they were nevertheless subjected over two days to a five-hour discussion of the law from Justice Denman. Try as he might and, in the view of many, he barely did, Denman's instructions tilted plainly to the Coleridge side. To Denman's mind, Adams and Mildred were "carrying out a game" with their "nominal engagement" scheme. With two daughters of his own, Denman believed Lord Coleridge faced "a state of things dreadful for a father to contemplate" and worthy of the strongest rebuke. Nonetheless, if the jury found that his lordship maliciously conspired to "unduly influence" the arbitrator, it was "an abominable charge" and Mr. Adams was due damages that "ought not to be stingy, small, or niggardly."

On the eighth day (!), 25 November 1886, the jury retired with 63 requested letters. They could hardly have done much reading. They went out at 27 minutes to one and returned just over an hour later at a quarter to two, cutting short Denman's lunch. "We find for the defendants," the foreman began when asked for their verdict. This prompted a burst of applause from the Coleridge partisans which the judge met with a commanding "Silence." Order restored; the foreman wished to continue. They had all agreed on a statement. Denman wouldn't hear it. This created something like "an angry scene." There was a mini-rebellion among the twelve and Denman gave in. "Very well, go ahead, but it's immaterial." The jurymen wished it known that their tedious ordeal was caused solely by the "careless and highly reprehensible manner" Lord Coleridge's solicitor bungled the document process. Adams was justified in bringing this action and had been put to great expense. While they found against him, the jury were agreed Adams should not be forced to pay the costs, as typically fell to the losing party. By now, an exasperated Denman "very snappishly" declared, "You have nothing to do with costs. I give judgment for the defendants *with costs*."

More cheering was heard and, this time, ineffectually suppressed. Lord Coleridge shook hands with his counsel and the many familiar clerks and court workers around him. He disappeared through his private exit. Adams stood with head bowed. Mildred had been in court for the verdict, looking "tall, thin and pale." She made her way to his side. Arm in arm, they left the courtroom in the company of "two or three friends." She looked, "as no doubt she felt, terribly hurt and annoyed." In the early darkness of a November afternoon, Charles and Mildred walked out into the roaring tide of humanity on the Strand. For days, a crowd gathered, at the Law Courts about four hoping to see the litigants of the hour, including one of the most beautiful women in England. Unfortunately, that wasn't Mildred. Lady Colin Campbell's divorce trial was running simultaneously. The crowd espied Adams immediately; he was "a giant in height, and by no means a knock-kneed giant either, but square-shouldered and burly." As usual. no one seemed to notice the pale woman at his elbow. They made their way past the stares and typical taunts from a few, and whether by foot or carriage, they departed the Law Courts, and – in reality – London, never to be seen again.

Few were really surprised by the verdict. Why was Adams allowed "the savage pleasure of torturing his father-in-law in court for eight days?" The central moment of the trial – Adams' cross-examination of his father-in law – was "contemptuous, not to say insulting." And over what? *The Times* declared: "A more frivolous and inexcusable action had seldom been brought before a Court of Justice." Denman talked too much and let Adams talk too much. The plaintiff was allowed to "fling mud and make claptrap sneers." The "Heathen Chinee" reference was tasteless. In the end, Adams had been exposed. "The more he said it wasn't about the money, he whined about the money." If anything, the flinty-hearted *paterfamilias*, crushed by the public reaction from the first trial, was restored in reputation. With a hint to 20th century advert copy, a headline writer declared, "Nine out of ten British fathers" would have done the very same thing. "It is unquestionably true that [Lord Coleridge] has never been more popular than he is to-day," assessed *The Saturday Review*. That may have been an overstatement. More restrained observers believed it was more the public turning its back on Adams. "Up to a certain point the general feeling was one of satisfaction that such an insufferably superior family as the Coleridge family and such a superhuman structure of eloquence, learning, piety, sarcasm and conceit, as the Chief Justice, should be rolled in the mire." But no longer. Instead, Lord Coleridge received "universal sympathy for the unmerited annoyance he has had to endure." He would return to the bench with an unsullied character.

On the Monday morning following the trial, there was anticipation in Court IV. Lord Coleridge was to return to his usual position, last occupied by Mr. Justice Denman. Moments before 10:30, his clerks entered carrying eight bouquets of flowers. There were so many the bench was filled and some were placed on the clerk's desks below. "Whence they came there was nothing to indicate; but their meaning was obvious." When the Lord Chief Justice entered the chamber, the waiting members of the Bar seemed to receive him with "more than their customary warmth." Coleridge appeared to be moved by the display and, for a moment, looked as if he might have some remarks for the occasion. Instead, he gently moved the central bouquet off to one side and bade the day's business to begin. The case of *Tucker v Mackie* was called. "Public curiosity was not gratified."

1  Certain men: "Builders of Our Law: Lord Chief Justice Coleridge," The Law Times, 7 Sept 1901.

2  Court IV: a helpful description of the Chief's courtroom, Frank H. Burt, "*A Morning in the London Law Courts*," Proceedings of the New England Shorthand Reporters' Association (1892) 61. The "great seal" mentioned was a large, wooden carving of the Royal Coat of Arms. It was placed in Court IV sometime after 1886.

3  "Practical fitness," "The New Law Courts," Times, 20 December 1883, 7.

4  Mrs. Weldon, "the well-known lady litigant," appeared often before Lord Coleridge. He once described her as "a person who has had wrongs, but who has taken advantage of them to weary the public about matters which are not wrongs." She answered, "My Lord, I know you think me a tiresome and misguided woman." He answered, "Mrs. Weldon, you may be a thought reader but I have not said so." For more, see Brian Thompson, *The Disastrous Mrs. Weldon: The Life, Loves and Lawsuits of a Legendary Victorian* (2002)

5  As mentioned previously, Iddesleigh was embarrassed by his sister's role in all of this. His only explanation was "by remembering in how unreal a world she has always lived, and how little she has ever entered into the natural life of an English family." CFP Add MS 86200.

6  Lord Coleridge's team wished to make it appear that he and Mrs. Bishop were old friends; letters between friends have greater privileges of privacy. Adams would challenge that, getting his lordship to admit he hadn't entertained Mrs. Bishop in his home, nor had he been to her residence in many years.

7  "My fears," Coleridge to Iddesleigh CFP 16 January 1885.

8  The Penny Illustrated Paper (27 November 1886) also included an unnamed veiled woman observing the scene. Today, under the long-standing Criminal Justice Act of 1925, courtroom sketching and photographs are prohibited.

9  Michael McDonagh, "*The Byways of Journalism*," Current Literature, Vol. 26, 13 (1899)

10  Harrison: one of the richest solicitors in Britain, was either working or yachting all the time. Lord Rosebery asked, 'When are the times and seasons at which Mr. Charles Harrison takes food or sleep?' (DNB).

11  Printing machines had been in vogue for some time but in the 1880s the documents still had to be hand fed, then collected and organised, "necessitating the employment of a large number of unskilled and frequently inefficient labour."

12  "Apt to be nervous," The Law Journal, 27 November 1886, 661.

13  Their "inky defence system" is why the cuttlefish is known as the chameleon of the sea.

14  Bret Harte's poem "The Heathen Chinee" (1870). Adams likened Lord Coleridge to Harte's Ah-sin (a smiling card cheat).

> Which is why I remark, and my language is plain,
> That for ways that are dark, and for tricks that are vain,
> The heathen Chinee is peculiar.

# 21. THE OLD MAN'S DARLING

ALL THOUGHTFUL SUBJECTS of the Queen were hopeful the last of the Coleridge family "jars" had been settled. Let the family return to that domestic obscurity sought by all. Adams still blustered, but "Mr. Adams is still Mr. Adams." Placid Mildred was said to be contemplating her own lawsuit. In December, "happily for the Coleridge family," a settlement of all grievances was announced. Mildred was, at last, "comfortably dowered" with £600 a year, affording Adams the luxury of upping sticks for Europe where they wandered for nearly a decade. They did not return to England until after Lord Coleridge's death. Their story will be told in the following chapter.

For his lordship, 1886 ended well but it had been a gloomy year, with the long-dreaded and dark second trial dominating all. He spent Christmas at Heath's Court with the usual retinue of Lawfords. There were no sightings of any of Lord Coleridge's children or grandchildren. The New Year was welcomed by a "merry peal" from the bells of St. Mary's. The Coleridges made no recorded public appearances and spent the holidays in quiet seclusion, returning to London on 11 January.

In 1887, the Lord Chief Justice and his young wife began to emerge from what was almost social seclusion. Her "exile" from the highest reaches of society must not be overstated. Lady Coleridge was not a courtesan, a Gaiety Girl, or, heaven forbid, an ex-barmaid. To be sure, the less known about her first marriage the better, and while it might disqualify her from a curtsey at the Palace, the greater social rules were a good deal more flexible. "We venture to predict her ladyship will be much sought after for her own sake and prove a very agreeable addition to London society."[1] The Coleridges were seen at the proper galleries and garden parties. Her first public appearance of significance came at the Royal Academy that May. All were agreed she was "exceedingly pretty." Wherever they went, people strained to see the "heroine of the abortive breach of promise suit which won her shapely head a coronet."

A charming report on this most interesting couple can be found in the diaries of Lady Monkswell who spent "a few days" at Heath's Court in October 1887. Mary, Lady Monkswell, was married to the son of the late peer, the former mediator. While in Devon, she admitted, "I sat in judgment on Lady Coleridge from Monday evening until Thursday evening." The young Baroness was not a tall woman but had a graceful pretty figure. Her hair was black and her skin was quite fair.

> She was a very gentle, pleasant, simple, pretty woman, without much individuality of character, but also without any swagger, and keen to do everything right and proper...It was beautiful to see old Lord Coleridge's admiration for her: I detected him several times sitting opposite her & simply worshipping her. Her beauty & sort of sweet gracefulness must be most delicious to him.

The Ottery days passed pleasantly, touring the countryside, and reading books in Lord Coleridge's charming library which was "not all given over to learned stuffiness." Lady Monkswell thought the other Lawfords were a bit tiresome with their "mangy fox terrier" nipping about. Mrs. Lawford, she wrote, was "old & seedy." Lord Coleridge referred to her as "Mother," which provided the Monkswells with "great amusement." After dinner, there was some music. Lady Coleridge and her sister were joined by "the Chief" as they sang "Blow, Gentle Gales." Lord Coleridge joined the chorus, in his "deep melodious voice with lots of feeling." Then prayers and it was off to bed. One afternoon, Lady Coleridge even brought her guest up to see their newly remodeled bedroom. It was a "glorious big old four-poster erected on a sort of a dais & what looked just like a communion rail dividing the raised bed from the rest of the room." All in all, Lady Monkswell found the mysterious couple to her liking: "They seem happy and she is quite the old man's darling."[2]

A few longtime friends did keep away from Devon. In one, rather pathetic, letter, Lord Coleridge pleaded with Mr. Gladstone: "If even for one night," he and Mrs. Gladstone would be most welcome at Heath's Court. They did not come. Others did and were made welcome. "There was never a guest who, when he was there, wished himself away."[3] Matthew Arnold was one of Lord Coleridge's oldest friends and he accepted an invitation to dine at Sussex Square. The aging sage reported to his wife, "Lady Coleridge improves in looks, though she was pretty to start with." He was happy for his old friend, "He is getting stout and looks much older than he did; but he is won-

"The Old Man's Darling"

derfully happy and she takes great care of him."[4] The age difference between the Chief and his beautiful young wife was striking. At the Royal Academy in 1888, "she looked like the Lord Chief Justice's grand-daughter." There was no more sought-after dinner invitation in London than from Lady Jeune's in Harley Street. Thomas Hardy was there one night in 1889 to admire Lady Coleridge's "really fine eyes." The evening was a pleasant one; the Coleridges departed early. Hardy recalled, "When Lord Coleridge and she had left, the ladies discussed her age."[5]

His lordship remained estranged from his sons. In hopes of establishing some *entente cordiale*, Bernard and his brothers were invited to dine at Sussex Square but the tone of the evening was spoiled when Lady Coleridge wore a necklace that had belonged to their mother. There was no scene but Bernard took great offence. "The necklace was my dear mother's, worn by her every day, sacred through many memories. I loved her. I love her still." He begged his father to ensure Lady Coleridge would never wear it again in the family's presence. Beyond the necklace, Bernard bridled at having to accept and defer to a woman not even his age. He avoided Heath's Court. Everywhere he turned, there was a Lawford. He could barely be civil to the interlopers. "You can hardly expect me to be cordial to them when we find ourselves crowded out by them from our old home." The Butterfield redo was hardly five years old but new renovations were underway to please the new lady of the house. Bernard could only fret that these changes would be "expensive to keep up in the future."[6]

The pinnacle of Lady Coleridge's celebrity arrived in 1891. Lord Coleridge presided over the trial of the Great Baccarat Scandal, a slander action involving the Prince of Wales in a tawdry card-cheating affair at a Yorkshire country house.[7] Until 2023, when Prince Harry testified in court, the baccarat trial was the last time a member of the royal family gave evidence. The crush to attend was intense and the Lord Chief Justice was delighted to serve as unofficial major domo.

"Had the Lord Chief Justice been welcoming all London to his own home he could not more blandly have enjoyed or taken part, in the show."[8] He placed the Prince of Wales on the bench to his right. Other select guests were given reserved seats with the best views. Lady Coleridge perched at her husband's left. The better to see and be seen:

> In all events, a beautiful woman is a pleasant sight, and Lady Coleridge is beautiful. There were other good looking ladies on the bench and in the galleries, and plenty of good millinery. But what chance had they with Lady Coleridge there? None at all.

It was a lengthy trial although the prince's presence was required on just two days. On those days, he lunched with Lord Coleridge in the Chief's private chambers. His lordship typically took no more than a cup of tea and a biscuit at midday, hardly enough for the rotund royal. Lady Coleridge could not keep away, popping in to ensure the prince was well fed. The Queen's snub had resulted in many London and country house hostesses closing their doors to the young baroness. Still, all the town knew the unquestioned leader of society was the Prince of Wales. Over lunch, HRH – ever attracted to pretty women – would have had an excellent, if brief, opportunity to consider the array of her Ladyship's charms and graces. The Marquise de Fontenoy, pen name for a relentless gossiper syndicated in papers outside the British Isles, went further.[9] Lord Coleridge, she wrote, knowing the prince's influence, decided to conduct the trial "in a way most likely to please the prince" and thereby to further his wife's aspirations for acceptance. A serious charge, if true. Some deference to the Lord Chief's impartiality must be paid. Nonetheless, all agreed, Lord Coleridge's charge to the jury was a call to reject the luckless Lt. Col. Gordon-

Cumming's case and the jury was out only thirteen minutes before doing just that. The prince emerged unscarred although his mother was furious with him (again.)[10]

The word "Great" was often overused to describe Victorian trials but it fit the baccarat affair. The "breakout star" was Lady Coleridge. Who was "the very piquant and pretty woman" seated so near the Lord Chief Justice? Her smart outfits, her "peach-like complexion," but, above all, her manner carried the week:

> The pleasant way in which she nods around the court to her friends, the delightful sense of property she has in the whole proceedings, the infinite amusement with which her smiles and dimples seem to show she regards the whole business, and above all the cheeky absence of awe with which she behaves under the very eyes of the great Lord Chief Justice, all make the court pleasant. But for her the great trial would have been a very dull business.[11]

So much attention was paid to Lady Coleridge that those in Court IV failed to notice his lordship's pet ferret that he kept hidden in his voluminous robes. (A family anecdote confided to the author Michael Scott by the 5th Lord Coleridge!)[12]

Ferrets aside, not everyone approved of her ladyship's "playful kittenish" antics. Lady Coleridge "brought herself into unenviable notoriety by the levity of her behaviour." A cheeky paper even dubbed her "the Lady Chief Justice." A young law student dared inquire why Lady Coleridge and her friends were allowed reserved seats. Would it surprise you to know that, once again, Lord Coleridge, rather than ignore it, felt the need to issue a full blast, published in the *Times*:

My wife has had at her disposal three seats and three seats only, including her own. The majority of persons on the Bench have been unknown to me, even by sight, but they have been persons to whom, for one reason or another, it seemed proper to grant the privilege. Exactly the same observations apply to my own small gallery and to a portion of the gallery opposite the Bench. The rest of that gallery and the whole of the body of the Court has been absolutely free, but I have given strict orders to prevent overcrowding, so that the quiet and orderly trial of the cause shall be secured.[13]

Lord Coleridge proclaimed that he would continue to allot the seats in his courtroom "when and as I see fit." It was good to be Lord Chief Justice.

An undated photograph of the Lord Chief Justice and his wife, Amy, Lady Coleridge, at Heath's Court, Ottery.

A longtime colleague, Lord Justice Mathew, said the Chief Justice's "later years seemed to be the happiest of his life." His second marriage brought Lord Coleridge much contentment, however much it seemed to rile many others. The relentless Fontenoy insisted smart society still closed its doors against the baroness, of "exceedingly bourgeois" pedigree. The story of her first marriage and the annulment was discussed in select salons but rarely publicly. Just once. In the summer of 1891, Thomas Terrell, a 40-year-old London barrister whose workload was not so heavy as to deny him the time to write, published his first novel, *Lady Delmar*. It was a book "calculated to create a great sensation." The plot defies summary but involves a "hotchpotch" of Russian nihilists, English socialists, marriages, murders, and tangled wills. A young swell named Sir Reginald Fantail (!) falls for a dancer named Polly and they gambol off for a hasty Scottish wedding. Their wedded life is soon miserable. Sir Reginald, meanwhile, has eyes on an heiress. His lawyer advises him to use the 21-full-day loophole, citing the Lawford case, "which every lawyer is familiar with from some curious circumstances which arose afterwards. You see the lady had it in her mind to marry again." In the early reviews, there were a few wink-and-a-nod comments on Terrell's book, which had "made some stir in the political and social world." The *Western Mail* in Cardiff, however, was more direct: "*Lady Delmar* is founded on a feature in Scotch marriage law to which one of our best-known judges owes his wife." Terrell was soon boasting his book was in its "fifth thousand" printing by early 1892. Such a novel was hardly worthy of shelf space in the serious library at Heath's Court. Still, Lord Coleridge had uncanny antennae for picking up any gossip at his expense. The book would not escape his attention. "Lord Coleridge is greatly incensed," the papers reported. However it was made to happen, *Lady Delmar* was in the remainder bins in very short order. At the Law Courts, meanwhile, Mr. Terrell was advised "to keep out of his lordship's way."[14]

Privately, the Coleridge rifts continued. The bitterness with the "dear boys" had worsened, more so with the older two, Bernard and Stephen. In October 1888, Lord and Lady Coleridge were in Torridon, a remote village in the Highlands of Scotland, for Gilbert's marriage to the eldest daughter of a local laird. The occasion passed off nicely, perhaps because the other Lawfords remained behind. An elaborate set of rules kept some civility in the relations between Lord Coleridge and his sons. The retinue of Lawfords especially nettled Bernard:

> I can never see you in town or country without feeling that they have usurped the place which we were all wont to occupy and when we hear, with your immense income, speaking so constantly as you do of your poverty, it of course raises speculation not favourable as to the conduct and motives of this family, utterly strangers to us, which is now so much dearer to you than your own.

By 1891, the rules broke down. Bernard complained to his father about the numerous slights his wife and children had received from the baroness. Lady Coleridge replied with a *28-page letter* defending

Lord Coleridge and "the Lawfords" at Heath's Court. Lady Coleridge is standing beside her husband. Seated on his left is "Mother" Lawford. Egerton Lawford stands to the right. One of the other two seated ladies is Flora Lawford. The extra woman is unidentified. Bernard complained of being "crowded out" of his family home by the Lawfords.

the hospitality she offered all the Coleridges. She even apologized for the necklace gaffe. She had tried to be friendly with Bernard but she would never forgive him for the slanderous gossip in Ottery. Those "sinister stories being freely circulated about the neighbourhood." She thought he was behind the horrid rumour Lady Coleridge may have left some "dear little ones" back in America?[15] Bernard answered curtly, denying his part in any tale-telling around the village. He appreciated her candour and her willingness to "express openly the hatred and animosity which I have long believed you cherish toward me and mine." In early 1892, Bernard informed his father he had given up, "As things stand, neither myself nor my wife can meet her."

Bernard had to think of his future. As his father's eldest son, he stood to inherit the peerage and its expenses. That was all well and good, but Bernard's only income came from the practice of law, a lucrative occupation which, traditionally, he would have to give up once he sat as a member of the Lords. The House of Lords was considered the highest appellate court and all lords were, in a way, judges and, hence, could not practice as an advocate. (But, see below note 21.) Bernard was troubled, then, to learn his father had rewritten his will. As had been established at the second Adams' trial, Lord Coleridge reserved the right to change his will. Bernard pressed Harrison for details but the solicitor declined to share them. Bernard wrote to his father, taking a tone with definite echoes of the departed Adams. Bernard insisted it was not about the money. "I have never been grasping," he wrote.[16] Still, he needed to know his future expectations better to manage his current expenses and lifestyle. Bernard eventually received some discouraging news from Harrison, "I may mention that the bulk of Lord Coleridge's property is settled on the Wife."

By 1892, the 72-year-old Chief Justice was clearly slowing down. He had mastered "the art of slumbering artistically" on the bench. Prime Minister Gladstone – an even older man – reportedly planned to offer Coleridge an earldom as enticement to retire, "but the LCJ positively declines to look at an earldom." His frequent absences from the bench "threatened to assume the proportions of a public scandal." He wrote to his close friend, Roupell, on the subject: "You say the time has come for me to go. Very likely it has, but if I can, I want to stay on the Bench till 1896, before which time I am not entitled to my full pension and my full pension is a serious object to me."[17] The death in 1893 of his brother was a depressing blow although the two remained separated by the Jesuit's opposition to the second marriage. Lord Coleridge attended Henry's funeral in Ottery; Lady Coleridge did not.

Lord and Lady Coleridge were among the "brilliant" crowd on hand on 2 May 1894, when the Prince of Wales used an 18-carat gold key to open the new Royal College of Music in South Kensington. It was a dull, cool, spring day and his lordship caught a chill. He was well enough two days later to attend the Royal Academy's private view at Burlington House, overshadowed again by his young wife, "very becomingly dressed in grayish fawn, completed with a charming bonnet." The next day, he missed court and again the following day. Sir William Broadbent, the leading man on Harley Street, issued a briefing: "There is every sign of His Lordship's recovering, but he is weak." Reports of an imminent retirement were contradicted. Coleridge lingered for almost six weeks. Daily bulletins were issued. "Lord Coleridge had a bad night and was not so well again yesterday." On the morning of 14 June, his youngest son, Gilbert, admitted they were "nearing the end." Lord Coleridge died that evening just before nine, "having been in a hopeless condition for the previous few days." A notice posted outside 1, Sussex Square revealed, "Lady Coleridge, who has never left him during his illness, was alone with him during his last moments." Very much alone. Bernard and Stephen believe they weren't summoned by Lady Coleridge until it was too late, and they arrived after their father had passed away. John Duke Coleridge was 73. The cause of death was reported as jaundice and liver failure.

The English papers mourned Lord Coleridge's passing with lengthy, respectful, but chilled tributes. "A silver-tongued orator, a student of literature, the companion of scholars and ecclesiastics, an apostle of culture," Lord Coleridge was a type now out of fashion. "He had a want of sympathy for most of what appeals to the average man." The old epigram resurfaced, "God intended him to be a Bishop. By accident, he became a judge." He did seem the ideal judge. "A tall column of manhood, it was a majestic sight to see him rise sweepingly from the Bench at the close of a sitting." People would "listen to him just read from the Bradshaw's Railway Guide." Those who appeared before him knew "he could say very nasty things in his gentle and delicately modulated voice." Critics found him pious, vain, and an elitist. He demanded respect from his inferiors and, "in his opinion, there were many such." His own chosen biographer admitted, "Outside the circle of his intimate friends, in middle life, at least, he was unpopular, at once admired and disliked."

A week later, a small cortege left Sussex Square, his lordship's coffin carried by open hearse to Westminster Abbey for a memorial service, mainly attended by members of the Bar. Justice Denman was one of the pallbearers. The body was moved by train to Ottery where it was placed for the night on a bier in the entrance hall of Heath's Court. The funeral was Saturday, all the shops in the town were closed. Workmen on the estate carried the coffin into St. Mary's church. Mourners were led by the grieving widow whose "devotion to the Judge during his long illness has won the admiration of all who have watched her." She was joined by the "Lawford suite." The three Coleridge sons and their families were also present, of course. "It was obvious to every observant person present" the two families mourned quite independently.[18] There were no scenes. His lordship's only daughter and eldest child, Mildred, and her husband were not seen in the crowd. The services were well-conducted. The flowers were beautiful, including a bouquet from the Victoria Street Society. The service was fully choral and Lady Coleridge's self-possession was respected by all. At the graveside, she briefly needed

Bernard's arm. It was a touching moment but undercut by the gossip already racing. Speculation about the will was on everyone's mind. The likelihood was considered quite high the family would soon be back before the courts, owing to "differences between Lady Coleridge and her late husband's family."

It was unfortunate but word spread round that Bernard Coleridge had not been left anything in his father's will. Bernard was now the 2nd Baron Coleridge and "seldom has a peerage fallen so heavily upon anyone." He would have to consider his new life; he had gone from being "a moderately prosperous working barrister to now an impecunious baron." Wills were frequently challenged on the grounds of undue influence, but the burden of proof was not easy to meet. However, given the "decidedly unfriendly feeling" existing between Bernard and Lady Coleridge anything might happen.

The final adjustments to Lord Coleridge's will had been made as recently as New Year's Eve 1893. The will was "proved" on 5 July 1894. The estate had been valued at £15,445, 4s 8d (roughly £2m today.) As a good Liberal, he would have appreciated that his estate was one of the first significant fortunes to fall under the new "death duties" of up to 8%. His widow would have that to deal with as she was the sole executrix. "Would it surprise you to know" that the Chief and Miss Lawford had a pre-nuptial agreement? In a settlement signed on the eve of their wedding in 1885, he agreed, in the event of his death, she would receive £600 a year for her life (exactly the portion he'd finally settled upon Mildred!). But there was more: Lady Coleridge was also left £10,000 in trust for her and their children. As there were no children of the marriage, the money was solely for her use (and the Lawford suite.) Bernard would get all the family real estate in London and Devon (and responsibility for the expenses to keep them up.) He was left all his mother's drawings and pictures (a few of which

Mildred had claimed), other artwork and furnishings, including the "Butterfield candelabra," no less. The Lord Chief's legal curios stayed in the family, the old seal of the Court of Queen's Bench, the chain of the Court of Common Pleas, and a chair from the Queen's Bench in Guildhall. There were numerous small legacies for his law clerks, there was £300 for Hannah Knott, his longtime housekeeper, all servants employed for at least three years received a year's salary, and small personal gifts to Stephen and Gilbert, although Mildred never got her pianoforte, apparently. Mildred was never mentioned in the will. The residuary legatee - that is, the person who gets "the rest," or everything not specifically devised to someone in the will - was the Dowager Baroness. Thus, she inherited the furniture and furnishings, carpets, the books in Lord Coleridge's library, the wine in his cellar, etc.[19]

"The details of the will of the late Lord Chief Justice have been almost the sole topic of discussion." Defenders of Lord Coleridge argued that – on the date of his second marriage – he settled certain sums of money on each of his sons. They were not cut off without a farthing. The will was only to ensure Lady Coleridge was well-provided for and to dispose of those items, such as furniture, bric-a-brac, etc, that his children didn't want anyway. But to those who read the will – and such was the interest it was printed almost in full in papers across Britain – it did not leave the Lord Chief Justice in a very favourable light. The veteran London correspondent for the *New York Times* told readers at home, "The great *paterfamilias* practically took from his children every penny it was possible to take away." The will managed to make the previously cold and distant figure of Bernard Coleridge into something of a sympathetic character. Many believed Bernard had been disinherited, "the old gentleman bequeathed [her] every vestige of the property over the disposition of which he had any control."

Bernard was now a peer, a very soft landing indeed, but he would succeed to his father's title "without receiving a single penny" to maintain the rank properly. Bernard made the effort, only the second of its kind, to decline the peerage. He had no more success than the first unwilling young peer and thus the 2nd Baron Coleridge took his comfortable seat on the famous red benches of the House of Lords. Westminster slumbered in August and the day of Bernard's investiture was a lacklustre affair witnessed by the few "stragglers" hauled out of the Lords' refreshment room. It was a fitting moment, somehow. Bernard would "have to take on his father's title whether he likes it not."[20]

The shocking will made it seem quite likely the Coleridge family would yet again provide "more washing of dirty family linen before the eager gaze of a nastiness-loving section of the community." A good indicator was Bernard's first move – he sacked Harrison, his father's solicitor who'd drafted the will. (Harrison quickly transferred his loyalties to the dowager baroness, besieging Bernard with demands and fees. Bernard confided to Stephen, "I begin now to see how lawyers are an unpopular race."[21]) Would the new Lord Coleridge challenge the will on grounds of the "undue influence?" In Bernard's mind, the will had been inspired by her ladyship's bitterness, playing off the estrangement between father and sons. Bernard believed his father's last will was prepared when "the Chief" was failing and unable to resist her machinations. She would get revenge on those who'd snubbed her from day one. Still, as Adams could tell his brother-in-law, proving "undue influence" was quite difficult. Of course, Lady Coleridge would have had influence over her husband but "undue influence" required evidence of coercion. Did Lady Coleridge get her elderly husband to do something he did not desire to do? The chances of winning such a chancery suit were not good. There was also the risk reward question. The Coleridges were not that wealthy; detractors thought the property was scarcely "worth the money which the suit cannot fail to cost." As for the dowager, she had little to gain from a public re-airing of her now mostly forgotten past. "She manifests such an anxiety to make people forget her first marriage."[22] The divided camps, warring but weary, quietly compromised on the details and coldly went about the business of severing all ties.

Amy, Lady Coleridge, the Lawfords in tow, arrived at Heath's Court in August. She spent several weeks taking stock of what she wanted to bring to London and what could be sold. A great sale was held in Exeter in mid-September: carpets, cabinets, couches, artwork, even the billiard table went under the hammer.[23] There may have been more lookers than buyers but "satisfactory prices were realised." Bernard lurked about but was outbid for anything he tried to salvage. His cousin, Arthur, commiserated with him over the loss of so much family property, gone "to fill the rapacious Lawford maw!"[24]

On 20 September, Amy, Lady Coleridge, left Heath's Court for the last time, leading a baggage caravan of wagons filled with a vast quantity of wine, several loads of the "best furniture," and "tons of books." The loss of the library rightfully enraged Bernard, writing to Stephen, "Our father (!!) left written instructions to Lady Coleridge to sell the library to prevent the chance, a slender one, of her giving it to me." Within hours of her departure, Bernard took possession of the family home. He found it had been "pretty well cleared out." Again, to Stephen: "The place is desolate." Anything that could be moved or removed was. "Meanness is everywhere displayed. I can see great expense before me," Bernard groaned.

By one estimate, the dowager's "haul" would, if well-invested, bring her between £2,000 and £3,000 a year. In London, she was now easily paying the rent at 1, Sussex Square, but not for much longer. Bernard was selling the place; he had no use for the old home as he was living in Wetherby Gardens, South Kensington. In October,

*The Morning Post* advertised, "To be sold, a bargain, the long lease of a handsome family residence, enjoying a southern aspect in this fashionable [Sussex] square." Sussex Square was listed for £8500. With a ready buyer, Bernard urged Lady Coleridge to find new lodgings. She complied but, at the last moment, decided the dining room paneling was meant to be hers and she would send the men to take it down. "Our beauty has excelled herself," Bernard wrote to Stephen; he thought she was intentionally trying to spoil the deal. The dowager (with her mother and family) moved across the park to 36 Hyde Park Gate. The remnants of Sussex Square were auctioned in May of 1895; the catalogue offers a glimpse inside the High-Victorian splendor of the Coleridge home:

> The costly contents to be auctioned include several Spanish mahogany bedroom suites, chests of drawers, bedsteads and bedding, elegant drawing room appointments in silk damask with curtains, brilliant chimney glasses and mirrors, marqueterie and fancy tables, antique French cabinets, handsome mahogany dining room sideboard, dinner wagons, extending tables, and a set of 24 chairs, library fittings, bookcases, Chippendale chairs, Brussels and Axminster carpets, pedestal clock, old Dutch timepiece, mantel clocks of the Empire period, crown derby and other ornamental china, choice bronzes, artwork done by Velasquez, F. Coleridge, Prout, Harrison, Sir William Boxall and other artists. Rare steel and wood proof engravings. A very fine life size marble figure of Hypatia by Williamson. A very fine porcelain dinner and dessert service, a very large and exceedingly choice cellar of wines, a capital landau, and miscellaneous effects.[25]

There were separate sales of the late chief justice's wines (600 dozen bottles) and his law books. A visitor to the library at Sussex Square was given tea by Lady Coleridge. "She seemed so much apart from the literary atmosphere pervading the place, that I could not escape from the impression that even the books felt it, and longed to slip away to some possessor who had a genuine affection for them."[26] The book sale, held in Chancery Lane, "excited considerable interest." All proceeds went, of course, to the dowager.[27]

There was a quiet victory in Bernard's war with his stepmother, "the beauty" as he had taken to calling her. Succeeding to his father's peerage entitled the new baron to be presented to Queen Victoria at Buckingham Palace on 5 May 1895. His wife, Mary, the new baroness, was graced to accompany him and curtsey before her sovereign. It was a much-coveted honour never afforded to Amy. The announcement appeared in the correct papers. Bernard wrote to Stephen, "I think we enjoyed the moment when the beauty opened the *Morning Post* the next morning."[28] He must have smacked his breakfast egg with a wide smile for the occasion. The fledgling peer took his family down to Heath's Court from which all traces of the interloping Lawfords were promptly expunged. Bernard began to entertain, although the local papers reported it was necessarily on a small scale. There was nowhere for guests to sit. "The late Lord Chief Justice, while leaving lands and houses to his son, left all the furniture to his widow, and this fact has made things a little slow for the new Peer - and his neighbours. But now the garden-party stage of entertainment, at any rate, has been successfully reached." By 1896, the Coleridges were in residence again, beside "the lonely Otter's sleep-persuading stream."

Lady Coleridge had been widowed at 41; for a few years it was almost required that the papers remark she was much too young to be a dowager baroness. After her period of mourning, she returned to society. "The Dowager Lady Coleridge, in widow's weeds and a black satin pelisse, was the admired of many eyes." Apparently, she abandoned the widow's weeds fairly quickly, adopting "a rather picturesque style of mourning garment." She never remarried. Sir Charles Cavendish Clifford of the Isle of Wight had been a longtime friend of Lord Coleridge, who once acknowledged Clifford's "warm heart and admiration for my wife." The wealthy bachelor left her £2000 in his will which was awfully nice.[29] By no means was the dowager ever prominent in society. In the early Edwardian days, she was frequently seen at the meets of "The Coaching Club," an elite set of rich men with their "splendid equipages" who trotted about the Park, almost always accompanied by one or two of the beauties of the day.[30] Her great friend was Sir Frederick Cook, a millionaire draper. She traveled with Sir Frederick (and Lady Cook) to his estate in Portugal where he held the euphonious foreign title, Viscount Monserrate.

Those heady days would fade. Amy, Lady Coleridge, lived quietly at Hyde Park Gate for many years, though she was still using her old Heath's Court stationery as late as 1919! Her unmarried sister, Flo, lived with her. Her mother died in 1905. That same year, her ladyship was "pleased" to present to King Edward VII a copy of *The Life & Correspondence of John Duke Lord Coleridge, Lord Chief Justice of England* by Ernest Hartley Coleridge.[31] Too heavy on the correspondence and not enough on the life was the justified verdict of most critics. Ernest worked more than merely closely with Lady Coleridge, thus the family friction following the second marriage went unmentioned. Ernest all but ignored Mildred and Adams as well. "The subject was, naturally, most distressing to (Lord Coleridge) and I know that, in thus putting it aside, I am doing what he would himself have wished."[32] Mildred's friend and cousin, Fanny Patteson congratulated the author. "Under the circumstances, you could not do better than ignore the family life."

Amy died at Hyde Park Gate on 27 May 1933. The death of the second wife of the first Lord Coleridge received only the briefest notice. The two families divided by acrimony for nearly fifty years came together for the day, anyway, at her ladyship's funeral. Stephen and Gilbert Coleridge attended the service at St. Mary Abbots, Kensington, along with the 3rd Lord Coleridge (Bernard's son.) Bernard, unreconciled to the end, predeceased her (q.v.) He would have not enjoyed hearing his stepmother died a very wealthy woman; her gross estate was £47,000 (more than £4m in 2023). In the will, besides her dependent Lawford relations, she left small gifts to the numerous Coleridge grandchildren and the residue to Miss Dulcie Dolores Bainbridge Barrington, spinster. Miss Barrington had been her companion for some years and was also named co-executor of the will. Amy Lady Coleridge was (apparently) buried in the churchyard at St. Michael's, Kirk Langley, in Derbyshire, where the Barringtons were well-known.[33]

Amy Augusta Jackson Baring Lawford Morse Davies Coleridge did have quite the life.[34] Assisted by her formidable mother, she got the Lord Chief Justice to come to "the scratch." As a baroness, she entered a world she never could have dreamed of. They had a happy eight years, proving the soundness of his lordship's belief that the looming risk of a breach-of-promise action probably led to more marriages than lawsuits. As he said, "Many marriages, fairly happy, took place in consequence."[35] His would seem to have been in that number. "All who enjoyed the intimacy and confidence of Lord Coleridge in his later years were witnesses of the abundant happiness which the marriage brought with it." The undeniable and sad consequence of this happy marriage was the resulting estrangement from his three sons. He had, of course, been previously estranged from his only daughter. What of Mildred?

1  Table Talk (Melbourne) 2 October 1885, 8.

2  Monkswell diary, A Victorian Diarist: extracts from the journals of Mary, Lady Monkswell 1873-1895.

3  Never a guest: *Life & Correspondence*, Vol 2, 393.

4  Matthew Arnold to daughter Lucy, 17 December 1887. Mrs. Arnold did not accompany her husband on that visit but the Arnolds did occasionally see the Coleridges together.

5  Hardy: Michael Millgate, ed., *The Life and Work of Thomas Hardy* (1985) 229. For Lady Jeune, Harry Furniss, Some Victorian Women, Good, Bad, and Indifferent (1923). In her memoir, Lady Jeune recalled his lordship as her "great friend," and the second baroness as his "affectionate and doting wife." *Memories of Fifty Years* (1909).

6  Bernard's letters are drawn from: (CFP Add MS 85925. 1889-1894. Correspondence relating to a prolonged family quarrel, including some letters from Stephen Coleridge and one letter from Amy, Lady Coleridge.)

7  The story of the Baccarat case: Havers, Grayson, Shankland, *The Royal Baccarat Scandal* (1988)

8  The St James Gazette compared the courtroom to "a theatre at a fashionable matinee." At one point, when Gordon-Cumming's counsel's speech was applauded, Lord Coleridge "angrily bawled out, 'Silence, this is not a theatre.'" Some bold soul retorted, "You have made it so."

9  Fontenoy: the pen name for a French-born American novelist, Mrs. Frederick Cunliffe-Owen, known as the "Lady with the Poison Pen" whose gossip "news" appeared in her husband's New York Herald Tribune and reprinted wherever. See The Catholic Standard and Times, Volume 32, Number 45, 10 September 1927.

10  The public was shocked; shocked I say, to learn their prince went about with his own baccarat set. Gambling on the turf, at cards, etc, was ever popular but the future king was "justly condemned by the stricter of his subjects." The Economist 13, June 1891.

11  London Correspondent, Retford (Notts) Herald, 6 June 1891, 6.

12  "The Baccarat Scandal: the last time a senior royal was questioned in court," The Guardian, 2 June 2023.

13  Coleridge's reply: "The Admission of the Public to the Law Courts," Times, 8 June 1891, 13.

14  Lady Delmar can be found on GoogleBooks. The Coleridge allusion is found on page 138. For a unique take on the Delmar novel, see "The Incredible Affair of the Secret Santa," by Christopher Wadlow in The Journal of Intellectual Property Law & Practice, 2012, Vol. 7, No. 12 (also available online.)

15  Lady Coleridge's letter/dear little ones CFP Add MS 85925.

16  Bernard grasping CFP Add MS 85925

17  Coleridge to C.M. Roupell, 29 August 1893, *Life & Correspondence*, Vol 2., 380.

18  "Obvious to every observant person," Brighton Gazette, 7 July 1894, 5.

19  The Coleridge will appeared in countless papers; e.g. The Daily Telegraph, 7 July 94, 5. The New York Times put it on the front page, 8 July 1894. "Sole topic of discussion" - Sheffield Evening Telegraph, 7 July 1894, 3.

20  Bernard's predicament – in the eyes of many – highlighted the "absurdity" of forcing a public man to accept a title he doesn't want. He once described the House of Lords as a collection of "the halt, the lame, the blind, the idiotic, those who had little sense and those who had a great deal." On the day he took his seat on the "red leather benches," Hansard, the official record, merely acknowledged the presence of "Lord Coleridge, after the death of his father." While Bernard agreed to succeed to the peerage he sought a ruling on the question of retaining

his career at the Bar. It was the Attorney General's "emphatic opinion" there was no legal reason to prevent it. The 2nd Lord Coleridge continued to work as a QC/KC until 1907, when he was appointed a Judge of the High Court, serving until his retirement in 1923.

21  Bernard re: lawyers – Sir Paul Coleridge's collection.

22  Fontenoy, New Orleans (U.S.) Times Picayune, 18 July 94, 7 "She can scarcely relish the prospect of having [her past] dished up afresh during the course of a sensational lawsuit for the edification of a scandal-loving public."

23  Heath's Ct sale: Devon & Exeter Gazette, 31 Aug 1894, 1.

24  "Rapacious maw:" Arthur urged Bernard to keep him posted on "the Cuckoos; what a mess they have made of the family nest." CFP Add MS 85968.

25  The house itself, 1, Sussex Square, is gone, lost in post-war rebuild.

26  Library visitor: Caroline Ticknor, *Glimpses of Authors* (1922) 299.

27  The sale of his lordship's books may have been overstated. When Chanter's House was on the market in 2019, the library still held "more than 22,000 historic books assembled by Lord Coleridge, one the UK's greatest legal minds." See "Take a Tour of Chanter's House," 24 January 2019, at KnightFrank.com.

28  Sir Paul Coleridge's collection.

29  Clifford died at Ryde on 22 November 1895. He was "for many years the glory of the Isle of Wight and the pride of its people." He left an estate worth a handsome £83,000.

30  The Coaching Club: "They meet at the appointed place, at the advertised hour, drive round the Park, and disperse."

31  Lord Coleridge's sons and cousin Arthur were critical of Ernest who wrote the biography much under the influence of the baroness. Arthur wrote to Bernard, "Ernest deserted us in the hour of trial." CFP Add MS85968. The EHC collection at Austin has 6 leaves of notes about the book removed from the Life and Correspondence. Patteson's letter is in the EHC papers at UT Austin.

32  Life & Correspondence, Vol. 2, 346.

33  Amy's will: Western Morning News, 15 August 1933, 9.

34  In the 21st century peerage books, there is still no mention of the fact that the baroness had been previously married.

35  "Fairly happy" marriages: Lord Coleridge's comment in Joslin v Otway, The Times, 6 December 1888, 3.

# 22. TO KEYHAVEN

THE SIMILARITIES ARE too striking to ignore. Both Mildred Coleridge and her father became involved in relationships with a person the rest of the extended family considered to be unsuitable. Mildred, in her darkened room, Lord Coleridge, in his private cabin on the *Britannic*, engaged in compromising behaviour complicating everything that followed. Who were these outsiders? Charles Warren Adams and Amy Lawford had no status or income. The larger

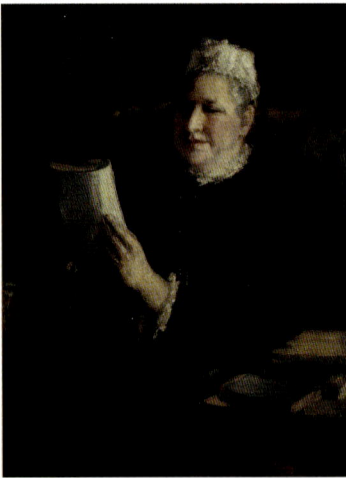

Portrait of Hon Mrs. Adams by Dame Ethel Walker. There was little of the "fashion plate" in Mildred's portrait. Seated in a "darkened room," of all places, she is posed reading a book without her eyeglasses. Mildred's portraits are not currently on display but they can be found online. For instance, search for "Cats in Art."

Painting of the second Lady Coleridge by Lord Leighton. Critics were divided on Leighton's work. Praised by some for the artist's "extraordinary verve and dash," others thought it was "unpleasantly suggestive" of a fashion plate (i.e. advertisement). Lord Coleridge didn't like it. "I shall not know what to do with the thing when it comes home."

Coleridge family viewed each, in turn, as a fortune-hunter. The family dug up any dirt they could find on the intruders. Facing implacable opposition, Adams and the Lawfords employed legal action (or the threat of it) to get what they wanted. In the end, the adage proved true. The more a marriage is opposed, the more likely it is to go forward. Adams married Mildred, dowered for life. Amy Lawford became a baroness, presiding over his lordship's possessions "in solitary aloofness." [1]

Now, what of Mildred? A biographer must regret the second half of her long life went all but unrecorded. Nor did her husband leave any significant record. Adams, who often described himself as a "literary man," wrote no memoir. The reading classes were not offered an autobiographical novel intended to settle his countless scores. Instead, when Mildred and Adams left the Law Courts that November day in 1886, they all but vanished for the rest of their lives.

As mentioned previously, there was briefly a fear Mildred would be next to litigate. At issue were paintings done by her late mother which Mildred claimed were left to her; she valued them at £1000. According to Adams, Lord Coleridge locked the artwork away while obstinately insisting he had no such pictures in his possession. *Adams v Coleridge* was threatening to be interminable. Please, no, the public cried as one. The mood had clearly changed. Lord Coleridge was now more to be pitied as "a father whose daughter has treated him badly for the sake of a son-in-law who has treated him worse." Adams needed to go away quietly. "Rarely has a man succeeded in alienating public sympathy from himself so rapidly and absolutely." After a few days' consultation among solicitors for the principals, a settlement of all claims was offered and signed. His lordship would pay Adams' court costs (and his own, of course), a not inconsiderable sum. Maybe even the paintings Mildred wanted were "found," at last.

The best news for the Coleridges was that Mildred and Adams were leaving England. It was either part of the settlement or Adams' belief that their money (Mildred's money, of course) would go much further on the continent. Whatever, their hovering presence in England – or, at least, Adams' - would have been too much for the family to bear. From the early days, Adams talked about taking Mildred to the continent for her health. He knew that Mildred, "whose health is very delicate" would be better off in a warmer climate. When pitching his proposed nominal engagement, he explained to Lord Coleridge such an arrangement would enable him to serve as Mildred's "recognised escort abroad." For him to dedicate his escort services to Mildred would mean giving up any chance to find employment in England. Couldn't people see why, then, he considered her a "white elephant?" His lordship and Adams never saw eye to eye on anything, certainly not on Mildred's health. "We are not agreed as to the state of my daughter's health," rejecting Adams' dire diagnosis she was on "death's door." Lord Coleridge always suspected Adams simply wanted to travel about Europe living on Coleridge money. By 1887, however, that prospect was no longer an unattractive one. Mildred was now married to the wretched man and never coming home; let them go wherever they want. His tormentors were soon to cross the Channel, his reputation had been somewhat refurbished by his triumph in court. He might be permitted a slight smile. "By the way, Lord Coleridge is much pleased with himself just now."[2]

The European move always made sense financially. The first of each month, Harrison posted £50 to Mildred's bankers. The continent was a cheaper place to live and travel. In France, where they stayed for most of nine years, £50 was roughly equal to 1250 francs and *Baedeker* expected English visitors with "moderate requirements" could live on fifteen francs per day, those with greater needs could make do at thirty.

Mildred knew and loved Europe – just keep her away from altitude and the bracing Engadines. As a girl, she and her mother and Aunt Maymie made annual trips. In her twenties, she frequently traveled to Italy with her cousin Mary, now and forever out of favour. Charles and Mildred first went to the south of France. They had only just arrived when Adams wrote to the London papers complaining a "report is being diligently spread that I have left England in order to evade payment of the costs in the late actions, amounting to £1500, and that poor Lord Coleridge has had to pay them." Adams wrote to both Harrison and Sir Henry James demanding clarification - but his blustering letters were now being ignored. The editors who once coveted his copy realized he'd become a rather tiresome figure; people were now "inclined to doubt that Adams was altogether an object for sympathy."[3]

Charles and Mildred spent time in Menton, a flourishing health resort on the Côte d'Azur, the French side of the Riviera border with Italy. Touted for the mildest winters in the south of Europe, Menton was crowded with English TB patients, and English doctors. So many, the local *médecin* rebelled. Mildred was delicate but never a consumptive and her time in Menton seems to have done her good. Adams wrote to the *Morning Post* in September 1889, while nearing the end of a "two year's tour" of France. He boasted that "we" walked from Menton on the Riviera, to Hendaye on the Bay of Biscay, 500 miles. The first bit, the fifteen miles from Menton to Nice via Monaco was "one those routes which must be walked over to enjoy in its perfection." Given two years, the entire walk could be done at a very leisurely pace but all the guidebooks remarked on the strenuous ups and downs. The walk was a memorable part of Mildred's life; she often spoke of the adventure and thinking what a strange couple they must have seemed. Adams was 6 foot 5 and dressed all in white, while she was 5 foot 11 and wore only black.[4] Mildred was fluent in French and they stayed at small, local inns, and found the people quite friendly. The *Boulangists* were on the rise in France at that time talking of "*Revanche*" against Germany, worrying many in England. Adams, in his "eyewitness account," found the people "curiously calm" and predicted (correctly) the belligerence would pass. If Adams hoped his occasional letters might scare up some kind of offer to be a "roving European curmudgeon" for some paper or news agency, it did not materialise.[5]

When off his feet, Adams launched a new anti-vivisection journal, *The Verulam Review*.[6] Their co-interest in "the cause" survived the litigation years. Frances Cobbe's biographer, Sally Mitchell, suggested Adams "found the funds" for the new venture: well, he found them, almost certainly, in his wife's bank account. It was very much an independent publication. Adams' disputatious final days at Victoria Street burned all bridges with the leaders of the London movement. He was "persistently boycotted" by the *Zoophilist* and other journals in the field.[7] He blamed "petty personal jealousies and self-seeking which have been so disastrous up to now." If no one would accept his submissions, he would go it alone. When he found few willing contributors, he wrote the *Review* by himself, cabling articles to his publisher in Paternoster Row. Adams preferred his name not appear on the masthead, "I enclose my name which you are quite at liberty to append if you like, to this letter. But as my personality has really no bearing on the subject, I shall prefer to sign myself simply as the writer of the article in the *Verulam Review*." Published quarterly, and priced at just a shilling, the review was hardly going to add much to their income.

They didn't spend all their time in France, visiting several other countries. Reputedly, Mildred was fluent in nine languages, but not including Norwegian. The familiar "splenetic" Adams resurfaced in the summer of 1891. Norway had become a popular tourist destination but, writing to the *London Daily News,* Adams warned English visitors about the shambolic logistics of travel in the fjord lands: "stick to the coastal boats as the number of post horses is inadequate." Mildred wasn't up to walking in that part of the world and she was not a bonny sailor. Whilst in Romsdalsfjord, Adams hired a *carriole,* an open horse-drawn carriage for two, driven by a local driver (*skyd*) who promised the horse would be changed out regularly. No relief horse to be found, it took the exhausted steed 11 hours to go 38 miles downhill. They arrived only just in time to get an essential boat but too late for the English language church services in Naes. In Adams' defence, these were frequent complaints.

Our last sighting of the traveling Adams' came from Italy in September 1893. Adams fired off a rant about an incident at the train station in Bergamo. They left luggage at the depot and returned to find it had been opened and items were missing. The local authorities refused to assist. Adams should have considered himself lucky; a newspaper warned: "Thefts are constant (in Italy) and not limited to the contents but often the baggage itself." Bergamo was on the line to the beauties of Lake Como but Adams was *non piace molto* with Italy. Mildred's experience, of course, was never discussed. She would have wanted to visit Italy, having done so many times, spoke the language, and formed "an intimate acquaintance with the literature and art and customs" of the new republic. Adams, regardless, pronounced his verdict: "I have no hesitation in saying that the pleasantest countries in Europe are Austria and Sweden, while the most odious, whether for dirt, discomfort, discourtesy, or dishonesty is unquestionably Italy."[8]

The last apparent contact between Lord Coleridge and his itinerant daughter and son-in-law came late in 1893. His lordship was in declining health and wished to resign from his role as trustee of his daughter's settlement. Nothing would ever be easy between Coleridge and Adams, chalk and cheese. After earlier requests were ignored, Coleridge sent a registered letter, opening stiffly, "Sir. You seem to think yourself privileged to disregard the common courtesies of life."[9] What should have been a routine matter instead became an excuse for another typical "display of foolish & ill-bred insolence entirely without provocation or cause."

As discussed earlier, the world was made well aware there were no Coleridges with him when his lordship breathed his last at Sussex Square in June 1894. Bernard and Stephen would always claim they were tardily sent for by the baroness, timed so they would not arrive until their father's death. Gilbert was in Scotland. Mildred, meanwhile, was not even mentioned. For more than a decade, Mildred and her father had not spoken; they hadn't seen one another but for those days across a courtroom. No one sought Mildred's comments on her father's passing. Adams must have stifled the urge to flood the newspapers with some discourteous barbed send-off to mark the occasion.

Great anticipation built for "the reading" of the will. Such scenes, however, seem to occur only in fiction. Any one in England could go to Somerset House and, for a shilling, could ask to peruse the paperwork. It was cheaper to the buy the evening paper, as many reprinted the will in full. There was much discussion about what her ladyship was getting and Bernard wasn't, but the most interesting revelation was, "His only daughter is not mentioned." Years after the fact, the scars of the Adams-Coleridge battles had not healed. For everyone who battered Lord Coleridge for pursuing Mildred "with a ferocity that could not but disgust sensitive people" there were defenders who thought Mildred should have expected nothing else. "She must suffer for her zeal for poisoning the last days of her aged father." As Shakespearean references were always prized, his lordship was twinned with Lear who denounced his daughter, Goneril, for "Ingratitude, thou marble-hearted fiend."[10] In fairness, Mildred's provision had been settled (finally!) and she and Adams received cheques the rest of their lives. But not a tuppence more.

Lord Coleridge's death meant Charles and Mildred could return to England. Clearly, they desired the same seclusion they enjoyed in Europe. If isolation was their goal, they chose wisely. In Hampshire, on the Solent, lay the "tything of Keyhaven," among the most inaccessible hamlets in southern England. Though only a few miles from Lymington and Milford-on-Sea, the approach to Keyhaven was "almost destitute even of a cart-track." Once there, the muddied traveler found a small cluster of a half dozen homes, one or two cottage farms, a pub and a coastguard station set amid marshes facing "a complete preponderance of grey sea and murky sky." A few boats sat moored in the mud, rising with the estuary tides. Peaceful, perhaps, but the coast was regularly battered by fierce storms, when "the sea ran so tremendously high that the village of Keyhaven was completely inundated." The only reasons anyone visited this isolated place were duck shooting or walking the windswept spit of shingle leading from Milford-on-Sea to Hurst Castle, where Charles I was briefly held prisoner. In sum, Keyhaven would well serve for anyone hoping to be left alone.[11]

Harewood House was north of the Lymore Road, the one road, and set on the edge of a tangle of channels and pools.[12] Built in the early 19th century, the house had been occupied for some time by a naval officer. The Adams' acquired it in 1896. It was "approached by a carriage drive through shrubbery, with a coach-house, stabling, gardens, and pleasure grounds." From the house, the views of the Isle of Wight and the Needles were unrivaled. The Adams' made some

Harewood House in Keyhaven, Hampshire. Charles and Mildred moved to the remote village on the Solent in 1896. He died there in 1903; Mildred remained in the house until her death in 1929. The house was pulled down in the 1950s.

immediate changes, reorienting the entranceway, and knocking out the walls of three smaller rooms to make a larger drawing room. Mildred ran the place. Years before, she walked away from keeping house for her father; in Keyhaven, she readily took up the same responsibilities for her husband. She managed the house and did all the hiring of staff. A typical advertisement:

Wanted, good Plain Cook; Churchwoman; wages £25. House-parlourmaid and gardener kept. Personal character indispensable. Hon. Mrs. Adams, Harewood House, Keyhaven, Milford-on-Sea, Hants.

The wages were rather on the low end but it was only a "small gentleman's family" to feed. It was hard to keep help, whether it was the pay, the utter remoteness and dullness of the village, latterly discovered failings of "personal character," or difficulties in pleasing the ever-irascible Mr. Adams. Similar job postings appeared steadily. Mildred and Charles took no prominent role in local affairs. Adams joined the New Forest Conservative Association and he and Mildred worshipped, semi-regularly, at All Saints Church in Milford. Keyhaven was not where people went to be social.

Adams was now in his sixties and despite a failing heart, he continued to edit the *Verulam Review*. His zeal for controversy was diminishing but he could still land broadsides on his enemies, including Miss Cobbe. She was retired and living in Wales and some thought her role in the movement was irreplaceable. Adams disagreed;

they could do without her "magnificent unscrupulousness."[13] Adams would never forget nor forgive. A case could be made Miss Cobbe ruined Mildred Coleridge's life. Cobbe's reaction to that darkened room set off the entire chain of events that drove Mildred from her father's house and 13 years later, found her alone with Adams in the sodden marshes of Keyhaven.

Adams blustered into his last public dispute in 1898. He remained obsessed about the certificates needed to perform medical experiments on animals and, in the *Verulam Review*, he accused the Home Secretary of failing to monitor the procedures. He accused several institutions and physicians of hiding the real horrors of their research. *The British Medical Journal* ridiculed Adams, "the irresponsible editor is either ignorant or careless," and had impugned dedicated professional men. It was time for a final libel action. Adams wasn't strong enough to be his own advocate anymore. He and Mildred retreated to the south of France, leaving the action in the hands of a barrister. Mr. Rawlinson QC told the court his client suffered from dilation of his heart and general weakness and was bedridden. It was impossible for Mr. Adams to appear in a London courtroom. Rawlinson admitted Adams wrote the article; he wrote almost every bit of the *Review,* dictating the material to his wife. Another brief Mildred sighting! The trial was brief and, unlike the Coleridge days, attracted no real attention beyond the medical press. In his closing argument, Rawlinson appealed for mercy; his client was in very poor health and has always been an "irritable old gentleman." The other side argued Adams was not due any consideration. "What ground had this individual living down in the country at Milford-on-Sea" to go about accusing distinguished men of "unrevealable abominations?" The verdict came quickly for the defence; the triumphant BMJ pitied Adams, a man "unnaturally sensitive to criticism." Which seems fair.[14]

On 30 July 1903, Charles Warren Adams died at Harewood House, a month short of his 70th birthday. A diligent search through the hundreds of digitized newspapers in the British Library's Newspaper Archive fails to turn up a single mention of his passing, not even in the perfunctory "Deaths" columns. He would have been disappointed. Perhaps the editors feared posthumous litigation should any comment on his eventful life irk his shade. The cause of death was syncope/*morbis cordis*, meaning a sudden fatal heart attack. On the death certificate, under occupation, Adams was listed without irony as a "man of independent means." *The All Saints Parish Magazine* did publish a very generous tribute. Could it really be the same man?

> It is with deep sorrow that we record the death of our dear Friend and Fellow Parishioner, Charles Warren Adams, of Harewood House, who fell asleep in Christ, on July 31st. He was a man of high culture and refinement, an accurate scholar of extensive reading and varied attainments, but above all, he was a man of deep and sincere piety, full of love toward God and generous sympathy with his fellow men. He was a true, loyal, and zealous Churchman, and his alms were truly bountiful.[15]

Adams was buried in an unmarked grave in the "old part" of the churchyard at All Saints.[16] In his will, Adams left everything to Mildred; by everything, he meant his effects valued at £323 0s 3d.

News of Adams' death reached the Coleridges, of course, and led to some hopes the dead man's "baneful influence" might have passed with him. Would Mildred be approachable again? "It was what dear Maimie was always crying for," but the aged aunt didn't live to have that opportunity. The old Coleridge generation was all gone; Aunt Maymie was the last when she died in 1898. Adams' death gave Mary Coleridge, Mildred's closest cousin, hope to seize her chance. Mary had never married; she was still living in London with her widowed father. By the turn of the century, she had written one or two "fantastical" novels that had been politely reviewed. She was also a poet, mostly unpublished until after her early death. According to a modern critic, Mary "wrote minor poetry to purge herself of her frustrations and unexpressed desires." A friend once wrote that Mary never hid her "passionate love" for her cousin Mildred.[17] She never forgave herself for her silence in 1883.

> Rebellion against her parents would have been unthinkable to her. But the breach distressed her very deeply and left her with divided loyalties and bitter self-reproach. She felt that, however little she could help it, she had failed a beloved friend and the smart remained unbearable and never healed throughout her life.

After Adams' death, Mary and her younger sister agreed it was time to reach out to Mildred. Mary's father, Arthur Duke Coleridge thought it best to inform Bernard (Lord Coleridge) as head of the family.

> Both Mary and Floss have written to Mildred; I mean to do so unless you had rather I did not. My letter would be entirely a suggestion to resume the old intimacy, as if the words 'I will never speak to you and cousin Minnie again' had never been written. I kept the document for a long time, it was the utterance of a woman hypnotised for the time by a splenetic ill-conditioned man. I am sorry to say this of a dead man, but it really is the simple truth. I should be truly glad to see M. again and in her right mind.

Bernard's reply has not been found but, no matter, as Arthur replied early that September: "I am sorry to say that Mary received yesterday a letter from Mildred of such a kind as to shut out all hope of the reconciliation and re-union which I had hoped for." It was 20 years too late but Arthur repented not speaking up for Mildred when the crisis came in 1883: "I thought it hard measure then, when I could not harbour her after she left Sussex Place (sic); I think it hard now."[18]

Mary Coleridge (1861-1907). Many of Mary's poems are said to refer to the heart-breaking end of her friendship with the cousin she idolized and loved. In Gone, for instance, a poem about friends who have come and gone, Mary ends with the line, "One door alone is shut, one chamber still."

Mary Coleridge was not willing to give up. Theresa Whistler, who annotated a collection of Mary's poetry, claims Mary decided to make an "in person" appeal. Whistler is vague about the time, saying it was "twenty years" after Mildred was turned away from Mary's London home, putting it in 1903, the year Adams died, making it quite possible. However, the author places the final confrontation not in Hampshire but in Somerset. Regardless, according to the story, Mildred would not even come to the door to see her visitor. Mary had to admit defeat to a friend; all her efforts to reach out to Mildred had failed. "It would have been better if we had not done so."[19]

Mary Coleridge was only 46 when she died in 1907 during surgery for appendicitis. According to a friend, Mary's "family troubles ... left their mark upon her spirit." A memorial volume of her poetry was published, including several that scholars believe show the influence of the lost companionship with her dearest older cousin. One is entitled, "Broken Friendship"

Give me no gift! Less than thyself were nought.
It was thyself, alas! not thine I sought.
Once reigned I as a monarch in this heart,
Now from the doors a stranger I depart.[20]

Fanny Patteson, another Coleridge cousin who befriended Mildred during the second trial, sent her a copy of Mary's posthumous collection and received a simple letter of acknowledgement, which was encouraging to Arthur. "[Mildred] was in my Mary's last thoughts before she lapsed into unconsciousness." He wrote to Bernard, "If I thought there was the faintest chance of Mildred returning to the family fold, I should press her to come to me when she likes, and for as long as she likes, but I fear I am forever in her black books, *denigre* hopelessly, though utterly unconscious of my sin against her!" Anyone who closed his door against her, Mildred would never forgive. There were no reunions at Heath's Court.

Mildred remained in Keyhaven after her husband's death. *The Verulam Review* was published until 1909; what role Mildred played is uncertain although all inquiries were directed to Harewood House, Keyhaven.[21] A contributor to the *Review* was Elizabeth Edith Abney Walker, of a wealthy Yorkshire family. In addition to anti-vivisection, the unmarried Walker was a prominent member of the Moral Reform Union, espousing sexual continence for men and women. It was through her that Mildred met the eccentric painter, Ethel Walker, and sat for two remarkable portraits. Ethel Walker was 40, born in Scotland, and with her female partner, established her studio in Cheyne Walk in Chelsea on the Thames (There was a coterie in the area, "the Cheyne Walkers," of course.) Ethel quietly painted female nudes and some portraits. In her two paintings of *The Honourable Mrs. Adams*, Walker posed Mildred seated in a chair, wearing a plain black dress with lace ruffles around the collar and cuffs. In each painting, one of Mildred's many cats sits in her lap. In one, Mildred is facing the artist; in the other, she is reading from a book held in her left hand. There were none of the signs of luxury, either in jewels or in the backdrop, as in the contemporary portraits of Sargent, Dicksee, etc. Miss Walker was famous (or infamous) for loathing female makeup; her models knew to remove all lipstick and polish before going to the studio. Mildred conforms - she appears to be wearing no makeup, and no nail polish. Two simple rings were permitted. Her face is rather masculine, her aquiline nose "Coleridgian." The artist thought the likenesses were "rather marvellous." Walker later became an associate of the Royal Academy and was titled Dame Ethel Walker but she is no longer in critical favour. The Tate has one of Walker's portraits of Mildred but it is not presently on display; the other is apparently in a private collection. Ethel Walker well remembered her visits to Keyhaven, "Many times I have bathed there in the nude."[22]

Harewood House was a sprawling pile that survived the occasional inundations. There was a mark in the drawing room cornice to indicate the high-water mark left behind by a flood during the Great War. There were 20 bedrooms in the house and Mildred often had guests. In the 1911 census, Elizabeth Walker was still in residence, as a "visitor." As Mildred grew older, the running of the place was left to Eva Adams, who was married to William Adams of Lymington, a half-nephew of Mildred's late husband. After William died, Eva moved into to Harewood House. In the village, Mildred was well-known if not particularly active. She donated to the local Cottage Hospital. She joined in the Shakespeare readings at Milford Vicarage. In 1918, Keyhaven, as did countless towns and villages across Britain, discussed a proper war memorial. The project was financed and completed thanks to "the interest and energy of the members of the study circle conducted by the Hon. Mrs. Adams," After the First World War, Mildred was, really, a guest in her own home. Eva Adams managed Harewood House "where guests came only by personal recommendation." And there, Mildred lived out her life. In her final years, she was tended by her devoted nurse Miss Peacock. Many locals recalled seeing "the old lady in her bath chair" being wheeled about. Mildred's sight, which had plagued her since childhood, gradually failed. Her religious devotion continued. Unable to get to Milford church, she took the sacrament almost each week at Harewood.

She outlived her brother, Bernard, who once found "good natured amusement" in his sister's numerous ailments. In 1900, Bernard opted to return Heath's Court to its historic name, Chanter's House. He wrote two books styled to resemble memoirs. *The Story of a Devonshire House* ends with his grand-father's time at Heath's Court. The other book, *This for Remembrance* is a strange, morose, little volume, despite – of all things - a lengthy chapter of jokes. Bernard mentions Mildred once or twice, his mother, and goes on at great length about his grand-father, John Taylor Coleridge, a man he much admired. As for his father, however, Bernard makes a single mention of the man, and that a passing reference to that long ago American tour. Of course, that was where his Lordship met Bernard's step-mother, she who must not be (and was not) mentioned. Bernard died of heart disease at Chanter's House in 1927. His will left the property et al to his eldest son, the 3rd Lord Coleridge.[23] The estate was significantly reduced by inheritance taxes and - as Bernard would argue - the depredations of his step-mother. There was no mention of Mildred in her brother's will, or in the guest lists and flowers at his funeral in Ottery. The dowager baroness, it should also be mentioned, was unable to be present, owing to an unstated "indisposition." Bernard's death was noted only in passing. At a tribute given by members of the Bar, a speaker remarked that the late Lord Coleridge suffered, "as many great men had suffered, from having, in some ways, a greater father."[24] Poor Bernard, even in death, he could not escape the spectre of the "Chief."

While it does not appear Bernard and his elder sister were ever reconciled, a few letters survive from Mildred to her "dear brother," Stephen. Ironically, Stephen – the *louche* youth - was the brother she most clashed with, even into adulthood. During the war, Stephen's son, Capt. Paul Coleridge, was badly wounded. Mildred wrote several letters to Stephen offering her sympathy and encouragement, signing herself, "your loving sister." It's fascinating to read in those letters, the few passing references Mildred made to "Father" without any hint of criticism.[25]

If Mildred still nursed grievances for her sufferings under her great father, they ended on 14 January 1929 at Harewood House. Dr. Maturin, who had signed the death certificate for Adams, a quarter-century earlier, did likewise for Mildred. The cause of death was old age and complications of chronic Bright's Disease. She was 81. A brief requiem service was held the same day in the little oratory in the house.[26] In the *Times*, the brief death notice incorrectly identified Mildred as "the widow of Charles Coker Adams." Adams would have been infuriated by the error; no doubt intentional, he would have believed. The papers got the rest correct, noting the deceased was the daughter of Lord Coleridge, "sometime Lord Chief Justice." *The Milford Magazine* afforded space for touching obituary:

> She was an exquisite and brilliant pianist, and as the favourite pupil of Sir Sterndale Bennett became a most accomplished musician, and passed the examination for Mus. Doc. Mrs. Adams also inherited the poetic gift of the Coleridges and was the author of much beautiful verse which however was never

published. In spite of her own outstanding talents, musician, poet, linguist, she never grudged time spent in helping with her interest and kindly criticism, the efforts of others. A gracious, dignified, striking personality, those who knew her well, will long think of her with gratitude and affection.[27]

In Mildred's will, as expected, she left her property, including the house, to Eva Adams, who continued to manage the property as a guest house. In the middle of the 20th Century, the novelist Elizabeth Goudge used Harewood House, where she had stayed on many occasions, as Damerosehay, the setting for her then popular books.[28] Harewood House, with "excellent cuisine," (and scads of cats) was in business until at least the mid-1950s. The house is gone today replaced in the 1970s by an "unfortunate intrusive modern small housing development on Harewood Green."[29] Keyhaven remains "a quiet place for quiet people."

Mildred Coleridge was an invisible daughter and spinster for the first 35 years of her life. She was described as "a very talented lady and (or, perhaps, because of it) she was still unmarried at 36." After her mother's death, she appeared well-suited and quite willing to be one of the "home daughters," caring for aged parents and manager of the family establishments. Of course, being Coleridges, there would be familial frictions. They could be sorted out. Mildred would walk the life path blazed, in many cases unwillingly, by the unmarried daughters of the upper classes, "the kind sister or aunt [who] will always be welcomed." The Victorian novelist Dinah Mulock Craik summed up the job description as being "the universal referee, nurse, playmate, comforter and counsellor."[30] Everyone expected her to succeed. They were all counting on Mildred.

Mildred was fine with that. And why not? She had an enviable life; it was quite opulent and she moved in elevated circles. She had her outlets: her music, charities, travel, and the VSS. She was not married and seemed untroubled by that. Charles Warren Adams then lurched into her world. He was nothing at all like any man in her limited experience. Suddenly, everything was unsettled at home and at Victoria Street. Adams became her fractious champion. She questioned things she never questioned before. She rejected her ordained role, "to be always there, ready to be counted on," a companion and caregiver for the father who still referred to his 36-year-old daughter as his motherless child. Despite universal opposition from her family, she made her decision to go off and partner in some fashion with a man who, though he "reverenced her above all others," did not love her. No matter. "I shall unhesitatingly obey him," she wrote in 1883. Her choice consigned her to three years as the unwilling focus of litigation and gossip. She never spoke for herself. It was always Adams, in his "slighting and supercilious, not to say patronising, tone, who ruthlessly dragged her before the public for his own objects." At last, after two trials and her strictly private marriage, she and Adams left England. Many people wondered along with Aunt Maymie, "Think what it would be like for her to be the wife of that man." It was safe to say, "No one envies Mrs. Adams."

Bernard had once (redundantly) predicted "a life of misery and unhappiness" for his sister. From the small footprints that can be traced, however, Mildred appears to have adjusted to her new realities. No London mansion or country house, no chasing her brother's grandchildren, or wearying dinners with her father's aged friends, colleagues, and wives. After nine years tromping about Europe, she and Adams settled in, a pair of hermits, at the end of a muddy lane by the sea. She was not the first spinster to make a late marriage, not heeding the warnings that "her habits, pursuits, society, sometimes even friendships, must give way to his." During 18 years as the Hon. Mrs. Adams and 26 more as his widow, Mildred makes scant appearances. She hired the servants, she took dictation, played the piano, and helped with local charities. Well played. She left a routine paper trail: census forms, death certificates, etc.

Her grave in Milford is also unmarked. Maybe unmarked graves are a "thing" in Milford; Admiral Cornwallis, whose command deterred Napoleon's navy in 1795 (Cornwallis' Retreat), also lies in unknown ground in All Saints churchyard. According to the parish registry, Charles and Mildred were both buried in the "Old Part" of the graveyard, but no exact location is given and "the old part" of the churchyard covers a large area. Also buried there is William Henry Adams, Eva's husband, who died in November 1920. They know where he was buried. Very near that grave is a wooden calvary, which is believed to be the prototype for the cross featured on the Keyhaven War Memorial. Mildred, as mentioned, had a leading role in that project. If the local memories are correct, the prototype was given by Mildred to All Saints church with instructions it be placed "somewhere" near her husband's grave. Bob Braid, the archivist with the excellent and helpful Milford-on-Sea Historical Record Society, explains: "It has come to be assumed that they are buried there. The resemblance of the wooden cross to the Calvary at Keyhaven and the fact that it is next to the grave of William Henry Adams, whose widow inherited Harewood, has led to this assumption."[31]

The author, who'd come all that way to delightful Keyhaven, cannot but agree. It seems fitting. Mildred rests a few hundred yards from the Solent, at All Saints, Milford, near her exasperating husband, in an unmarked grave "somewhere around here."

She was not as others.

All Saints Churchyard, Milford-on-Sea
This wooden cross, given to the church by Mildred Coleridge Adams following
her husband's death, is presumed to mark a proximity to his unmarked grave and,
eventually, hers. On a more melancholy note, in 2024, Bob Braid emailed the author:
"I am afraid that the wooden calvary in the churchyard, that I am convinced is the
site of Mildred & Charles' grave, has seriously deteriorated recently and all that now
remains is the the main upright of the cross that now leans rather drunkenly."

1   Aloofness: Ticknor, Glimpses, 298.

2   "Much pleased with himself," Ulster Echo, 1 December 1886, 4.

3   "The Costs in the Coleridge Case," Pall Mall Gazette, 8 March 1887, 8.

4   All Saints Parish Magazine, September 1929. Milford on Sea Historical Record Society collection.

5   Morning Post. 20 September 1889, 3.

6   Verulam Review - Sir Francis Bacon of Verulam was one of the historical supporters of vivisection, as he called it, "the dissection of beasts alive." Animal Experiments in Biomedical Research: A Historical Perspective Published online 2013 Mar 19. NCBI.NLM.NIH.Gov.

7   CWA boycotted: French, op. cit., 224n.

8   Adams letters: from Norway, London Daily News, 21 July 1891; from Italy, Cheshire Observer, 23 September 1893.

9   "You think yourself privileged," CFP Add MS 86211.

10   Goneril: Shakespeare, *King Lear*, Act 1, Scene 4.

11   Keyhaven: RH Hutton, Holiday Rambles in Ordinary Places, (1880) 269-272. See also The Diary of Col. Peter Hawker, the legendary duck hunter. His Instructions to Young Sportsmen was the shooting bible of the 19th Century. He lived the last half of his life in "my healthiest of homes, Keyhaven."

12   Harewood: milfordhistory.org.uk. See acknowledgements.

13   Cobbe's "unscrupulousness," Verulam Review iii, 1892-1893 201. Miss Cobbe outlived Adams by less than a year. "When she died, by an appropriate and beautiful coincidence, a dog was the only witness of her last breath." S. Coleridge, Great Testimony, op. cit.

14   Adams' last trial: Morning Post, 1 May 1900. The BMJ enjoyed vindication: 5 May 1900.

15   All Saints Parish Magazine, (September 1903) Milford on Sea HRS.

16   In January 1904, Mildred gifted a stained-glass window in the chancel of Milford Church in memory of her husband. The glass features the figures of Charles the Martyr and of St. Charles Borromeo. "The design is tasteful and the colouring very rich."

17   "Passionate love:" Violet Hodgkin, quoted in D.E. Stanford, *A Critical Study of the Works of Four British Writers* (2006) Mary Coleridge: Edith Helen Sichel, Gathered Leaves from the Prose of Mary E. Coleridge (1910)

18   Arthur & daughters reach out to Mildred: CFP Add MS 85968.

19   Mary Coleridge papers, Eton College Library MS 683 01 01, letter to Ella Coltman, 18 October 1903. After Mary's death, her letters to and from Mildred were left to Coltman; Mary's sister, however, was "sure they should be burnt." Undated letter, October 1907, Mary Coleridge papers, Eton College. There is some indication that Mary's father, Arthur, may have burned some of her papers but Eton holds "quite a large collection.." Email 18 January 2024.

20   Mary Coleridge, *Poems* (1908) 162.

21   The Verulam Review ceased publication in 1909. "We leave the field to those younger and stronger than ourselves. We leave it, as we entered it, with full conviction in the righteousness of our Cause."

22   Alicia Foster, "Ethel Walker: painter of women," (9 June 2021) artuk.org. Claude Summers, T*he Queer Encyclopedia of the Visual Arts*, (2012), 338.

23   In 2006, Chanter's Court was sold by the 5th Lord Coleridge, it was "the poignant sale of the year." The house is still there, a modern critic described it as facing the road "Like a solemn fossil in a High Victorian cliff face." *The Victorian Country House: From the Archives of Country Life* (2009).

24   "A greater father," Western Morning News, 6 October 1927, 4.

25   Letters courtesy of Sir Paul Coleridge. Capt. Coleridge had earlier won the Military Cross for "conspicuous gallantry."

26   Mildred's death: Times 16 January 1929, 1; "Death of (3rd) Lord Coleridge's Aunt," Western Times, 18 January 1929, 2. Her funeral: Western Morning News, 18 January 1929, 4.

27   Milford Magazine, Milford on Sea Historical Record Society collection.

28   Christine Rawlins, *Beyond the Snow: The Life and Faith of Elizabeth Goudge* (2015).

29   "Unfortunate" development, NewForestNPA.gov.uk Buckland, Keyhaven & Ashlett Creek, 70.

30   Craik, quoted in, Judith Flanders, *Inside the Victorian Home*, 217-18.

31   Bob Braid e-mail, 4 December 2023. I owe so many thanks to Bob and his colleagues.

# INDEX

Victoria R.I. - Mildred's presentation to 13, and Amy, Lady Coleridge 194, LCJ's opinion of HRH 195, Bernard's wife presented to 241

Victoria Road (42) 129, LCJ and Amy Lawford married at 180

Victoria Street Society (VSS) - history of 37, Mildred joins 38, Adams employed 39, working relationship 44, 72 Ferrier case 44-6, Owen controversy 49-51, the "darkened room" 54ff, entrapment claim 159

Wales, Albert Edward, Prince of - 44, Baccarat trial 227-8, 234

Walker, Elizabeth 259-60

Walker, Dame Ethel 259-60

Weldon, Mrs. Georgina 208, 223n

Whistler, Theresa 258

"White elephant" Adams refers to Mildred as 72, Bernard and 111, Adams defends 146, damages for Bernard's letter 192

Woolf, Virginia quoted 122

Yates 135 138n denounces LCJ 154-7

Yates, Edmund Hodgson - (journalist, creator of the gossip column) sent to jail by LCJ 135-6, 138n, attacks LCJ 154-7, 167, "the pretty story," agrees to hold fire on 2nd wedding 176-9, 182, death 187n

Yarnall. Ellis, American correspondence with LCJ, 136, 194,

Yonge, Charlotte, concerns for Mildred

7, 14, 21, 127, 165 Goslings 8-9, Maymie's concerns 9, 109

*Zoophilist, The* founded 1881 39, Mildred and Adams at 44, 49-51, Adams sacked 61, Adams boycotted by 250